A Portrait of Contemporary U.S. Teachers of Piano

A Portrait of Contemporary U.S. Teachers of Piano

A Musical Journey

Barbara Ann Stolz

LEXINGTON BOOKS
Lanham • Boulder • New York • London

Published by Lexington Books
An imprint of The Rowman & Littlefield Publishing Group, Inc.
4501 Forbes Boulevard, Suite 200, Lanham, Maryland 20706
www.rowman.com

6 Tinworth Street, London SE11 5AL, United Kingdom

British Library Cataloguing in Publication Information Available

Library of Congress Cataloging-in-Publication Data

Names: Stolz, Barbara Ann, author.
Title: A portrait of contemporary U.S. teachers of piano : a musical journey / Barbara Ann Stolz.
Description: Lanham : Lexington Books, 2019. | Includes bibliographical references and index. | Summary: "Drawing on historical and social science literatures and interviews with current piano teachers, the book explores the contemporary U.S. piano teacher through a social science lens"—Provided by publisher.
Identifiers: LCCN 2019045575 (print) | LCCN 2019045576 (ebook) | ISBN 9781793603012 (cloth) | ISBN 9781793603029 (epub) ISBN 9781793603036 (pbk)
Subjects: LCSH: Piano—Instruction and study—United States. | Piano teachers—United States. | Piano—Instruction and study—History. | Piano—Instruction and study—Social aspects.
Classification: LCC MT220 .S87 2019 (print) | LCC MT220 (ebook) | DDC 786.2/193071073—dc23
LC record available at https://lccn.loc.gov/2019045575
LC ebook record available at https://lccn.loc.gov/2019045576

*To my dad, who first introduced me to music and
awakened my passion for the piano.
To Sister Rose Cecilia from whom I learned the joy of a new piece.
To Alan who kept me studying for more than thirty
years—Chopin, the Russians, and arias.
To Cathy who set the challenge—you can do more.
To Andrew who provided the guidance and tools
to do more and inspired this book.
To Carlos who continued to foster my development as a musician and
offered the insight, motivation, and support needed to complete this study.*

Contents

Preface

Images of the childhood music lesson are etched in the memories of many, although few pursue careers as teachers or performers of music. Whatever the musical instrument studied—violin, clarinet, trumpet, guitar, piano, or voice—the one-on-one lesson is viewed as an "indispensable, intense, and intricate" part of the learning experience (Gaunt 2008, 230). At the core of the lesson is the unique relationship between teacher and student. The piano and the piano lesson provide the context for this book, because they are what I know best. The central character is the piano teacher—the individual who chooses a career, characterized by an intense personal relationship, and decides to make the commitment to not only pass on the knowledge, skills, and traditions of earlier generations of pianists but also, perhaps most importantly, the joy of music.

Recalling childhood piano lessons may evoke warm feelings, but for many the weekly half hour of instruction at the keyboard provided a stage for the adult/child conflict. Often prominent among the memories are the sights and sounds of the lesson—the teacher, the room, the discipline, and sometimes life lessons. Memories of first piano teachers may be positive—a kindly older woman who lived in the neighborhood, taught from her home, and rewarded her students with chocolates or stickers. Memories may also be negative—the draconian task master who drilled scales and arpeggios, the dreaded pencil used to enforce proper technique and behavior, the daily parent/child struggle over practicing, and the drama of misplaced or lost music books. Piano lessons, including the time spent going to and from the lesson, may have interfered with other activities—sports, games, and just playing outside with friends.

Although my father was a professional pianist/organist, who taught me how to read music, the first recollections of my piano lessons are of a nun dressed in a stiffly starched Dominican habit smelling of laundry soap; with long, pale fingers; and wearing granny glasses. Fortunately, she did not use her pencil for disciplinary purposes and the lessons were pleasant. The room, located in the convent, was bright, furnished with a Steinway grand piano and harp, and separated from the inner sanctum by a glass door with white opaque curtains. Whether the student loved or disliked his or her piano teacher or considered lessons to be fun or a chore, the experience is usually not forgotten. Perhaps we remember because of the unique character of the piano lesson.

Despite my family background, career as a university professor, and having taken more than thirty years of piano lessons, the question "Why does someone choose to teach piano?" never crossed my mind. Perhaps I viewed teaching piano as just one of those tasks that pianists do to make a living. Two events during the winter of 2013 elicited the question and precipitated my writing this book—rereading Thad Carhart's book *The Piano Shop on the Left Bank: Discovering a Forgotten Passion in a Paris Atelier* and working with a new piano professor. Chronicling his foray into the inner sanctum of an unassuming neighborhood piano shop in Paris, Carhart relates his reentry into the world of the piano—purchasing his own piano and undertaking piano lessons as an adult. Reading his recollections of childhood piano teachers and lessons evoked thoughts of my own childhood and lifelong love of playing the piano. The unexpected retirement of my professor of many years, an academic colleague, led to my studying with a new professor, providing the opportunity to compare and contrast teaching approaches. Over the next few months, I began to view my lessons and practicing differently.

From these experiences emerged the central topics of this book—deciding to become, becoming, and being a piano teacher. In researching this book, I became a participant observer through my continued study of piano, interviews and conversations with piano teachers, and observing. Not all students will become great, even good musicians, but all can learn to appreciate music, which is to the benefit of any society. Accordingly, viewed as a social and cultural experience, the study of piano and the piano teacher is an appropriate topic for social science inquiry.

Acknowledgments

As the title suggests, this book is a story of a musical journey from student to teacher. Because of the unique character of the piano lesson, the musical journey is a deeply personal experience. Therefore, I would like to express my gratitude and respect to the twenty contemporary piano teachers who agreed to be interviewed. I thank them for their willingness to give of their time, share, and delve into themselves. While many of the memories they shared were happy, they also revealed painful experiences. Taken together, the stories of individual journeys create a picture of the contemporary piano teacher, very different from the portrayals in modern fiction. As agreed to prior to the interview, the participants remain anonymous. Without the assistance of Melinda Baird and Lois Narvey at the Levine School; Marilyn Nonken at New York University; Danielle La Senna at the Juilliard Evening Division; and referrals from interviewees, finding participants would have been much more difficult.

Additionally, I would like to thank those who assisted me in the research and development of the book. My friend Harold Wechsler, whose research prowess identified numerous resources, enhanced the depth and richness of this study. His personal support was vital during the early stages, but sadly he did not live to see its completion. Many thanks go to Blair Ruble and Ruth Nielsen-Jones, who read drafts, shared their wisdom and experience, and provided moral support through the writing process. The librarians in the Performing Arts Room of the Library of Congress not only provided assistance in researching the historical pedagogical literature but also friendship and a place to work each day—thank you Robin, Susan, Bob, Sam, Karen, Melissa, Paul, and Walter. The editorial and contract staff at Lexington Books provided valuable assistance, contributing to the final publication.

I am grateful to my family and so many friends from whom I learned to love music and with whom I continue to share the experience. They provided continuous support and encouragement. Coming from the many facets of my life, they are my village.

Finally, I owe much to the piano teachers along my journey—Alan Mandel, Cathy Campbell, Andrew Harley, and Carlos Rodriguez—and my friends from Piano'scape. I am indebted to Andrew, an exceptional piano teacher, who inspired this book. And, I am grateful to Carlos, who spent many hours reading chapters, discussing my observations, recommending new sources, and being there through the writing process while continuing to guide my piano studies.

Introduction

The invention of the piano is generally attributed to Bartolommeo Cristofori, in approximately 1709 (Wier 1940, 31). Keyboard methods, existing since the invention of the keyboard, and the one-on-one piano lesson, one of the most enduring forms of the tutorial tradition, are fundamental to the sociocultural history of the instrument.[1] Among the earliest master piano teachers were the Italian-born Muzio Clementi (1752–1832) and Austrian Carl Czerny (1791–1857). Nevertheless, even the greatest pedagogues are usually recognized only within the music world (Sand 2000, 41). Moreover, the roles of the piano teacher, the piano lesson, and methods explaining how to play the instrument have changed over time (Uszler 1982–1983, 12 and 1983). For example, during the eighteenth century, many masters called on a student every day to give a lesson (Parakilas 2001, 111). Yet, changes notwithstanding, individual instruction has been and remains essential to the teaching and study of piano, usually hinging on a relationship between the teacher and the student (Parakilas 2001, 112).

This book is perhaps best characterized as a social scientist's exploration of the purveyors—the piano teacher—of a widely shared sociocultural phenomenon—the piano lesson. The unique relationship between the piano teacher and student has been and continues to be part of the lives of many children and, today, even adults. The level of intimacy of the one-on-one piano lesson is not typical of most contemporary general educational experiences (e.g., classroom learning or athletic coaching) but carries on the master-apprentice tradition (Uszler 1992, 584). While very personal, the study of piano is a social and cultural experience not only for the individual but society in general. Accordingly, the study of piano and, in particular, its central figure—the piano teacher—is a matter for social science inquiry. The historical and contemporary social science literatures provide insight into the lives of

1

selected piano pedagogues, musician as performer, and music educator within schools. Focusing on the factors contributing to the process of deciding to become, becoming, and being a contemporary U.S. piano teacher—the journey, the current study situates the piano teacher and teaching within its social science context.

THE STUDY

Ultimately, the piano teacher bears the responsibility of passing on the love of music and the traditions associated with the study of piano, which extends beyond the individual piano student to society, in general. The overriding purpose of the current research is to develop a portrait of the U.S. piano teacher and teaching, situated within its historical and social science contexts. Memoirs and early treatises on piano pedagogy set the historical stage. Drawing on pertinent social science literatures and interviewing a judgmentally selected cadre of contemporary U.S. piano teachers, the piano teacher and teaching profession are examined as subjects of social science inquiry. Viewed through a social science lens, it is possible to develop systematically a portrait beyond the anecdotal and idiosyncratic, identifying common themes and patterns, and thereby enhance our understanding of both the piano teacher and the profession.

Approach in Brief

Using a three-pronged approach, the book explores three topics: (1) deciding to become, (2) becoming (i.e., factors contributing to the development of an approach to teaching piano), and (3) being (i.e., the qualities of a good piano teacher and contemporary piano teaching, in practice) a contemporary piano teacher.

1. The literatures: Reviews of selected popular, historical, and social science literatures;
2. Qualitative methods: Interviews with a judgmentally selected cadre of current U.S. piano teachers; and
3. Analysis and synthesis: Exploring interviewees' experiences using the factors identified from the historical and social science literatures.

The Literatures

To establish the current study within its popular, historical, and social science contexts and frame the analysis and synthesis of the primary information and observations gathered through the interviews, the objectives of the literature searches and reviews were to identify (1) fictional and nonfictional literature depicting piano teachers, (2) historical literature on piano pedagogy, and (3) pertinent social science research.

Contemporary fictional and nonfictional works and historical memoirs are explored to ascertain the images of the piano teacher. Readily available not only to the scholar, piano teacher, student, or music enthusiast but also to the general public, the popular literatures communicate messages that frame, reflect, and reinforce general societal beliefs and attitudes about piano teachers, lessons, and teaching, for better or worse. The portraits of noted historical pedagogues, usually written by former students, describe the personal characters and teaching approaches of individuals, who have had a major influence on piano teaching, and highlight qualities of the piano teacher.

Exploring selected treatises on piano pedagogy situates the contemporary piano teacher and teaching profession in an historical context. These resources describe requisites of piano teaching, fundamental to creating beautiful music (e.g., fingering, pedaling, sound/tone, daily practice, and artistic image) and present diverse perspectives on the roles, responsibilities, and qualities of a piano teacher. Considering interviewees' observations regarding the development of an approach to and the practice of piano teaching, within an historical context, demonstrates both continuity and change.

Selected studies from the literatures on career choice, achieving success, and the study and teaching of music provide the social science foundation for the study of the piano teacher and piano teaching. The career choice research offers some direction as to the factors that may affect the decision to pursue a particular career path (e.g., family and education). The achieving success literature examines the role of talent, hard work, and other factors that may contribute to professional success. U.S. and British research on developing the talented young musician confirms the relevance of the factors, extracted from the general literature, to a career in music and highlights additional factors reported to affect musical growth and development (e.g., listening to music and personal commitment). Social science studies on teaching music describe factors that may contribute to the development of an approach to piano teaching (e.g., early teachers and formal pedagogical training) and qualities of a good piano teacher (e.g., knowing each student). Additionally, U.S. and British research on the teaching and study of music is explored to ascertain what is known and not known about the contribution of the identified factors to the decision to become, becoming, and being a piano teacher.

Qualitative Methods

A qualitative methods approach is used to study the contemporary U.S. piano teacher and piano teaching—specifically, what actually is involved in deciding to become, becoming, and being a piano teacher. Grounded in that social science research tradition, which views those who have experienced a situation as meaningful informants regarding that situation (Stolz, 1985, xiv–xv), the primary source of the firsthand evidence, presented in this study, is a cadre of classically trained piano teachers. Each interviewee is considered to be an expert on his or her experience.

Twenty U.S. piano teachers with diverse backgrounds were interviewed using a semi-structured interview schedule, designed to elicit information on their respective experiences as a piano teacher. All were engaged in teaching one-on-one lessons and had been teaching for more than ten years. Interviewees were selected considering the following criteria: gender, age, educational training, national origin, and country of piano study and training. Variations in types of students taught and institutional affiliation were also sought. While pedagogical "lineage" was not a criterion, unexpectedly, several interviewees either studied with a pedagogue or student of a pedagogue discussed in the historical literatures. Geographic locations included Washington, D.C.; New York; Pittsburgh, Pennsylvania; and Baton Rouge, Louisiana. To maintain anonymity, as agreed in advance, each interviewee is referred to by a unique identification number (e.g., I#).

Analysis and Synthesis

The factors identified from social science and historical literatures frame the analysis and synthesis of interviewees' responses under each of the three topics of inquiry. While the importance of these factors to the pursuit of a career in music is evident from the review of the literatures on the study and teaching of music, the gaps in this research provide fertile ground for the current study of the contemporary piano teacher and teaching. Viewed through a social science lens, interviewees' personal experiences and perceptions, although not generalizable to the total population of piano teachers, provide insights into what occurs in the course of deciding to become, becoming, and being a contemporary piano teacher. Taken together, the patterns and common themes that emerge should create a portrait of the contemporary piano teacher and teaching, situated within its historical and social science contexts. A detailed discussion of the methodological approach is presented in chapter 5.

ORGANIZATION OF THE BOOK

The organization of the book emerged from the historical and social science context of this study. To set the current study within historical and science contexts, the five chapters in Part I: The Piano Teacher: Setting the Stage consider the following: (1) images of the piano teacher in popular fiction and nonfiction and historical student memoirs; (2) selected historical treatises on piano pedagogy; (3) pertinent social science literature; (4) extant research on developing the talented young musician and teaching piano; and (5) qualitative methods approach. Part II: A Study of the Contemporary U.S. Piano Teacher explores the development of the pianist as teacher—deciding to become, becoming, and being a piano teacher—through interviews with contemporary U.S. piano teachers. Chapters 6 and 7 focus on the early formative years of the pianist and the decision to teach piano. Chapter 8 explores the process of becoming a teacher, specifically factors contributing to piano teaching approaches. Chapters 9 and 10 consider the professional life of the piano teacher, including the demands of a music career; qualities of a good teacher; and being a piano teacher, in practice. The final chapter presents the author's conclusions.

NOTE

1. See, for example, Uszler 1982–1983, 12, and 1992, 584.

Part I

THE PIANO TEACHER

SETTING THE STAGE

Situating the current study within historical and social science contexts, part I sets the stage for the study of the piano teacher and teaching in the United States, today. Drawing from contemporary popular fiction and nonfiction and historical memoirs portraying notable piano pedagogues, chapter 1 presents images, communicated through word and film, which help frame our beliefs about and perceptions of the piano teacher. In chapter 2, examples of historical pedagogical treatises highlight requisites of piano teaching and the roles, responsibilities, and qualities of a good piano teacher, as viewed by famous pedagogues. From social science research on career choice, achieving success, and the study and teaching of music, factors that may contribute to deciding to become, becoming, and being a contemporary piano teacher are identified in chapter 3. To ascertain what is known and not known about the contribution of these factors to the pursuit of a piano teaching career, chapter 4 explores selected social science studies on developing the talented young musician and teaching piano. Having identified gaps in the extant literature, chapter 5 lays out the methodological approach used to study the contemporary teacher and teaching of piano.

Chapter 1

Popular Literatures and Historical Memoirs

Images of the Piano Teacher

Beyond our personal experiences, popular literatures and memoirs describing early piano pedagogues help to form our images and expectations of the piano teacher. The first section of this chapter considers images of the piano teacher in examples of children's literature, adult fiction and nonfiction, and film. Readily accessible not only to academics and students of piano but also to the general public, these works are one source of the messages that frame and reinforce general societal beliefs and attitudes about piano teachers and piano lessons. The second section examines selected historical student memoirs and correspondence of piano pedagogues, dating back to the 1800s. While probably read less frequently than the more lurid modern novels and exposés, these writings offer a picture of the personal character of individuals who shaped piano pedagogy. Written from the perspective of the student, the memoirs highlight qualities of the piano teacher, although certain examples should probably not be emulated today, and the arenas in which piano study and teaching occur. These portrayals provide a sociocultural context within which to begin to explore the contemporary piano teacher and piano teaching.

THE PIANO TEACHER IN POPULAR CONTEMPORARY FICTION AND NONFICTION

A search of the Library of Congress online catalog, using the terms "piano teacher" and "piano lesson" generated a list of contemporary children's fiction and adult fictional and nonfictional depictions of the piano teacher and piano lesson. Sometimes positive but more often negative, the portrayals are complex and ambivalent at best. The children's literature typically describes the piano teacher as a not very exciting mature female, while images in the adult literature range from "monsters" to "angels," as may be found in real life (See, for example, Bernstein 2002). Depictions of the piano teacher may be positive (Conroy 1993; Tunstall 2008; and Goldsworthy 2010), but the literature search revealed disturbing portraits in both popular fiction (Lee 2009; Jellinek 2010; and Grant 2014) and nonfiction (Burns 2014). Given its general availability, this literature contributes to perceptions of the piano teacher and lesson, for better or worse.

Children's Fiction

From our earliest reading, we are typically presented with at least ambivalent pictures of the piano teacher and piano lesson. As portrayed in the children's literature, the piano teacher is a mature woman, who lives in the neighborhood, teaches in her home, and is kind to her students. The child protagonist complains that practicing is a bother; scales are boring; and lessons interfere with childhood pursuits, such as playing sports, even if rewarded with candy or stickers (Macmillan 1943 and Delton 1994). Taking piano lessons may also negatively distinguish the child—"playing the piano is for sissies" (Delton 1994).

In *The Curse of Rafferty McGill* (Macmillan 1943), for example, Ryan O'Connor, running late for his piano lesson and fearing a lecture for not practicing, exclaims: "I wish I didn't have stupid piano lessons!" Unfortunately it is Saint Patrick's Day and an unscrupulous leprechaun hears and grants Ryan's wish. All disappear—the teacher; her house; and Angela Morgan, the "goody goody" piano student who was having her lesson. To reverse his wish and restore things to normal, Ryan must devise a plan to meet the leprechaun's condition—a new pair of shoes. In *My Mom Made Me Take Piano Lessons*, Archie itemizes all the reasons a boy does not want to take lessons: "I have games to pitch; a bike to ride. I'll hit the wrong keys. I'll lose my music book" (Delton 1994). By the end of each story, events lead the child to decide that playing the piano and taking piano lessons are not so bad, the teacher is okay, or playing an instrument in school productions has its rewards.

Audio recordings and movies—now CDs and DVDs—send a similar message. *Rusty in Orchestraville* not only introduces the instruments in the orchestra and major classical works of music but also directly addresses the issue of practicing. The story begins with Rusty banging on the piano because he hates playing scales, practicing, and the piano itself. Frustrated, he curls up in the large chair and is carried off to Orchestraville, where the instruments talk and serious pieces can be played on any instrument without practicing. The conductor introduces Rusty to members of the orchestra—the strings, woodwinds, and brass—except "Peter the piano" whose feelings Rusty has hurt. In the end, Peter and Rusty reconcile and Rusty experiences the joy of playing Chopin's *Minute Waltz*. Waking from his dream, he vows to practice scales so that someday he can play the *Minute Waltz*. We never meet Rusty's teacher.

In the full-length feature *The Thousand Fingers of Dr. T*, screenplay by Dr. Seuss, the piano teacher, Dr. Terwilliker, is a villainous tormentor of young boys. Bored from practicing, the nine-year-old protagonist, Bart Collins, dozes off and dreams that he and his widowed mother are held captive in an old castle. Having musicians of all other instruments banished to the castle's dungeon, the diabolical Dr. T recruits 500 young boys who practice 24 hours a day, 365 days a year, using the *Happy Fingers Method*—the best method for teaching piano. At the grand opening of the Terwilliker Institute for the study of piano, the boys are to perform Dr. T's colossal concerto, *Ten Happy Fingers*, on the grandest of pianos. The message is conformity and compliance with Dr. T's method, not individuality. Aided by his friend, Mr. Zabladowski the plumber, Bart thwarts the doctor's plans and rescues his mother. Awakening from his dream, the story ends well for Bart, his mother, and the plumber, but there is no redemption for the evil piano teacher.

The piano teachers of children's literature and film range from unexciting to diabolical; piano lessons and practicing are boring, evidenced by the tendency of young students to fall asleep at the keyboard. Such images seem to resonate with the experiences of many. The kindly Signor Ravelli, portrayed by Chico Marx in *The Big Store*, is the exception. His four young Gotham Conservatory of Music piano students, who joyfully greet news of the construction of a real conservatory, offer a sharp contrast to the predominant image of the piano student. They perform a highly spirited eight-hand two-piano rendition of Schubert's *Moment Musicale #3*, imitating, in tandem, the "shooting the keys" action of their beloved teacher. Clearly these boys love music, the piano, and their teacher. The intent of the children's literature and film may be to reassure the young piano student and demonstrate the value of piano lessons. Nevertheless, the images of and feelings toward the piano teacher and the lesson usually articulated in the story lines seem to reinforce youthful concerns and offer a litany of excuses and arguments for not taking lessons.

Contemporary Popular Adult Fiction

Although portrayals of the piano teacher in adult fiction are mixed, negative images of the piano teacher, both male and female, abound. Nefarious motives, including sadism and pedophilia (Grant 2014 and Jellinek 2010), underlie the pursuit of a teaching career; or, the character is flawed—kleptomania (Lee 2009). Perhaps, the idiosyncratic makes more interesting reading.

In Katherine Grant's novel *Sedition* (2014), the pianoforte and the male piano teacher are essential to the plan of four 1790s social-climbing London fathers to marry off their five eligible daughters. The girls are to learn to play the piano in preparation for a concert before an audience of potential husbands—titled, but fortune-less, young Englishmen. The fathers buy a pianoforte, made by a man, whose talented but disfigured daughter will never marry, and hire a French piano teacher, Monsieur Belladroit, to teach the girls. Monsieur sabotages the girls' performances and seduces them, one by one, as part of their training.

> Monsieur would steal the girls' virtue and be away before the new husbands discovered the cherry picked, the goods secondhand. He quite envied these husbands. What a favor he was doing, enabling them to ditch the wife as sullied but keep the marriage settlement. Should he demand a cut? (49)

The plot unfolds, but the image of the disreputable piano teacher and the sad commentary on the relationship between piano teacher and student is set.

Fictional female piano teachers do not fare better than men. In *Die Klavierspielerin* (*The Piano Teacher*), set in 1980s Vienna, Austrian Nobel Prize winning author, Elfriede Jellinek, depicts Erika Kohut as a late thirtyish piano teacher at the Vienna Conservatory who lives with her overbearing mother (2010).[1] Erika's underlying violence is expressed by "accidently" banging into other trolley passengers with her string or wind instruments and large musical scores or kicking and stepping on people but blaming someone else. She and a young engineering student Walter Klemmer, who becomes her piano student, are obsessed with each other. Initially resisting, Erika relents but the relationship is stormy, as Walter resists her sexual masochism. Driven by her jealousy over a female pianist's contact with Walter, Erika destroys the young woman's prospects by hiding shards of glass in the girl's coat pocket, resulting in permanent damage to her hand. The story ends violently. While the book's message extends beyond the pathology of an individual to the position of female piano teachers in Austria's musical culture, the lasting impression is a mentally unbalanced almost middle-aged single woman who teaches piano (Introduction).

The film version (2001) of the novel, which may be more familiar to the American audience, underscores that film is no kinder to the piano teacher than literature.[2] Negative depictions of music teachers in popular movies are not limited to piano. The 2015 film *Whiplash* relates the story of a young drummer's musical studies under a professor with a sadistic teaching approach. For his portrayal of this unsympathetic character, J. R. Simmons won an Academy Award.

Set in Hong Kong in the 1940s and ten years later, Janice Y. K. Lee's novel *The Piano Teacher* (2009) paints a sympathetic figure of Claire Pendelton, the title subject. Young, married to a civil engineer, and newly arrived in Hong Kong in 1952, she takes a position teaching piano to the daughter of a successful Chinese businessman; but she is a kleptomaniac.

> It started as an accident. The small Herend rabbit had fallen into Claire's purse. It had been on the piano and she had been gathering up the sheet music at the end of the lesson when she knocked it off. It fell off the doily (a doily! on the Steinway!) and into her large leather bag. . . . It wasn't until she was downstairs and waiting for the bus that she grasped what she had done. And then it had been too late. She went home and buried the expensive porcelain figurine under her sweaters. (Lee 2009, 3)

The novel is a story of romance, intrigue, and the tragic consequences ten years after the Japanese occupation during the Second World War. The piano teacher and the piano lesson are used as literary devices to move the plot, rather than subjects.

In contrast, a generally positive portrayal of the piano teacher is Frank Conroy's somewhat historical novel *Body and Soul* (1993). Set in New York City in the 1940s, the plot follows the rise of a young prodigy, Claude Rawlings. Raised by a less than stable single mother, who drives a taxi to support them, five-year-old Claude spends his days plinking around on an old white upright piano. His life changes when he ventures into a music store run by Weisfield, a European refugee who becomes his first piano teacher. Along Claude's musical journey, we meet three piano teachers, each more illustrious than the preceding.

The first teaches him technique, the second passion, and the third to transcend himself. From Professor Menti, a prematurely balding slender man with a large nose and heavy lips, for whom technique is paramount, Claude learns finger strength; little was said about interpretation, drilling was constant, and scales were to be practiced two hours a day using a contraption screwed to the piano (Conroy 1993, 87, 89). From Herr Sturm, a short man with a large square head and fierce expression, who lived in the neighborhood, 10-year-old Claude learns to get inside Bach's Well-Tempered Clavier, but the incessant talking and wandering around the room throwing up his hands on the beat are unsettling (90–92). For Mr. Fredericks, who lived in the suburbs, dynamics were a crucial element to make such magically pure music; three hours of work with total concentration was sufficient (94–97). "Anything you can imagine clearly, you can play. That's the great secret" (101). Each of Conroy's fictitious pedagogues is someone we might encounter in life.

Contemporary Popular Nonfiction

Modern popular nonfiction offers a mixed picture (Goldsworthy 2010; Tunstall 2008; and Burns 2014). The accounts range from warm memories to the horrific, mirroring recent scandals in the Catholic Church—an adult in a trusted position of authority violates the most vulnerable.

On a positive note, Australian classical pianist Anna Goldsworthy's memoir, *Piano Lessons* (2010), invites the reader into the close, personal teacher-student relationship with a good teacher; the world of the piano lesson; and the author's journey to a career as a concert pianist. Recalling her early studies over a decade from age nine, Goldsworthy describes Mrs. Eleanor Sivan, a Russian émigré and world-class pianist, as a warm and dedicated teacher. Most relevant to the current study are the memories of Silvan's philosophy of music, life, and the importance of piano teaching—words that continued to haunt Goldsworthy:

> "We are not teaching piano playing. We are teaching philosophy and life and music digested." (3) "We have a huge responsibility to future! Of passing this spirit to next generations. Always remember: only what you give is yours." (175)

Mrs. Sivan's thoughts on the importance of piano teaching to society in general echo those of several great European pedagogues. "Not all students will be professional pianist . . . but equally important to educate audiences" (*sic*, 175). That is, teaching piano is not just about teaching genius; it is also about enhancing the culture of a society.

Tricia Tunstall's *Note by Note: A Celebration of the Piano Lesson* relates her generally positive memories as a student and piano teacher (2008). Reminiscing about her first piano teacher at the Peabody Conservatory—a woman who was maybe fifty, dedicated to the art of pianism in the European tradition, firm and methodical, and gracious and cheerful but strict, Tunstall observes: "I was transfixed and intimidated" (4–5). In contrast, she describes a first lesson with her own students as chattier, asking them about their musical experiences, sharing jelly beans, and teaching each child how to play the beginning of a tune (6–11). Looking for a piano teacher after her family moves to a new community, she describes trial lessons with several excellent teachers: Mrs. Bernstein—too excitable, Mademoiselle Combs—too rigid, and Mr. DeGray—too far away. She chooses Mrs. Gordon, after watching her play scales during the first lesson—"I knew I was in the presence of real virtuosity." Mrs. Gordon had light blue eyes clear as lake water, a beautiful aquiline nose, an easy smile, and astonishing fingers; the Steinway grand stood at the end of her sparsely furnished living room (122–23). "My lessons with Mrs. Gordon gave me my first clear image of musical mastery" (125).

Amy Jo Burn's memoir describes the horrific. *Cinderland* is essentially an apology to correct her testimony, denying being inappropriately touched by piano teacher, Howard Lotte, during his 1991 sexual molestation trial. Lotte, a piano teacher in a steel town between Pittsburgh and Erie, Pennsylvania, was accused of molesting his female piano students. Seven girls testified to the truth regarding his "feckless hands"; others, including the author, then ten years old, lied (2014, 1 and 7). They chose to protect a criminal, as it was their best chance for survival in the town (3). Although Lotte was convicted, those who told the truth were ostracized by the community. The memoir takes the reader from the case through the author's adolescent years, reflecting on life in small-town America, and examines her feelings of guilt for not admitting the truth. The image of the piano teacher is despicable; the image of the student is tragic.

PORTRAITS OF HISTORICAL PEDAGOGUES: FROM THE STUDENT'S PERSPECTIVE

To assume that piano teaching—the teacher, the lesson, and daily practice—as we know it was established at a point in time and has remained the same would be a mistake (Parakilas 2001, 112–15). For example, many eighteenth-century music masters called daily on their students to give them their lessons; consequently, some teachers preferred the student not to practice to avoid "wrecking" the good done during the lesson (111–12). Nevertheless, not only did these early pedagogues establish expectations and practices that continue to influence the teaching of piano, but their personalities, as teachers, have contributed to the images of the piano teacher. Because the individual relationship between teacher and student was essential to even the earliest piano teaching, perhaps the best source of information about the early pedagogues is their students. Fortunately, students of a number of well-known early and contemporary pedagogues took the time to describe their experiences.

Through searches of the Library of Congress and New York Public Library online catalogs, using the terms "piano teacher" and "piano pedagogue"; names of early pedagogues, particularly those mentioned by interviewees; and references listed in several publications on the history of the piano (Wier 1940; Kochevitsky 1967; Parakilas et al. 2001; and Soderlund 2006), writings by students of early piano pedagogues were identified. These accounts, often written by American piano students, who studied abroad, describe the personalities and teaching approaches of noted teachers. Table 1.1 references the memoirs and biographies, portraying the selected historical pedagogues discussed in this section.

The memoirs and published letters usually present a more balanced image of the pedagogue. Reflecting the close teacher-student relationship, these writings highlight the positive and the personal, although the content varies

Table 1.1 Selected Memoirs and Biographies of Historical Piano Pedagogues

Author/s	Memoir/Biography	Description	Pedagogue	Nation
Jean-Jacques Eigeldinger Jeremy Nicholas	*Chopin: Pianist and Teacher As Seen by His Pupils.* 1986. *Chopin: His Life and Music.* 2006.	Biographies drawing on correspondence	Frederick Chopin 1810–1849	Poland
Charlotte Moscheles	*Recent Music And Musicians, As Described in the Diaries and Correspondence of Ignatz Moscheles.* [1873] 1970.	Moscheles's wife draws from entries in his diary (1814 to his death) and letters to relatives and friends	Ignaz Moscheles 1794–1870	Bohemia
Auguste Boissier	*A Diary of Franz Liszt as Teacher 1831–1832—Auguste Boissier.* [1928] 1973.	Boissier's notebook details her daughter Valerie's lessons with Liszt at age twenty-one	Franz Liszt 1811–1886	Hungary
Amy Fay	*Music-Study in Germany.* [1880] 2011.	Memoir of American Fay's six-year musical journey beginning in 1869, describes German pedagogy and study	Ludwig Deppe 1828–1890 Franz Liszt 1811–1886	Germany Hungary
William Mason	*Memories of a Musical Life.* 1901.	Memoir of American pianist and teacher	Franz Liszt 1811–1886	Hungary
Elisabeth Caland	*Artistic Piano Playing as Taught by Ludwig Deppe.* 1903.	A student's description of Deppe's methods.	Ludwig Deppe 1828–1890	Germany
Ethel Newcomb	*Leschetizky, As I Knew Him.* 1921.	Memoir of American student and assistant of Leschetizky	Theodor Leschetizky 1830–1915	Poland

Author/s	Memoir/Biography	Description	Pedagogue	Nation
Joseph Rezits	*Beloved Tyranna: The Legend and Legacy of Isabelle Vengerova.* 1995.	Rezits' personal memories and interviews with students of Vengerova	Isabelle Vengerova 1877–1956	Russia
Douglas Ashley	*Music Beyond Sound: Maria Curcio, A Teacher of Great Pianists.* 1993.	A student's biography of Curcio	Maria Curcio 1919–2009	Italy
William Brown	*Menahem Pressler: Artistry in Piano Teaching.* 2009.	A former student describes Pressler's approach to teaching	Menahem Pressler 1923–	Germany
Seymour Bernstein	*Monsters and Angels.* 2002.	Includes the American pianist and teacher's accounts of his teachers	Seymour Bernstein 1927–	United States

because each relationship is unique. Nevertheless, descriptions of certain qualities—personality and temperament, knowing each student, methods or lack of, recognizing the individuality of each student's playing, and responsibility of the student—recur and are demonstrated in the arenas of the lesson and beyond the lesson.

Qualities

Personality and Temperament

While giants in the field of music, the pedagogues were, nevertheless, human beings with different personalities and temperaments. Some were understanding and patient; others were moody and prone to emotional outbursts. The portraits of Chopin, Moscheles, Liszt, and Deppe reveal patient and caring individuals and teachers. In contrast, Isabelle Vengerova had her partisans and critics: "there were people who idolized her and those who feared her—or worse! The very mention of her name stirs a strong emotional response. There is no neutrality in this reaction" (Rezits 1995, 8). The theme of patience recurs, although even the patient teacher might display a temper. Moreover, they had likes, dislikes, and complaints—"pet peeves." The vignettes portray very human beings.

Largely self-taught, Chopin pursued his teaching career during the latter part of his life (Wier 1940, 382). Although his main source of income, he recognized the importance of the task and showed a human understanding of his students' personal, musical, and technical problems. He knew how to inspire self-confidence and to find the right words of encouragement to free the pupil's inner resources at the right moment (Eigeldinger 1986, 6–7 and 10–11). Nevertheless, on days of illness or irritability, his playfulness and courtesy could give way to "fits of anger, as violent as they were brief"; male students were more prone to these "leçons orageuses" than were the women (Eigeldinger 1986, 11; and Nicholas 2006, 88–89).

The nineteenth-century Bohemian concert pianist, composer, and eminent teacher at the Leipzig Conservatory, Ignatz Moscheles, is remembered as having friendly ways. His wise discipline was invariably tempered with kindness, and he enforced obedience by sympathy (Wier 1940, 399–400; and Moscheles [1873] 1970, 358–59). Although his health seldom prevented him from attending to his duties at the Conservatoire, when indisposed and confined to the house, he would have the pupils at home rather than allow them to miss their lesson (Moscheles [1873] 1970, 358).

Hungarian-born, Franz Liszt was not only a composer and pianist but also a teacher. He did not take beginners and looked askance at child prodigies but put the finishing touches on a good number of pianists of the nineteenth century. His teaching consisted of advice and illustration (Schonberg 1987, 255–56). Madame Boissier describes Liszt as an incomparable teacher. Blond, thin, of elegant bearing and a very distinguished face, he was a unique and good-humored person ([1928] 1973, xi). He was an eminently meditative and reflective individual; his is the mind of a thinker. During the lesson, his conversation was filled with musical revelations (xiv). Nevertheless, she also describes another side of the artist:

> Lesson a little more than mediocre: Liszt was in a bad mood, rough, refractory, with no heart. He showed us his artistic whimsical aspect. There was a dryness in his soul. . . . He is a whimsical and unsteady young man, but full of whit, of magnanimity and talent. (xx)

Mississippi-born and Louisiana raised, Amy Fay chronicled her studies in Berlin with German pedagogue Ludwig Deppe, who developed a system of instruction involving careful attention to muscular movement and is considered by many as the father of the weight technique (Fay [1880] 2011; Uszler et al. 1995, 312; and Caland 1903, 31). Asking to study with him in 1873, Fay describes the encounter: he was of medium height, with a great big brain, keen blue eyes, and a most cheery and sunny expression. The front room of his two-room apartment was much filled with a grand piano cover with music, as were the chairs and other furniture. She notes that Deppe taught more for the love of art than for love of money—"a rare thing in these materialistic days!" (Fay [1880] 2011, 285–86)

A student of Karl Czerny, Theodor Leschetizky was a major pedagogical figure in late nineteenth- to early twentieth-century Vienna. Ethel Newcomb observes that some portrayed him as moody, but the students who knew him longest and best did not think so (1921, 97). Nevertheless, she also reveals that students referred to the small room where they waited for lessons as the "torture chamber." If one heard shouts of rage, students feared what might be their fate later; good playing was also alarming for fear of not being able to retain his good and cheerful mood. Rages usually meant that the pupil was playing unrhythmically; this had the worst possible effect on Leschetizky (22-23). Perhaps he was passing on the tradition he inherited from his studies with Czerny as young boy. Many times he had had a music book thrown at his head or been seized by the collar and thrown from the room (Gardner 1901, 87). He found no virtue in suffering of any kind, and very little in patience. Something, he thought, was radically wrong if one needed patience and his patience lasted only as long as it took to correct a wrong (Newcomb 1921, 177).

Emigrating from Russia in the 1920s, Isabelle Vengerova, a student of Leschetizky, brought her teaching approach to Philadelphia's Curtis Institute and Manhattan's Mannes College. From interviews with Vengerova's former students, Joseph Rezits paints a picture of the "beloved tyrant." Pianist, author, and musical director of New York City's radio station WQXR (1946–1965), Abram Chasins describes her as such an elegant lady, but

> when I began to hear her yelling at her pupils, and when I would recall her fierce anger and nothing short of it, even hostility, and bitter sarcasm, this was another Isabella! I did not know that person until I heard her with pupils. She was so anxious for them to do their best, and I realized that musical integrity was her wish for all of them. (Rezits 1995, 53)

In contrast, Seymour Bernstein[3] characterizes Vengerova as the "incarnation of evil" (2002, 162), who like many European pedagogues used terroristic tactics to dominate her young, inexperienced pupils and behaved like a warm, supportive colleague toward older, more experienced artists who came to her for advice (171). His studies at Mannes ended with her ultimatum to the school's director—"either he leaves the school, or I do!" Expulsion—Bernstein was devastated (174).

Twentieth-century Italian-born pianist Maria Curcio was urged by her teacher Artur Schnabel[4] to make the effort to teach (Ashley 1993, 11). By 1965, she had decided to devote herself to teaching and, with the help of the composer, Benjamin Britain, settled in London. Her student and biographer, Douglas Ashley, describes her as businesslike in her use of the allotted hour and accepting students on the basis that she thought it professionally worthwhile for both. Shouts and screams were not imaginable with her—it was contrary to her nature, philosophy of teaching and music making, and goal of recreating the inspiration of a masterpiece (16–17).

As reported by his student, William Brown, German-born Indiana University professor Menahem Pressler describes tailoring his temperament to the student. "With some I can yell, which I do, but with some you can only speak nicely" (Brown 2009, 47). The need to adjust one's temperament and temper to the student remains a challenge for the contemporary piano teacher, particularly in the U.S. context.

"Pet peeves" are usually a matter of personal preference, taste, or even expectations and the historical pedagogues were no exception. For Leschetizky, for example, the most serious fault was bad phrasing and failure to listen to one's own playing so as to judge the relationship of one tone to another (Newcomb 1921, 29). He would exclaim: "Thou shall not be stupid." Upon this text he would often deliver sermons (68–69). Yet, certain "peeves" run through the historical student memoirs—parents being perhaps the most common. Newcomb cites Leschetizky's tirade on parents—American and European:

Oh these mothers and fathers! They drive me insane! I don't mean only the American parents—they are peculiar in that they always appear to be so glad to get away from their husbands. In Europe the husbands come along, too, and I generally have the fathers as well to attend. (81)

Isabelle Vengerova is reported to have had as much trouble with some of the mothers as with some of the children (Rezits 1995, 84). Parents—although perhaps in different ways and for different reasons—continue to be a challenge to today's piano teacher.

Knowing Each Student

Reflected in the teaching approaches of the historical pedagogues is knowing each student. The student memoirs frequently describe the attention paid by the pedagogue to the individual student—the total student. Knowing comprised analysis and correction, personality, beyond personality, identifying individual needs, and tailoring one's approach to the student.

Deppe appears not only to have analyzed a student's difficulties but believed in his ability to correct limitations (Fay [1880] 2011). Listening quietly without interruption, as Fay played during her first lesson with him, he told her on finishing that her difficulties were principally mechanical ones. She had conception and style, but her execution was uneven and hurried; her wrist was stiff and her third and fourth fingers were very weak; her tone was not full and round enough; she did not know how to use the pedal; and she was too nervous and flurried. He concluded—"You have talent enough to get over all your difficulties if you will be patient, and do just as I tell you" (287). Moreover, he observed: "Gifted people play by the grace of God; but everybody could master the technique on my system" (301).

A student's personality was of great importance and interest to Leschetizky, although the absolute correctness of every musical and technical detail was the supreme test in the first lesson (Newcomb 1921, 96). Characteristic of Leschetizky was to become more interested if he saw that the pupil was trying doggedly to overcome a difficulty. Bringing to bear complete concentration and all the resources of his ingenuity, he only became more and more determined to succeed in solving the problem. Time did not count with him (131).

Curcio wanted to know her students very well musically, pianistically, and personally. She felt that helping them discover their musical personality was an important part of her work, because if they feel her concern and interest, they open up to her, which in turn helps them open up to an audience (Ashley 1993, 18). Moreover, it was necessary to know each pupil musically and psychologically to grow as a teacher. The teacher must truly care for the student, be devoted not only to music but also to the student. Caring for the student opens the teacher's vision of what is the best approach for each individual (30). Feeling so strongly about the moral responsibilities of teaching, she advised young teachers never to look down on a student: we must keep our idealism high or else the quality of teaching deteriorates. One cannot give a less good lesson just because the student is not the greatest talent. We are free to choose our students; but if we are serious about the music and our profession, then we must take each student seriously (18–19).

Vengerova worked out very carefully what each student needed and the time he or she needed to develop it. Chasins describes her attitude toward pupils as scientifically precise. There was no blanket treatment for all students; for each she had an entirely different approach, different treatment, because she was sensitive to personalities, their degree and state of development, and their needs. Rezits replies: "Her relationship was, in fact, unique with each individual; there were literally hundreds of these relationships" (Rezits 1995, 56).

Pressler underscores the importance of a teacher tailoring demands to the student, noting that very often the teacher can be harmful by demanding that all students do certain things but a particular student cannot do it that way. People have different physiques—long arms, short arms, big, small, heavy, no weight whatsoever. People also have different personalities (Brown 2009, 47). Pressler further explains that he always takes students who may not be the best players but who might make good teachers. What will make a good teacher?: character, the attitude—"a sense of inner discipline," a force that will help the student succeed (44).

Methods or Lack of

The term "piano methods" usually refers to a method of playing—the technique (Uszler et al. 1995, 113). Whether a pedagogue actually taught according to a precise, systematic "method" or what we know of his or her "method" is only what has been passed down through a student is an open question. Nevertheless, the descriptions of methods found in the student memoirs provide a basis from which to identify requisites of piano study—fingering, pedaling, sound/tone, and daily practice.

Although Chopin did not create a school or institute a set tradition, his collected writings and those of his students suggest his views on elements of technique and methods (Eigeldinger 1986, 4 and 27–63). Regarding position at the keyboard, sit high so as to be able to reach both ends of the keyboard, with the right foot on the sustaining pedal, and elbows level with the white keys with hands turned neither to the left or right (28). Place the fingers on the keys E, F#, G#, A#, B; the long fingers will occupy the high (black) keys, and the short fingers will occupy the low (white) keys (28–29). Have the body supple right to the tips of the toes—suppleness was his great object (29). Chopin played only with finger touch, no weight from the arms (30). Concerning pedaling—"The correct employment of it remains a study for life" (57). The goal was not to play everything with equal sound but a well-formed technique that can control and vary a beautiful sound quality (31).

Deppe's principle was to not learn a piece completely the first time but to master it three-quarters and then, "as you would fruit that you have put on a shelf to ripen," take it up again and finish it. Sit very low, not higher than the common chair, which will work the fingers a great deal more (Fay [1880] 2011, 293). Contrary to the general principle of lifting the fingers high, Deppe advocated lifting the fingers moderately high, letting the finger just fall to allow the muscle from the whole arm to come to bear, thereby producing a fuller, less loud but more penetrating tone (288). Among the refinements of Deppe's teaching was pedaling, revealing that with careful study it was possible to get as great a virtuosity with the pedal: "The pedals are the lungs of the piano" (297).

Leschetizky claimed to have no method. There was only one goal—good piano playing. He did not believe a teacher could be a good teacher who could not play himself (Newcomb 1921, 244). He advised his assistant that it was better to leave her mind blank for the pupil to fill in; each hand is different. "Write over your music-room door the motto: 'NO METHOD!' Adopt with your pupils the ways that succeed with them, and get as far as possible from the idea of method" (107). Nevertheless, one of his students prepared an approved text of his methods (Breé 1913).

Vengerova developed a technical approach that, when applied correctly, gave the player an almost uncanny physiological advantage. The approach, based on the carefully planned use of the wrist, was her means to the ultimate in interpretative control and greatest efficiency in a purely technical sense. Another factor was the production of a beautiful tone (Rezits 1965, 2). In her interview with Rezits, Brooklyn-born pianist and teacher, Blanche Abram identifies the many things in her teaching that carry over from her studies with Vengerova.

> Emphasis on a flexible wrist, a fluid legato, planned and appropriate movement of the wrist "up" or "forward" or "down" to help shape the musical line, sensitivity to the relatedness of different segments of the score, the hidden bass line or the long melodic line, a singing tone free of an unintended hard-edged attack, and, above all, a musical intent. (Rezits 1995, 26)

Curcio viewed technique, not as a goal in itself but as the equipment essential for communication and projection and realization of the composer's intentions. It is not just a question of hands and arms, but it involves the whole body (Ashley 1993, 22). She was a firm believer that a solid, working technical basis comes from the studies of Cramer,[5] Czerny, and Clementi. A fine working technique is also an enormous asset for good sight-reading, a skill which a responsible teacher should encourage—she encouraged her students to sight-read every day, something not too difficult so as to be able to keep the rhythmic pulse and play as many notes as the eye can catch (24).

Describing his first year of teaching, Pressler explains that he had to first learn what each student needed—some students could not read music. Being able to teach has more to do with one's desire to transfer knowledge than knowledge—to understand the psyche of the person to whom you are trans-ferring the knowledge, what the person is capable of receiving, and even how much that person needs (Brown 2009, 37). He underscores the need for the teacher to express what you know about a piece in words in order to com-municate to a student what you want: "This is This" (47). To help students discover how to apply arms, wrists, and fingers to passagework he used the first of the Hanon exercises (60).[6] For years he provided his students with photocopied pages of exercises that promote finger independence and proper action of the wrist, while maintaining a relaxed arm (56).

Recognizing the Individuality of Each Student's Playing

Stemming from the discussion of methods is the question, to what extent is allowance made for individual creativity or is the expectation that the stu-dent will simply follow the master? Listening to a pianist, do we recognize the style of the teacher with whom he/she studied; or, stated somewhat dif-ferently, do the students of a particular teacher all sound alike? During the twentieth and into the twenty-first century, the importance placed on winning a major piano competition, as the road to a successful performance career, raised a related question: Has the emphasis on winning competitions led to a decline in the individuality of playing? To win one must play it safe and fol-low the rules; thus, competitors tend to play the same piece in the same way.

Liszt was said to advise students to cultivate their individuality, rather than to imitate (Uszler 1995, 317). To refute the charge that Leschetizky failed to develop the individuality of his students, Gardner asserts that one only need listen to Leschetizky's students who play in public: whatever one may think of their playing, no one can hold that they play in the least alike, as would be the case had their master "crushed out their individuality" and made their ideas entirely subject to his own (1901, 87–88). Pressler observes: "When you have three students playing the same piece, they couldn't all play it the same because they're different." He observes that while it is not written anywhere, you learn that each student has a fire inside them but there are "places that you don't touch because it hurts them and it will hurt you" (Brown 2009, 46).

Treasuring individuality, Curcio considered each student in terms of individual goals, possibilities, and procedures. She had an uncanny ability to grasp a student's musical personality. An important part of her work was synthesizing the paradox between the composer's conception and the expression of a student's own artistic individuality, which she resolved by working with the student to reach the composer's meaning and level of inspiration and then finding the means to project the student's vision (Ashley 1993, 81).

Responsibility of the Student

Success in studying piano depends not only on the teacher but also on the student. The primary responsibility of the student is to practice.

While the recommended length of time and regime differed, the early pedagogues were aware of the hazards of mindless or over-practicing. Chopin advised practicing no more than three hours a day; not working too long at a stretch; breaking up the time by reading a good book, looking at masterpieces of art, or taking an invigorating walk; and not playing exercises merely mechanically but with the intelligence and entire will of the pupil (Eigeldinger 1986, 27). Liszt required Valerie to practice two hours on mechanical studies daily, apart from the rest (Bossier [1928] 1973, xiv). For the purpose of making each finger perfectly equal and independent, he insisted that each finger be exercised for a quarter of an hour daily by raising it very high and releasing it downwards, not on its tip but instead upon the ball of the finger. This exercise might be done while reading in order not to become bored, but he considered it most important for the greatest development of the mechanism (xix). Leschetizky also did not advocate long hours of practice—four hours of well-considered practice was quite enough, although to keep familiar with a large number of pieces, a player may spend one or two more hours memorizing. Piano practice should never become thoughtless throwing off of exercises by the hour or by the number. To gain good results, it must train the head and hand alike (Bree 1913, 57).

The later pedagogues also underscore the importance of concentration when practicing and the link between practicing and the lesson. Curcio counseled five or six hours of practice for someone studying for a professional goal. Some work with such concentration that after four hours they cannot practice more; some do seven or eight. Discipline is important (Ashley 1993, 77). Brown cites Pressler's response to the question: "What is practicing for?"

> Practicing is for creating within you how you would like the music to sound. And obviously, it is very seldom that we come to the ideal, but we come close because we create something that leads us toward that ideal.

Pressler expected students to master all the details covered in the previous lesson and go beyond his instructions in technical and musical preparation (Brown 2009, 87).

Arenas

The teacher-student relationship fundamental to the study of piano transpires within the arena of the piano lesson and also in activities that extend beyond the lesson. Despite changes over time, the one-on-one lesson remains the pillar of piano teaching. The student memoirs also offer evidence that the education of the student occurred beyond the time and place of the lesson. Situating the lesson and beyond historically, by way of examples from the early pedagogues, provides background and perspective for exploring the contemporary piano teacher and teaching.

The Lesson

Reconstructing what usually occurred during an eighteenth- or nineteenth-century piano lesson or practice session would be difficult, but from a review of early methods texts, one may deduce what was expected to take place (Parakilas 2001, 110–11). The content of a lesson, for example, the extent to which the teacher demonstrated by playing, varied generally from teacher to teacher. The basic structure of the lessons described by the students of the noted pedagogues, while focused on an individual student, might take place in the presence of other students as audience. Leschetizky held class sessions during which time a student would perform in front of the other students—150—as a class, with the professor himself sitting at the other piano (Newcomb 1921, 32). Student populations differed. Assistants might be used to prepare students for a lesson with the master (Bomberger 2001, 129).

Chopin did not accept children or beginners as students. The core of his students consisted of ladies of the Faubourg St-Germain or the Slavonic aristocracy exiled in Paris, whose social status effectively forbade them from performing in public except for charity functions (Eigeldinger 1986, 4–5 and 9). Each lesson lasted theoretically between forty-five minutes and an hour, but sometimes extended over hours, particularly on Sundays, for the benefit of the gifted student whom he particularly liked (6). During the lesson, the student sat at the large Pleyel,[7] while Chopin sat at a small upright piano. Preferring students to play from the score rather than memory, he would mark the score as it lay on the music stand (11). He worked simultaneously with music and words and might play a piece from beginning to end (12).

Valerie's lessons with Liszt were usually two hours. The content varied, as did Liszt's mood. Lesson seven, for example, was about fugues. During the lesson, Liszt discovered that Valerie's timing was not quite precise and that she dragged her fingers for no apparent reason. On this occasion he explained his system of legato (Bossier [1928] 1973, xii). For the most part, however, Liszt used the plan of the master class; all could play for each other while benefiting from the master's wisdom (Dubal 1989, 169). American pianist William Mason recalls playing for two or three hours during his first lesson with Liszt. He explains that Liszt never taught a regular lesson in the pedagogical sense. He would notify "the boys" to appear at a certain hour at which time he would call on a student to play for him (1901, 98).

Amy Fay's lessons with Deppe usually lasted three hours, as he liked to have time to express himself and did not like to be hurried. "He likes to have plenty of time to express all his ideas and tell you a good many anecdotes in between!" (Fay [1880] 2011, 304). She characterizes her lessons as a genuine musical excitement, always. In every one is something so new and unexpected and something I've never dreamed of before that I am lost in astonishment and administration (318). Instead of saying "Oh you'll get this after years of practice," he showed how to conquer the difficulty now (319). To overcome her difficulties in playing, he counseled her to be patient and "do what I tell you" (287).

Having more than 100 students in his school, Leschetizky's students were initially taught by an assistant until ready for a lesson with him (Newcomb 1921, 95–101), although not all pupils had a lesson or had only one or two with him (Gardner 1901, 89). There were all kinds of lessons—poor lessons by good pupils and good lessons by pupils he expected little of; however, if a pupil had no rhythmic sense, it was better to study with someone else unless one had real heroism (Newcomb 1921, 23). Often, little playing occurred. Sometimes Leschetizky listened to a piece through in silence and then asked if the student liked it that way; more often there was a great deal of conversation. If played well, he would ask whether the student wanted to play the piece in class, recommending it as good practice (26). During the lesson, Leschetizky rarely refrained from expressing himself with the utmost frankness and honesty, according to his impressions (97).

Recalling his lessons with Vengerova, Rezits describes her as listening passively to his playing during his first three lessons, allowing him to review some of his old pieces, and offering a number of general suggestions. For the fourth lesson he was assigned a Beethoven sonata, and

> from the moment I started to play on that fateful day, Madame's wrath was upon me. Everything was wrong—phrasing, tone, finger movement, arm movement, wrist movement, shoulder movement, articulation, dynamic structure, balance. I was especially thankful that I hadn't played too many wrong notes.

From that time on, the essence of Madame's teaching was to "infiltrate my musical being, and to this day I am often guided by either a direct application or a newly discovered interpretation of her musical principles." In one word, the essence of her teaching was "perspective"—constantly evaluating and reevaluating in order to place every aspect of music—or of life—in proper perspective (Rezits 1965, 2).

Curcio was adept at tailoring each lesson to the individual student (Ashley 1993, 17). She is reported to have said that she had never given two lessons alike because no two students are the same (30). Generally, however, the student had the opportunity to play through the piece, or a large section in the case of a multi-movement composition, without interruption. Then after some general comments, they would begin working from the opening, proceeding thoroughly and, at times, very slowly. Frequently, she would demonstrate, sitting next to the student and practicing the troublesome spot together. A physical problem would be analyzed until the student could do it; if a musical problem, she would show what she meant and have the student try to be sure the idea was understood. She did not believe in just saying more practice but believed in staying with the passage until the student grasped it. Ashley characterizes the lessons as often exhausting but also exhilarating (17–18).

Pressler's lessons were demanding. The basic requirements for the student included arriving on time; providing two copies of the score—one for him and another for the student—the student's own copies, not from the library; bringing pencils and a way of recording the lesson; knowing all the markings; and if an ensemble, having time to practice together and learn each other's part. If the basic requirements were not met, the lesson got off on the wrong foot (Brown 2009, 49). Within a lesson, Pressler would model the depth of tone needed for melodies, suggest fingering and redistribution of the hands, shape the desired musical inflection for musical lines, voice the chords, and use the pedals to create a multitude of effects (50–51). Additionally, Pressler explains that he does not have visitors in his lessons, because "when you are alone with a student it is different from when someone is there" (46–47).

Beyond the Lesson

For the historical pedagogue, the responsibilities of teaching and musical learning did not stop at the end of the lesson. The interactions between teacher and students often extended to other activities beyond the lesson. Moscheles delighted in organizing small fetes, where his pupils could meet him on equal terms and the classical musician would cheerfully put aside Beethoven and Mozart and play a waltz or polka for the merry dancers

([1873] 1970, 358–59). Leschetizky's classes were great occasions—singers, actors, and painters were usually present (Newcomb 1921, 33).

Moscheles was a true friend. To any deserving pupil about to leave the Conservatoire he gave credentials, which were sure to be of value to the recipient. These were honestly and scrupulously worded, and thus became the best passports for an aspiring artist. From his diary:

> As regards my pupils, I don't allow myself to be trifled with; I have fought a battle for some of them. In the composition of the programmes for the Pupil Concerts, I will not stand any favoritism; each and all shall have their turn, according to their merits. ([1873] 1970, 359)

He also listened to artists visiting Leipzig who called on and played for him. In an 1847 diary entry, he writes:

> It is my duty to show that one can play the piano without hammering; that such a thing as a pianissimo can be obtained without a soft pedal. The pedals are auxiliaries; whoever makes them of primary importance puts in evidence the incapacity of his own fingers. (338)

Leschetizky wanted his students to become musicians, as well as "mere pianists." His approval required the serious cultivation of chamber music; the study of composition; and, among other things, the ability to accompany singers. "To play the piano, one must understand composition and be a singer and accompanist all together" (Newcomb 1921, 228).

Vengerova insisted upon a constant improvement in the student's general and musical culture and tried to foster a strong sense of application.

> When you play a Beethoven sonata, you must also form an idea of all other Beethoven sonatas. While playing a work of a certain composer, you must become familiar with the historical era of his time, his biography, his ideas, and the musicians who influenced his creative imagination. You must also study scholarly and literary works devoted to this composer. (Rezits 1995, 39)

Curcio had a strong sense of mission in developing pianists who wanted to teach and do it well, knowing the difference that good teaching makes in one's progress and possible career (Ashley 1993, 19). Acknowledging that it takes so much energy and patience to teach properly, she tried to make her students aware of the problems they would encounter as teachers and inspire them to the level of dedication required of good teaching. She spoke of teaching as "such an enormous responsibility to the student, the composer, and the great musical achievements of our heritage" (29–30).

SUMMARY AND CONCLUSION: IMAGES
OF THE PIANO TEACHER

Popular fiction and nonfiction and student memoirs describing historical pedagogues establish the contemporary piano teacher and teaching within a sociocultural context. The kindly elderly woman and unwilling student of the children's literature mirror the experiences of many piano students. The adult fictional and nonfictional depictions of extreme personalities, common in the literature, are a sad commentary on the profession of piano teacher. In contrast, Conroy (1993), albeit fiction, and Goldsworthy (2010) and Tunstall (2008) describe flesh and bones human beings with strengths and weaknesses. Historical memoirs reveal the personalities and teaching philosophies of major figures in piano pedagogy, who were very human, even challenging personalities. Pervading these accounts are personal qualities of commitment, dedication to profession, love of music, joy in developing talents of another, desire/even obligation to pass on the tradition, and caring about students. The identified qualities of a good teacher (i.e., personality and temperament, knowing each student, methods or lack of recognizing the individuality of each student's playing, and responsibility of the student) and arenas of the lesson and beyond the lesson remain relevant to piano teaching, today.

NOTES

1. Although preferring her work not to be seen as autobiographical, Jellinek, who was a conservatory student, has said in interviews that the book contains many autobiographical elements (2010, Introduction).
2. Another contemporary documentary, albeit focused more on a love of playing than teaching, is the 2014 Academy Award winning film *The Lady in Number 6*, which chronicles the life of Czech pianist and Holocaust survivor Alice Herz-Sommer.
3. Seymour Bernstein (1927) may be familiar to the reader from the recent documentary *Seymour Bernstein: An Introduction*, directed by Ethan Hawke.
4. Artur Schnabel (Austrian 1882–1951) was a child prodigy, student of Leschetizky, and successful pianist. He taught at Berlin Hochschule für Musik. From 1939 until his death he lived in New York (Randel 1978, 449).
5. Johann Baptist Cramer, concert pianist and teacher, established a music publishing house in England, composed numerous piano works, and wrote a pedagogical series *Grosse Praktische Pianoforte Schule* in 1815 (Randal 1978, 124).
6. Reference is to Charles-Louis Hanon's (1819–1900) compilation of piano technique exercises. He suggested playing through his entire book of exercises daily, promising that working the fingers vigorously for this hour (or more) would result in evenness and security (Uszler et al. 1995, 310).
7. Ignaz Joseph Pleyel (1757–1831), pianist, piano manufacturer, and composer founded a well-known piano factory, bearing his name, in London in 1807 (Randel 1978, 395). Reference is to the piano bearing his name.

Chapter 2

Historical Pedagogical Treatises

*Perspectives on Piano Teaching
and the Piano Teacher*

An excursion into a music store or Internet search of Sheetmusicplus.com reveals numerous piano instruction series, color- or number-coded according to the level of difficulty; materials geared to the adult student; and books on specific topics (e.g., finger power, scales, rhythm, and technique) available to contemporary piano teachers.[1] Pedagogical tools for piano are, however, not a recent development. Exploring selected early pedagogical treatises, identified through library searches on such terms as piano teaching and piano pedagogy, this chapter situates the contemporary piano teacher and teaching within its historical context. From the treatises on piano pedagogy (1) generally recognized requisites essential to creating beautiful piano music and (2) historical pedagogical perspectives on the roles, responsibilities, and qualities of a good piano teacher are extrapolated. Influenced by changes in the physical properties of the instrument; research interests; and prevailing philosophies, the methods[2] advocated and expectations of the piano teacher and piano teaching vary over time. Differences notwithstanding, the requisites and qualities identified are fundamental to the development of an approach to and the practice of teaching piano, whatever century.

IDENTIFYING HISTORICAL TREATISES
ON PIANO PEDAGOGY

Even until the end of the nineteenth century, the majority of piano teachers applied texts on keyboard methods to the study of piano (Kochevitsky 1967, 3). Changes in the instrument, however, demanded new and exclusive techniques for teaching piano (Parakilas 2001, 113). Early piano resources might include exercises for the student; brief descriptions of the goals of each exercise (e.g., equal force of fingering or acquiring flexibility); or explanatory commentary with exercises on notes, clefs, and scales. Among the earliest master teachers of piano to publish teaching materials were the Italian-born Muzio Clementi ([1801] 1974) and Austrian Karl Czerny ([1837/43] 1982), a student of Beethoven. During the nineteenth and twentieth centuries, the sciences of anatomy, physics (mechanics and acoustics), psychology, and neurophysiology (brain and central nervous system) influenced piano pedagogy and methods, although the underlying science was not always accurate (Uszler et al. 1995, 295–96).

Searches of the Library of Congress and New York Public Library online catalogs and databases (RISM, RIPM, RILM),[3] using the terms "piano teaching," "piano lesson," "piano pedagogy," and "piano instruction" identified piano teaching treatises by pedagogues of different nationalities and keyboard traditions, dating back to the 1800s. A further search of these catalogs and databases using the names of influential piano pedagogues, particularly those mentioned by interviewees, yielded additional titles. Examples of nineteenth- and twentieth-century publications on piano pedagogy with explanatory text, shown in Table 2.1, were reviewed.[4] Although not an exhaustive list of schools of piano pedagogy, each is a systematic study of piano.[5] Appendix A provides additional information on the named pedagogues.

Table 2.1 Selected Historical Piano Pedagogical Treatises

Pedagogue	Dates	National Origin	Publication
Muzio Clementi	1752–1832	Italian	*Introduction to the Art of Playing on the Pianoforte.* ([1801] 1974). Primer for beginning piano students.
Carl Czerny	1791–1857	Austrian	*Letters to a Young Lady, on the Art of Playing Pianoforte.* ([1837/43] 1982). Letters to a fictitious pupil describing methods and process for piano study.
John Freckleton Burrowes	1787–1852	British	*The Piano-Forte Primer: Containing the Rudiments of Music: Calculated Either for Private Tuition or Teaching in Classes.* (1840). Basic concepts of music.

Pedagogue	Dates	National Origin	Publication
Louis Plaidy	1787–1852	German	*The Piano Teacher* (Der Klavierlehrer). (1875). Rules and principles essential to playing (e.g., reading notes, techniques, and musical delivery) to master.
Theodor Leschetizky	1830–1915	Polish	Malwine Brée. *The Leschetizky Method: An Exposition of His Personal Views.* (1913). Leschetizky's methods, published by his teaching assistant with his approval.
Ludwig Deppe	1828–1890	German	Elizabeth Caland. *Artistic Piano Playing as Taught by Ludwig Deppe.* (1903). Student's description of Deppe's methods.
Tobias Matthay	1858–1945	British	*The First Principles of Pianoforte Playing.* (1905). Method of teaching based on the observation of physical and psychological aspects of playing.
Hans Schneider	1863–1926	U.S.	*The Working of the Mind in Piano Teaching and Playing.* (1923). Piano playing as mind work first and muscular second.
Josef Lhevinne	1874–1944	Russian	*Basic Principles of Pianoforte Playing.* ([1924] 1972). Statement of principles based on experience in performance and teaching.
Josef Hofmann	1876–1957	Polish	*Piano Playing: With Piano Questions Answered.* ([1920] 1976). Tricks of correct piano playing (e.g., touch, practicing, and pedaling).
Abby Whiteside	1881–1956	U.S.	*Indispensables of Piano Playing.* (1961). A synthesis of piano teaching.

(*Continued*)

Table 2.1   Selected Historical Piano Pedagogical Treatises (*Continued*)

Pedagogue	Dates	National Origin	Publication
Heinrich Neuhaus	1888–1964	Russian	*The Art of Piano Playing.* (1973). Thoughts on music and methods written in conversational style.
Seymour Bernstein	1927–	U.S.	*With Your Own Two Hands.* (1981). Practicing, discipline, and fulfillment of performing, directed toward the amateur and professional pianist.

Memoirs by American pianists and teachers, William Mason (1901) and Louise Stroud (1989), and collections of interviews with contemporary great pianists, although focused primarily on performance careers (Marcus 1979; Mach 1991a; and Grindea 2009), offer additional reflections on piano teaching.

PIANO TEACHING: PERSPECTIVES ON FINGERING, PEDALING, SOUND/TONE, DAILY PRACTICE, AND ARTISTIC IMAGE

Good fingering, pedaling, sound/tone, and daily practice, alone, do not make a pianist, but they are requisites of playing to be mastered by the piano student. Beyond good technique is that additional "something" that marks the virtuoso—the artistic image (i.e., the meaning, content, expression, the what-it-is-all-about) (Neuhaus 1973, 7–29). Opinions regarding each requisite vary over time, geographically, and by pedagogical school and individual pedagogical preference. For example, emphasis on the mechanical side of playing is found in many mid-nineteenth-century pedagogical publications (e.g., Plaidy 1875) (see Uszler et al. 1995, 310–11). Additionally, whether and to what extent a text addresses each requisite varies with the age and/or instructional level of the intended student audience. While Clementi's primer, believed to be directed toward the inexperienced student, does not mention pedaling ([1801] 1974, Introduction, xiv), Leschetizky emphasized the relationship between proper pedaling and good playing (Brée 1913, 49–50). Pedagogical perspectives on these requisites demonstrate continuity and change in piano teaching.

Fingering

As a keyboard instrument, the point of contact between the player and the piano is the fingers. Most performers agree that good fingering[6] is the sine qua non in expressing music on an instrument, for it not only affords you ease and accuracy at fast tempos but also comfort and control in slow passages (Bernstein 1981, 46–47). Accordingly, an understanding of touch and the movement of the fingers on the keyboard is basic to the creation of the desired musical effect.

Position at the Keyboard: Body, Hands, and Fingers

Early piano teaching drew on the general keyboard literature, for example, the works of Francois Couperin ([1717] 1933) and Daniel Gottlob Türk ([1789] 1982).[7] Written for harpsichord and clavichord, respectively, these texts consider the position of the body and fingers relative to the keyboard (Couperin [1717] 1933, 11–14; and Türk [1789] 1982, 31–32 and 129–42). Couperin recommends choosing a chair that allows the elbows, wrists, and fingers to all be on one level ([1717] 1933, 11). To use hands and fingers without constraint and with the necessary ease, Türk advises: sit exactly in front of one-lined c, so that the highest and lowest notes may be comfortably reached; position the body approximately ten to fourteen inches from the keyboard; and sit in such a way that the elbow is noticeably higher by several inches than the hand ([1789] 1982, 31–32). Pedagogical thought on the physical aspects of playing continues to develop in the piano texts.

The Body. The earliest treatises on piano teaching provide instructions on how to sit when playing the piano. Clementi advises holding the hand and arm in a horizontal position, neither depressing nor raising the wrist; the seat should be adjusted accordingly; and all unnecessary motion must be avoided ([1801] 1974, 14–15). Czerny counsels his imaginary student, Cecilia, to sit exactly facing the middle of the keyboard; the seat must be just so high that the elbows, when hanging down freely may be a very little less elevated than the upper surface of the keys ([1837/43] 1982, 3–4). Deppe required the use of a low chair so that the elbow is a trifle lower than the white keys when the hand is laid on the keyboard; the forearm should form a right angle with the keyboard (Caland 1903, 26). Leschetizky compared sitting at the piano to riding a horse: "Sit easy and erect at the piano, like a good rider on his horse, and yield to the arm movements, as far as needed, just as the horseman yields to the movements of his steed" (Brée 1913, 5).

Hands and Fingers. Placement of the hands and fingers relative to the keyboard is fundamental to playing the instrument. Ideas about and approaches to finger strength, finger technique, and the relationship of the wrist, forearm, and total body to the production of sound change and evolve not in isolation from the historical and social context. By way of example, during the nineteenth century (the so-called Machine Age), the idea that piano playing was a machine-like activity, emphasizing the development of equality of finger strength, appeared in piano texts and extended to piano teaching (Parakilas

2001, 116–17; and Uszler et al. 1995, 310–11). Czerny instructs Cecelia on how to employ the various degrees of power of each finger to produce the most exact equality of strength, in point of quickness, and in holding the notes down ([1837/43] 1982, 16–17). The emphasis on developing uniform finger strength led to the invention of a variety of devices, such as the chiroplast, designed by Johann Bernhard Logier for the supposed purpose of strengthening weaker fingers to the level of others (Parakilas 2001, 118; and Rainbow 2009).[8]

The influence of science on the evolving piano pedagogy is reflected in efforts to apply scientific principles to the playing of the piano. Among the leading advocates of a scientific approach to piano playing was the early twentieth-century British pedagogue, Tobias Matthay, who expounded through his writings and teaching what he regarded as compliance with the laws of science (Siek 2012, 2; and Uszler et al. 1995, 329–31). Matthay developed a complex analysis of the physical aspects of piano playing—finger movement, hand movement, arm movement (e.g., 1905 and [1912] 2012). He asserts that "finger-technique" or "finger individualization," depending on the correct application of the forearm rotational adjustments, is a paramount requirement of the pianist ([1912] 2012, 414). His writings are not easy to read, nor encompass (Uszler et al. 1995, 330).

With the assistance of the device or the correct application of principles, a student, any student, could learn to play the piano or correct bad habits. Playing the piano was not restricted to the genius. Logier claimed a student could play without knowing a note of music by merely observing the marks of his machine (Rainbow 2009, 117; and Loesser 2015, 295–98). Matthay asserted that any pupil found to be lacking or unsound as to power and control of "finger" must set it right by understanding the requirements. "[H]owever bad the pupil's technical habits, and provided he is not below average intelligence, he can hereby *at once* be made to provide perfectly correct and easy technique" (Matthay [1912] 2012, 414).

Fingering to Produce the Best Effect

A recurring theme in the keyboard and piano literature is that the best fingering is that which produces the desired effect. As a general rule, the easiest fingering, requiring the least movement, is considered the best. Türk asserts that the most comfortable fingering—what requires the least movement of the hand is generally regarded as being the best ([1789] 1982, 129). According to Clementi, the great basis of the art of fingering is to produce the best effect, by the easiest means ([1801] 1974, 14). Czerny directed—choose that mode of fingering by which one most easily and naturally is able to maintain a tranquil and fine position of the hands, firm and perpendicular percussion, as well as a correct holding down of the keys, and a beautiful and connected performance of the melody and of the scales and runs ([1837/43] 1982, 25–26). Leschetizky held that a fingering that is easy may be taken as correct, if the effect of the music is not injured (Brée 1913, 56). Lhevinne favored the easiest position as always the best. The fingering must be the best possible for the given passage; it must be adhered to in every successive performance ([1924] 1972, 34). Neuhaus's third principle of fingering is that it should be convenient for the hand in question taking into account the peculiarities of the pianist's intentions (1973, 145). A contemporary reference is "economy of fingering."

While generally recommending adherence to the prescribed fingering, historical and contemporary pedagogues recognize that there may be exceptions. Leschetizky advocates using the given fingering, or that usually adopted, if it seems good but to seek new fingerings suited to special hands only when it proves necessary or advisable. He notes that fingering cannot always be printed on a piece because the hands of different size and reach will take the same passages differently (Brée 1913, 56). Similarly, Hofmann admits that the great diversity of fingering prohibits a universal fingering, all the variety of fingering ought to be based on the principle of natural sequel ([1920] 1976, 36).

Nevertheless, rules are not to be broken without careful thought—effect is most important. Clementi lays out a process:

> The effect, being of the highest importance, is first consulted; the way to accomplish it is then devised, and that mode of fingering is preferred which gives the best effect tho' (*sic*) not always the easiest to perform. ([1801] 1974, 14)

Leschetizky cautioned that rules must not be broken by mere caprice; there should always be an improvement in effect or facility to justify an irregular fingering (Brée 1913, 56). Hofmann counsels, if a player is confused, a teacher should be consulted; a good one will gladly help ([1920] 1976, 36). To determine good fingering for a difficult passage, Bernstein advises taking it up to tempo even if the student cannot negotiate it correctly: Be daring! Even if you make mistakes, you will nonetheless find out whether or not the fingering in your edition or the one devised by your teacher will eventually work (1981, 47).

Pedaling

Often, particularly during the early years of piano study, pedaling is considered only as a matter of down and up—when to depress the (right) damper pedal to hold the sound and when to raise it. Inattention to the pedal is not a new issue. Amy Fay notes that Deppe was the first to teach her the intricacies of pedaling ([1880] 2011, 297–98). Even less discussed is the (left) soft pedal—una corda.[9] Hofmann advises: "Train you ears and then use both pedals honestly" ([1920] 1976, 48). Seymour Bernstein observes that a skillful use of both pedals can spell the difference between a good and a truly artistic performance (1981, 143).

Damper Pedal Touch

As with fingering, the pedagogical treatises direct how to position the foot and use the pedal. Deppe's one general rule of pedaling was that the foot, hovering lightly over the pedal, should be so under the control of the player that its impact thereon is inaudible. The manipulation of the pedal should be so noiseless, so unostentatious, that no thought of its mechanism is obtruded on the sight or hearing of the listener (Caland 1903, 61). Bernstein advises positioning the right foot on the pedal with the heel firmly rooted to the floor. The heel must never leave the floor; it not only enables you to depress and lift pedal with greater control but serves as a fulcrum for grounding the body (1981, 146). The pedagogues emphasize the importance of pedal study both to produce the desired and avoid negative effects. Lhevinne specifies that the pedal should be used with the same intelligence and definiteness as the fingers and should be applied in the fraction of a second and released at just the right moment ([1924] 1972, 47). Leschetizky notes that for many good people (but bad performers) the pedal is a device for trampling on good taste and crushing it under foot (Brée 1913, 49).

Learning to use the pedal to produce the desired effect demands careful study and attention, including understanding the relationship of pedaling to fingering and sound and tone. Leschetizky underscores the great assistance of the pedal to fingering, as it links intervals that cannot be stretched by the hand alone, allowing the hand to leave the chords in time to play the next one (Brée 1913, 56). In coordinating fingering and pedaling, the pedal may be depressed simultaneously (regular)—when the note or chord is struck—or syncopated (legato)—after the note or chord is struck (e.g., Neuhaus 1973, 158; and Lhevinne [1924] 1972, 47). The damper pedal may be used not only to reinforce the tone and link separate notes together but to produce special effects sought by the performer. Lhevinne writes that pedaling is all in the knowing how ([1924] 1972, 47). That "know how" is reflected in the instructions of Lhevinne, Neuhaus, and Bernstein, among others, on depressing the pedal to different levels—full, half pedal (partially down), or quarter (minimum depression), or just touch—to produce different effects (Lhevinne [1924] 1972, 47; Neuhaus 1973, 157; and Bernstein 1981, 147).

Soft Pedal, Una Corda

The use of the soft pedal requires careful study as well. Nevertheless, very often students must discover for themselves how to use the right pedal since teachers all too frequently neglect to discuss its use (Bernstein 1981, 143). The pedagogues held different opinions on the use of the soft pedal, ranging from no use to judiciously, and not only to lessen sound but as a coloristic device. Emphasizing the importance of the performer having power and control over playing pianissimo, early pedagogues, including Burrowes and Deppe, might recommend its use only when expressing indicated by the composer (e.g., Burrowes 1840, 32 and Caland 1903, 64). In contrast, Leschetizky notes the value of the soft pedal for the veiled quality of the tone that it produces, which is useful in pianissimo passages and of value in ending a diminuendo with extreme delicacy (Brée 1913, 50).

Later pedagogues highlight the soft pedal's value as a coloristic device. Whiteside observes, while of very little value for merely playing more softly, the soft pedal can be used most effectively in producing a subdued passage, followed by a sparkling passage when it is released (1961, 64). Bernstein advises using the soft pedal judiciously to create effects otherwise impossible to achieve with two hands. Its purpose is not simply to lessen sound but as coloristic device, lessening the percussive effect (1981, 150–52). Hofmann explains that the left pedal should not be regarded as a license to neglect the formation of a fine *pianissimo* touch or cloak or screen a defective *pianissimo* but should serve exclusively as a means of coloring where the softness of tone is coupled with what the jewelers call "dull finish" ([1920] 1976, 48).

Sound/Tone

Fingering, pedaling, and other aspects of technique affect the creation of sound/tone. Instructions on how to produce beautiful tone reflect the principles and emphases of the various traditions. Deppe emphasizes the "feather-light" hand: "Your elbow must be *lead* and your wrist a *feather*" (Caland, 1903, 46). Leschetizy stresses the relationship of the fingertips to tone: Notice the fingertips carefully and see that they strike the keys accurately, for that is the only way to obtain a full, strong tone (Brée 1913, 7). Matthay asserts that correctness in expression (correspondence of tonal-result with that intended) depends on applying one's work in answer to the key's resistance, and before it is too late to do so (1905, 128).

An emphasis on sound and tone is attributed to Russian pianism. Neuhaus specifies that the subject is not sound in general, but the tone produced by the pianist's hand on the piano; tone is the substance of music; in ennobling and perfecting it we raise music itself to a greater height. He defines the mastery of tone as the first and most important task of all the problems of piano technique that the pianist must tackle, noting that three-quarters of all work with his students is on tone (1973, 56–57). For Lhevinne, a beautiful tone involves mind and body, that is, in addition to the ability to conceive a beautiful tone mentally, the richness and singing quality of the tone depend very largely upon the amount of key surface covered with the well-cushioned part of the finger and the natural "spring" which accompanies the loose wrist ([1924] 1972, 25).

The question arises: Can less-favored musicians with ordinary, normal talents attain the production of beautiful tone and artistic interpretation of the composition? Noting how we delight from the natural grace and unassuming simplicity with which the great artists render the hardest and most involved passages, Deppe argues that if certain laws underlying this beauty of executing could only be discovered and systematized, then less-favored musicians could at least hope to do so (Caland, 1903, 15–16). Handed down through the pedagogues, the advice to the student wishing to create a beautiful tone is to "listen" carefully and well during your practice, as well as during a performance. Deppe advises Amy Fay: "Horen Sie Sich spielen" (Listen to your own playing) ([1880] 2011, 287). Bernstein writes, "when you practice, nothing must escape you. For if your practicing is to be productive, you must be aware of every sound you produce. Moreover, you can train yourself to listen inwardly to sounds which originate in your mind's ear. . . . All of this demands the greatest concentration possible" (1981, 116). Listening properly during your practicing is an art (117). Self-criticism is a further step in correct playing, according to Leschetizky: "He who can criticise his own work as keenly as he would that of another is well advanced" (Brée 1913, 58).

Daily Practice

Originally part of the piano lesson, practicing became an activity in itself. Instructions in pedagogical texts vary on the length and regime of practice recommended.

Length of Practice

Despite differences of opinion regarding the desirable length of practice time, the recommendations reflect common pedagogical concerns—the goal of the student, quality of practicing, dangers of over-practicing, and maintaining concentration. Czerny advises Cecelia that practicing an hour, possibly two in addition to her daily hour lesson, would enable her to forever conquer all that is difficult or tedious in the elementary branches of playing but with only three hours of practicing with the determination to excel she would be able, by degrees, to attain a very commanding degree of excellence ([1837/43] 1982, 9 and 29). Leschetizky warns that piano practice should never become a thoughtless throwing-off of exercises by the hour or by the number (Brée 1913, 57). Deppe required his students to practice two hours daily but no more than three; practicing any longer was no profit whatever to the player because it became mechanical. Progress in music is dependent largely on the mental vigor which the student brings to bear on his daily task and excessive keyboard work is as prejudicial to mental freshness as it is injurious to physical health (Caland 1903, 54).

Similarly, twentieth-century pedagogues emphasize the necessity of concentration for effective practicing and the dangers of over-practicing. Hofmann underscores the importance of the quality of the time spent practicing, specifically, concentration: remember that in studying the matter of quantity is of a moment only when coupled with quality. Attention, concentration, and devotion will make unnecessary any inquiries as to how much you ought to practice ([1920] 1976, Questions 49). Lhevinne advocates four hours a day of practice, advising that over-practicing is just as bad as under-practicing. He counsels the reader to avoid worry and distraction while practicing, as the value of practicing is lessened if the mind is not every minute on what you are doing. By intense concentration, love of your work, and the spirit in which you approach it, you can do more in a half hour than in an hour spent purposelessly. "Do not think you have been practicing, if you have played a single note with your mind on anything else" (1921, 151–52; and [1924] 1972, 43–44). "You must be happier while you are practicing than when you are doing anything else" (152). Bernstein dedicates an entire chapter to concentration and how to acquire the facility of concentration in practice (1981, 39–61).

Practice Regime

Expectations regarding how practicing time is to be spent—activities and time spent on particular activities—also vary. For Plaidy, the lesson provided a model for the student's practice—begin with finger exercises; followed by etudes and pieces for performance; and, if time, playing with four hands (1875, 29–30). Lhevinne advised always dividing practice periods—doing technic (*sic*) at one time and pieces at another ([1924] 1972, 44). Neuhaus advocated spending about four hours working on repertoire and technique and two hours on getting acquainted with music in general (1973, 194).

While daily practicing was usually to include exercises (e.g., scales, finger exercises, and memory drill); review of old work; and learning new pieces, opinions differ as to how to practice them. Clementi advises daily practice of scales in all the major keys, with their relative minors ([1801] 1974, 15). Leschetizky recommends playing all the finger exercises with a light touch at first, and above all play them evenly, with all the fingers giving equal power of tone (Brée 1913, 7). Viewing piano playing as mind work first and muscular second, Schneider, describes practicing as the coordinations and exchanges between mind and muscle; constant repetition results in habit, reflex action, and in economy of muscular energy (1923, 78). To the contrary, Whiteside asserts that practice should never mean working without any of the fun that is attached to playing, and, therefore, advocates completely discarding Czerny and Hanon, as there is no time to waste on dull literature. The mechanism can be coordinated expertly only when there is excitement and intensity of desire for accomplishment in the practice period (1961, 50).

Artistic Image

Beyond technique, the Russian pedagogue Neuhaus asserts that artistic image—reflection on the emotional content of the music as well as its intellectual context—is quintessential to making a pupil who plays well, plays as an artist (1973, 24–29). Whoever is moved by music to the depths of his soul, and works on his instrument like one possessed, who loves music and his instrument with passion, will acquire virtuoso technique; he will be able to recreate the artistic image of the composition; he will be a performer (29). The real task of the teacher is not merely teaching the student to "play well," but making the student more intelligent, more sensitive, more honest, more equitable, more steadfast—a task that is dictated by art itself (23). The main error of the majority of pedagogues is focusing only on the intellectual aspect of artistic activity, forgetting the other side—the inconvenient X— necessary to recreate the artistic image of the composition (24). Almost a century earlier, Plaidy similarly defined the challenge of the music teacher: the problem is to lead the pupil to that degree of artistic insight, which his musical talent and his mental endowments, generally, enable him to reach (1875, 3). Perhaps leading the student to artistic insight—grasping the artistic image of a piece—is the greatest responsibility of the piano teacher.

THE PIANO TEACHER: ROLES, RESPONSIBILITIES, AND QUALITIES

What are the responsibilities and qualities of a good piano teacher? Pedagogical texts detail the finer points of piano teaching—what needs to be taught, in what order, and what is to take place during a lesson. For purposes of the current study, becoming entangled in the weeds of these technical debates is unnecessary. What are most important are the reflections of the historical pedagogues on the roles; responsibilities; and qualities of a good piano teacher, including, lacking such qualities, who should not teach. Although not all the pedagogical texts reviewed include such philosophical reflections, those that do provide perspective on the piano teaching profession, historically, and remain relevant to any discussion of the profession. Such reflections consider the challenge of finding a good teacher, temperament, knowing the individual student, rational method, reciprocity, beyond the instrument, and promoting the general culture.

Finding a Good Teacher

The early literature identifies the challenge of finding a good teacher. As the issues raised have not lost their salience in two hundred years, Türk's sage remarks about the importance of finding a good teacher are worth repeating.

> The most important thing in the beginning is to find a good teacher. Usually it is
> in this respect where the first mistake is made, for the opinion that the rudiments

can be learned from anyone is almost general. It is believed that money can be saved and the cheapest teacher is engaged which results in actually costing far more than the most experienced teacher. For experience shows that a skilled and conscientious teacher can bring his students further in a few months than a bad teacher can in a whole year. ([1789] 1982, 17)

Having to repair the damage of poor teaching is costly in time, energy, and money.

Moreover, how much time and energy is saved, thereby. For usually the student has to begin over again with a more skilled teacher, after being instructed for several years without correct principles and after much labor finally seeing how ignorant he and his instructor are! And how difficult it is to get rid of old faults which have now become mechanically ingrained. (17)

Seymour Bernstein chronicles his errors in looking for a teacher (2002). Predicating his search for a teacher on one criterion—improving his musical technique—it never occurred to him to weigh a teacher's personal credentials as his or her musical ones (59). Once recognizing that one's teacher is a monster, one rationalizes that this situation does not matter so long as you are making progress. Yet, in the end not only your emotional world but also your musical world is affected by a "monster-teacher" (60). The underlying message is that "musical growth at the expense of one's psychological and emotional stability is simply a losing proposition" (69).

Moreover, reputation alone must never be the chief criterion for choosing a music teacher, just as one would not want to entrust the development of musical talent to an incompetent teacher who is "such a nice person!" (69)

Neuhaus observes that the fullest possible understanding between teacher and pupil is one of the most important conditions for fruitful teaching. "Like unto like" is one of the wisest principles in solving the teacher-pupil problem. That is, "a talented teacher and an ungifted pupil are just as unproductive as an ungifted teacher and a talented pupil" (1973, 170). Who is the "right" piano teacher for a particular student? Even the "best" teacher is not the "right" teacher for every student. Continuing the discussion of the qualities of a good piano teacher, begun in the previous chapter, from the perspective of the pedagogue, provides additional historical context for exploring the qualities of the contemporary piano teacher.

Temperament

Türk, Plaidy, and Schneider counsel patience, a calm temperament, and even love as the essence of the teacher. Türk emphasizes the importance of understanding the weaknesses of others; patience; and knowing how to keep the pupils' respect, not be dull and sullen with them. He notes that with most pupils calm dignity will avail more than angry reproaches and the like ([1789] 1982, 18). Plaidy advises: Let the teacher be quiet and composed, and constantly encourage the pupil; if he makes no progress in one way, let him try another way (1875, 4). To ensure the successful communication of advice from teacher to student, Schneider considers the manner of communication—with sufficient force absolute sincerity—and the receptivity of the student. "Talking to an unwilling, balking child is a useless waste of breath until the mood is changed favorably" (1923, 69). Without being sentimental, perhaps the most important quality of the good piano teacher is love of student, as well as love of music. Plaidy concludes that "it is plain that the teacher who surrenders himself with entire love and self-sacrifice to his scholars is the true artist" (1875, 6).

Recognizing the uniqueness of the teacher-student relationship, fundamental to the teaching of piano, the concern arises that the relationship does not become a long-term dependency. Historical pedagogues articulated awareness of both sides of this issue. Türk notes that the earnest concern of the teacher is to fashion his pupils into able musicians as rapidly as he can ([1789] 1982, 18). Neuhaus considered one of the main tasks of the teacher to be ensuring that as quickly and thoroughly as possible, he is no longer necessary to the pupil and ceases to be a policeman, trainer. The student is to be inculcated with independent thinking, method of work, and knowledge of self and ability to attain his goal (1973, 172). The teacher who is only a teacher may be more vulnerable to developing such a dependency than the teacher who is also a performer (169–70).

Considering temperament raises the question, who should not teach? Central to the world of piano performance is the method of verbally handing down musical ideas and traditions from generation to generation of piano pedagogues (Grindea 2009, vii). Not all pianists, no matter how talented or well-trained, have the temperament to teach. Türk advises—if he is at all lacking in diligence, facility, and natural talent, he should not teach ([1789] 1982, 18). Contemporary British psychologist Roland S. Persson observes that the formidable artist and the formidable pedagogue may be attributes of the same individual but describe different roles and different skills in different contexts (1994, 89).

Knowing the Individual Student

The importance of understanding the individual student not only in terms of musical capabilities but emotional makeup is a recurring theme. The literature emphasizes the teaching of the individual, although providing some advice on how to approach different categories of students (e.g., children and adults).

Capabilities and Person

Focusing on the individual is first a matter of addressing the different capabilities of the student. As Türk observes, because of each student's different capabilities, the teacher must not teach all pupils according to the same plan. Some understand everything quickly, while others require more time and reminders to understand. The pace at which one proceeds and length of the assignments given vary accordingly. With the former the teacher must go at a faster pace so the student keeps in constant practice and the latter must be given shorter assignments ([1789] 1982, 18).

Knowing a student's individuality extends beyond musical ability to the very person. As Neuhaus suggests: How different is the work of a teacher, depending on the person he is teaching (1973, 182)? I think every experienced teacher considers his pupil first and foremost as a personality in spite of the many characteristics he may have in common with others (203). Much earlier Plaidy similarly observed that the teacher must become acquainted with the pupil's individuality, as well as musical capacity. Only when the teacher has gained a clear judgment of the natural endowment of his student can he fix the goal for him, and give a definite direction to his instruction (1875, 3–4).

Later pedagogues introduce the consideration of a student's physical and mental health on piano studies. Focusing on the central nervous system, Schneider observes that it is often necessary to influence the whole temperamental makeup, the whole way of thinking before the student can do musical work. That is, progress is not always bound to the music and keyboard; nothing can be done unless the whole system of the pupil is in a healthy condition and that is as much the work of a competent physician as the music teacher (1923, 65). More recently, Bernstein characterizes the aim of practicing to be good mental health, as defined in principle by psychologists—a balance between emotion and reason within the framework of a healthy, functioning body (although psychologists tend to neglect the body). He believes that it is possible to teach his pupils to harmonize themselves through the techniques of practicing, tackling their emotional problems in the way he knows best—through music (1981, 18–19).

Age of the Student

Children and adult students present different challenges to the teacher, as evidenced by the variety of methods texts available. Adult piano study, as we know it, was not common in all countries and not all early pedagogues taught children (e.g., Chopin and Liszt did not). Nevertheless, specific mention of the differences between teaching adults and children are found in selected historical pedagogical texts. Schneider (1923, 69) underscores the necessity of giving clear and sharp suggestions in language a child can understand—based on the facts of the child's life. He further recommends using a little story leading to the proper point. Leschetizky advises that children should not play exercises for as long a time per day as adults, nor should they be made to attempt intervals suited only to adults (Brée 1913, 75).

Lhevinne counsels that not teaching certain things in the early years results in enormous disadvantages later. Emphasizing the importance of early music education, he compares and contrasts instruction in Russia and the United States. In Russia the teacher of beginners is often a man or a woman of real distinction. The work is not looked upon as ignoble, worthy of only the failures or inferior teacher. These teachers are well paid. In contrast, he observes that in America in the past there must have been some ridiculously bad teachers of elementary work, judging from a few of his so-called advanced pupils, but further notes that many teachers of beginners who have had real professional training for this work are being developed (Lhevinne [1924] 1972, 2).

Matthay focuses on the necessity of teaching technical aspects and content differently to children and adults. For example, in dealing with adults, it is best to devote the first two, three (or more) lessons to general consideration of the main principles and laws that must be obeyed during practice and performance if one would succeed technically and musically, after which the actual teaching of the various touch methods must be proceeded to at once (1905, 121–22). With an intelligent child, one may start with the facts to be learned, as adults but in the simplest and barest outline and focusing on what has to be done not why it has to be done. A child is interested to know "the rules of the game" before starting to play. The teacher must make plain the immediate and practical applications of these rules to hold the child's interest (125). Matthay's impressive success as a teacher may be attributed to his building a rapport with each individual student, providing answers to musical, technical, and psychological problems (Uszler et al. 1995, 330).

North Carolina school music and private piano teacher, Louise Stroud perhaps epitomizes the generally held image of the first piano teacher—the kindly, elderly woman from the neighborhood. She taught hundreds of students from her home (Stroud 1989, 1–6, and 39). Embedded in her memoir are anecdotes, describing her relationships with students and "lessons learned." For example, watch what you say to children even in fun, children will take it quite seriously ("I think I'd like to take a nap. You go ahead with your lesson, but be sure to wake me up when you leave, if I don't hear the bell") (57).

Rational Method

Plaidy emphasizes the need for a rational method, leading quickly to the goal and persistence in following the end set before him (1875, 4). Yet, texts and treatises notwithstanding, well-known pedagogues denied having a method.

Leschetizky is reported to have exclaimed: I have no method and I will have no method (Newcomb 1921, 107). As to method in teaching, he thought that there had always been a deplorable tendency to found systems and methods upon one point of technique—how he himself had suffered from that tendency (99). Yet a monograph on his method, subtitled "an exposition of his views" was published by his student, with his approval (Brée 1913). Matthay, who became known for a technical approach, rather than musical concepts, claimed not to have a method, meaning undoubtedly that he gave neither the same regimen nor the same advice to all of his students (Uszler et al. 1995, 330).

Reciprocity

The discussion of roles and responsibilities has focused on those of the piano teacher. As a reciprocal relationship, the interaction between piano teacher and student is a two-way street. The pedagogical literature highlights not only the responsibility of the student, as part of this equation but the rewards to the teacher.

Türk lays out the responsibility of the student in the two-way interaction. He advises the student to follow assiduously the instruction of the teacher and never to act according to his own judgment; trust in the master, receiving instructions with gratitude; and if directed to repeat certain passages until they are executed directly, do not become vexed. Additionally, if the student does not understand why this or that is to be, ask the teacher for the reason or further explanation, so as not to become a mechanical musician ([1789] 1982, 18–19).

Bernstein considers the responsibilities and reward of the reciprocal relationship. On the one hand, the teacher must care not only about the student's practicing but the individual response to music. Such caring draws student and teacher into a closer bond, transcending mere music instruction; it means the teacher cares about the student personally. The teacher must earn the student's respect by being an example of excellence, both musically and personally, and practicing so as to remain the eternal student throughout his or her teaching career. Just as the teacher encourages the student's best self, so can the student strive to do so for the teacher—all relationships flourish in reciprocity. The most effective way in which the student can encourage the teacher is by practicing (1981, 14–15).

The fruits of reciprocity—gifts from student to teacher are acknowledged by Neuhaus, who observes that his students gave to him no less, if not more, than he gave to them. Expressing gratitude for their joint striving to know and master art, which was the foundation of our friendship, intimacy, and mutual respect, he characterizes these sentiments as among the best that one can experience on this planet (1973, 203).

Beyond the Instrument

Historical pedagogues recognized that even within the lesson, the role of the teacher extends beyond the transference of skills. While defining the primary challenge of the music teacher to be that of leading the student to artistic insight, Plaidy also identifies other conditions indispensably required of a good teacher, including not only a most thorough knowledge of the musical instrument but a comprehensive musical culture and the gift of making himself intelligible (1875, 3–4). Similarly, Schneider (1923, 69) defines teaching as leading, making a pupil do what he generally would not do by himself, arousing interest in matters which are foreign and new to him.

Twentieth-century pedagogues of different nationalities and traditions acknowledge that the role of piano teacher extends beyond the transfer of skills, beyond the instrument. Neuhaus distinguishes between mere teaching and educating the student.

> I believe that the task of consolidating and developing the talent of a pupil, and not merely of teaching him to "play well," in other words, of making him more intelligent, more sensitive, more honest, more equitable, more steadfast . . . is a real task which, if not fully attainable, is none the less dictated by the times we live in and by art itself, and is at all times dialectically justified. (Neuhaus 1973, 23)

Pressler defines teaching as giving, giving to his students what he has received.

> An artist is the outcome of one's tradition and background, and I want to pass this on to younger musicians, to bring in them an awareness of what the instrument demands, how to develop an understanding of styles, as well as the skill to interpret what the composers mean to convey, and many other aspects of teaching. (Grindea 2009, 240)

English pedagogue Fanny Waterman, whose students include a number of prize-winning artists, characterizes teaching as the greatest profession and a piano teacher, especially, has very special trust and great responsibility because of the one-to-one relationship. "The teacher is expected to be a good musician, a good psychologist and know the craft, how it has to be done and how to express this clearly to the pupil" (Grindea 2009, 23).

Promoting the General Culture

The role of the piano teacher was also considered to extend beyond teaching the genius to society, as a means of raising the culture of the entire society. Plaidy notes that quicker and better results may be obtained by instruction with a pupil who has talent but still something must be reached in the end, even with the less gifted who strive to make good what is wanting through preserving diligence in study (1875, 4–5). Neuhaus was convinced that a dialectically designed method and school must encompass all degrees of talent— from the musically deficient (since such, too, must study music, for music is a vehicle of culture just as any other) to natural genius (1973, 8–9). The end is not only the individual but society. One cannot create talent, but one can create culture, which is the soil on which talent prospers and flourishes (171). What is general in our task and from which all particular aspects and details flow, is the need to create a high level of musical culture worthy of our people and the great times in which we live (203).

The relationship between piano teaching and the general culture in the U.S. context is complex. Early students of piano often traveled abroad for advanced piano studies, as described in the memoirs referenced in the previous chapter. At the turn of the nineteenth century, American pedagogue, William Mason, observed that it was no longer necessary for piano students to study abroad, as piano teachers of first rank, including his former students, could be found in the principal U.S. cities. Moreover, these teachers were able to secure better results with American students than foreign teachers do "because they have a better understanding of our national character and temperament" (1901, 261). The relationship between the broader socioculture context and approaches to piano teaching, in practice, remains a consideration of contemporary U.S. teachers of piano.

SUMMARY AND CONCLUSION: PAST AND PRESENT PIANO TEACHING—COMMON THREADS

The early treatises on piano pedagogy provide an historical context within which to explore contemporary piano teaching. Among the factors considered in developing an approach to piano teaching, the requisites extrapolated from the historical pedagogical literature (fingering, pedaling, sound/tone, daily practice, and artistic image) are fundamental. Accordingly, the identified requisites inform the description of contemporary piano teaching approaches. Given the unique relationship between teacher and student, which lies at the core of the piano teaching profession, the roles, responsibilities, and qualities of a good piano teacher articulated by the historical pedagogues are recurring themes in the literature on the study and teaching of piano. Although definitions and descriptions may vary over time, finding a good teacher, temperament, knowing the individual student, rational method, reciprocity, beyond the instrument, and promoting the general culture are factors relevant to the description and analysis of the contemporary piano teacher and teaching practices. Setting the contemporary piano teacher and teaching within its historical context highlights continuity and change.

NOTES

1. Uszler 1983 and Uszler et al. 1995 explore the development of piano methods books in the United States.

2. The chapter does not trace the development of piano pedagogy, present a comprehensive review of piano methods, resolve debates over the best approach, or situate the piano within modern social history. Others have taken on these tasks. See, for example, Wier 1940; Kochevitsky 1963; Schonberg 1987; Parakilas 2001; Soderlund 2006; Uszler 1982–1983, 1983, and 1992; Uszler et al. 1995; and Loessor 2015.

3. RISM—1800–1950 online archive of musical periodicals, RIPM—inventory of musical sources after 1600, and RILM—abstract of musical literature 1969–present.

4. Nineteenth-century piano methods books generally focus on technique, including technical commentary, exercises, and études. Later nineteenth- and early twentieth-century American piano methods offer advice and commentary on technique. In the next decades (1930–1950) books on technique were published as supplementary to a series or separate books or series (Uszler et al. 1995, 113–14).

5. A notable omission is the Spanish School, especially the academy in Barcelona, established by Spanish pianist and composer, Enrique Granados (1867–1916), and then directed by pianist and teacher, Frank Marshall (1883–1959). In the United States, Alicia deLarrocha (1923–2009) is perhaps the best known student of Marshall and graduate of this school (see Sadie 2001, 10:277, 14:277, and 15:898).

6. Fingering—the act of placing the fingers on the keys, as well as the notation on the music indicating where to place the fingers (Music Dictionary 2008, 43).

7. Francois Couperin (1668–1733) was a French organist, composer, and writer of books on the harpsichord (Randel 1978, 123). Daniel GottlobTürk (1750–1813), born in Saxony, was a violinist and organist, music director at Halle University, and composer. He published books on methods and music theory (527).

8. The chiroplast consisted of a wooden framework extending the whole length of the keyboard; two parallel horizontal rails into which the hands of the pianist were inserted into to keep the wrists at working levels; and a brass rod with the finger guides—two flat brass frames containing slots into which the thumb and fingers were to be inserted (Rainbow 2009, 116 and Loesser 2015, 297).

9. Una corda refers to the use of the left pedal—moving the entire action, keyboard, and hammers to the right causes the hammers to strike a single string (in modern instruments usually two strings) instead of three (Randel 1978, 530).

Chapter 3

Situating the Study of the Piano Teacher within a Social Science Context

The academic literatures on career choice, achieving success, and the study and teaching of music provide the social science foundation for studying the contemporary piano teacher and teaching in the United States. In the first section of this chapter, selected studies from the career choice and achieving success literatures are reviewed for the purpose of identifying general factors that may contribute to the pursuit of a career as a piano teacher. Contemporary U.S. and British social science research on the study and teaching of music reveal factors associated with musical growth and development, arenas of music education, and challenges and barriers to the pursuit of a career in music. The second section of the chapter lays out factors, extrapolated from the social science literatures, in conjunction with the historical memoirs and treatises on piano pedagogy, to be used to explore systematically each of the topics addressed in this study—the deciding to become, becoming, and being a piano teacher. While the one-on-one piano lesson continues to be the primary arena in which the study of piano occurs, the literatures highlight additional arenas relevant to contemporary piano teaching.

ACADEMIC LITERATURES: CAREER CHOICE, ACHIEVING SUCCESS, AND STUDY AND TEACHING OF MUSIC

Situating the current study within a social science context involves a snowball approach. Considering first the question of what factors might contribute to the decision to pursue a career teaching piano, factors generally associated with choosing a career are identified from the literature on career choice. Closely related to the question of choice is that of achieving success: What distinguishes the most successful? Contemporary U.S. and British social science research on music study and teaching is explored to corroborate the relevance of the factors, extrapolated from the career choice and achieving success literatures, and identify additional factors that contribute to musical growth and the pursuit of a career in music.

Career Choice: General Literature

What factors enter into the choice of a career—the choice of a vocation rather than simply a job? Modern theories and perspectives about career choice and development dating back to the beginning of the twentieth century are found within the academic disciplines of psychology and sociology (Brown 2002, 4–7 and 18). An assessment of the diverse theories and perspectives presented in this literature is beyond the scope of the current study. Rather, the research on career choice provides a starting point for systematically identifying factors that may be relevant to the decision to pursue a career in music and specifically teaching piano. Johnson and Mortimer's synthesis of the general sociological career choice and development literature highlights factors contributing to career decision-making and potential structural challenges and barriers to career choice (2002, 37–81).

Factors

The factors affecting career choice include family, especially parents; educational experiences; adolescent employment; and community labor market conditions (Johnson and Mortimer 2002, 37–81).

   Family. The research on career choice considers the influence of family of origin (i.e., parents) and the destination family (i.e., adult family roles) on the choice of a career (Johnson and Mortimer 2002, 37 and 51–54). Parents may affect vocational choice by providing opportunities and socialization (53). For example, parental working conditions, especially those of the father, may affect child-rearing behavior, which, in turn, may affect children's and adolescents' development of interests, values, aspirations, and work values (51–52). Supportiveness in the parent-child relationship may influence attitudes that facilitate socioeconomic attainment (e.g., close father-son communication fosters greater self-confidence of sons) (52–53). In early adult years, family formation, education, and career are interwoven; for example, the age at which young men and women enter adult family roles has historically had important consequences for occupational attainment (62).

   Education. Beyond the family, sociological studies of career choice consider educational structures thought to perpetuate existing social inequalities in career outcomes across generations and produce additional inequalities

(Johnson and Mortimer 2002, 43). For example, the research examines possible consequences of (1) internal differentiation within schools—how tracking and "ability groupings" shape educational and career outcomes (43–46) and (2) structural differences between schools (e.g., average socioeconomic status composition, size, and racial composition) for student achievement and postsecondary and occupational opportunities (47–48). The jobs people hold, as well as wages and other rewards, are a function of workers' educational credentials, preferences, and skills (48).

Adolescent Employment. Adolescent employment is generally defined as after school activities to earn money, concentrated in the retail and service sections, and not related to a career track. While such jobs may still provide opportunities to learn useful skills on the job (e.g., how to accept responsibility, get along with people, be on time, manage money, and follow directions), the research points to both positive and negative consequences for educational attainment (Mortimer et al. 1996, 1406 and 1411–14; and Johnson and Mortimer 2002, 54–58). Adolescents who were stably employed during high school, but limited their work hours, achieved more secondary education and were more successful in obtaining baccalaureate degrees; however, long hours of work in adolescence may ultimately hinder educational attainment (Shanahan et al. 2002, 112; Mortimer and Johnson 1998; and Johnson and Mortimer 2002, 57).

Community Labor Market Conditions. Community labor market conditions, including the types of industry, vary widely. Research has found that the presence and range of industries within a community affect employment. Additionally, the likelihood of employment and level of earnings achieved are affected, in part, by local unemployment rates and wage levels, and the size and racial composition within central cities. Occupational segregation—the tendency for men to work in different careers from women—and the gender gap in wages also play an important role in shaping occupational choice and attainment, particularly at the time of labor force entry (Johnson and Mortimer 2002, 58–60).

Barriers and Challenges

Structural barriers, specifically racial, ethnic, class background, and gender are found to affect the selection and pursuit of a career (Johnson and Mortimer 2002, 69). Additionally, the effect on career choice of any of the identified factors may be negative. For example, family support, if absent, or an inadequate teacher may have a negative effect. The negative impact of the lack of employment opportunities in industry within certain communities has been studied (57–60). Consideration of opportunities within a profession, such as aeronautical engineering or music, is necessary to understand career choice.

Insufficient Picture

As in many careers, family, education, and economics (i.e., adolescent employment and community labor market conditions) can be expected to contribute to the choice to pursue a career in music, generally, and piano teaching, specifically. Nevertheless, while these factors provide the starting point from which to explore the decision to teach piano, they are not sufficient to explain either the choice of a music career or to teach piano. Considering the relatively few piano students who decide to become professional musicians, the question arises what distinguishes those who choose and are successful? What factors might affect achievement and success in one's chosen career?

Achieving Success

Fields such as sports, for example, Olympic swimming (Chambliss 1989); music (Tsay and Banaji 2011); and business (Tsay 2016) are ripe for exploring the question of achieving success. Often the response to the question—what distinguishes the successful in these fields—is reduced to a simple dichotomy. Is it talent or hard work? Is the source of achievement the "natural"—with early evidence of high innate ability—or the "striver"—with early evidence of high motivation and perseverance (Tsay and Banaji 2011, 460)? Advocates on both sides of the question hold strong opinions. The purpose is not to resolve the debate but to explore how each may contribute to the choice of a career teaching piano.

Factors

Talent. Perhaps the most commonly expressed explanation for success, whether it be that of the athlete, artist, or entrepreneur, is "talent." Stanford psychologist Carol Dwek attributes the emphasis on talent to sports. That is, from the study of success in sports comes the idea of a "natural"—someone who looks like an athlete, moves like an athlete, and is an athlete, all without trying (2006, 83). Similarly, sociologist Daniel Chambliss, who studied the success of Olympic swimmers, observes that talent is perhaps the most pervasive lay explanation of athletic success.

> Great athletes, we seem to believe, are born with a special gift, almost a "thing" inside of them, denied to the rest of us—perhaps physical, genetic, psychological, or physiological. Some have "it," and some don't. Some are "natural athletes," and some aren't. (Chambliss 1989, 78)

Recent research on the question of whether a preference of "naturals" over "strivers" exists in performance judgment in the domains of entrepreneurship and music found a preference for "naturals" over "strivers." Tsay and Bana-ji's study of professional musicians' perceptions of "naturals" and "strivers" exposed (1) a bias among expert decision makers, who favored "naturals" over "strivers" even when the achievement of the two pianists (actually the same person) was equal, and (2) a dissociation between the experts' stated beliefs about achievement and actual choices (2011, 460). Similarly, participants in a study of business proposals found those of the "natural" to be superior to the "striver" on multiple dimensions of achievement and success, although the entrepreneurs were equal in achievement. The conclusion to be drawn from this research is that people tend to pass over better-qualified individuals in favor of apparent "naturals" (Tsay 2016, 40–42).

Hard Work and Other Factors. The theme that emerges from the social science research, however, is that talent, alone, does not explain achievement and success. Reflecting the different social science disciplines, some studies of success and achievement focus on concrete influences (e.g., geography), while other studies emphasize the more psychological.

Studying excellence—consistent superiority of performances—among Olympic swimmers, Chambliss observes that talent (quality, gift, or natural ability) fails as an explanation for athletic success (1989, 71 and 78). He concludes that in the case of Olympic swimming, geographical location (i.e., living in Southern California where the sun shines year round); height, weight, and proportions; the luck or choice of a good coach, who can teach the skills required; and having parents who are interested in the sport, more precisely explain athletic success (78).

Dwek emphasizes what she calls the "growth mindset," which is based on the belief that your basic qualities are things you can cultivate through your efforts (2006, 6–7). Specifically, while initial talents and aptitudes, interests, or temperaments may differ, everyone can change and grow through application and experience; it is impossible to foresee what can be accomplished with years of passion, toil, and training. A person's true potential is unknown (and unknowable); the view you adopt for yourself profoundly affects the way you lead your life. The passion for stretching yourself and sticking to it, even (or especially) when it's not going well, is the hallmark of the growth mind-set (7).

Often a complex set of factors are found to contribute to success and achievement. Psychologist Angela Duckworth asserts that an obsession with talent distracts us from the simple truth that what we accomplish in life depends tremendously on our grit—our passion and perseverance for long-term goals (2016, 269). Passion consists of interest and purpose. Interest, which begins with discovery, needs time to develop. Purpose is the intention to contribute to the well-being of others (100, 114–15, and 143). Perseverance constitutes the second component of grit—quiet determination to stick to a course once decided and the tendency not to abandon tasks in the face of obstacles (77).

Practice is one form of perseverance—the daily discipline of trying to do things better than we did yesterday—the focused, full-hearted challenge-exceeding-skill practice that leads to mastery (Duckworth 2016, 91). Although interest or purpose may come first, the mature passions of gritty people depend on both (143). Research has shown that talented children typically feel passionate about their activities and do not need constant coaxing to practice but, having an obsession or rage to achieve in their domains, are fiercely persistent (Greenspan et al. 2004, 120–21). Passion and perseverance are two parts of a whole (Duckworth, 2016, 57).

Perhaps the strongest case in support of the position that factors in addition to talent affect achievement and success can be made by considering the genius. In a study by British psychologist Michael Howe, geniuses themselves were asked to account for their exceptional abilities. Howe observes that even geniuses have to devote very substantial amounts of time to training and practicing activities (2004, 111).

> The experiences and insights of geniuses suggest that little of enormous significance is achieved in the absence of diligence and the capacity for sustained hard work. (117)

Barriers and Challenges

The factors identified from the literature on achieving success may also be considered from the perspective of barriers and challenges. Lack of talent or disinclination to hard work may inhibit success in most fields. In contrast to the "growth mindset," Dwek posits the "fixed mindset"—the belief that qualities are set in stone. Believing one has only a certain amount of intelligence, a certain personality, or certain moral character creates an urgency to prove oneself over and over (2006, 6). Viewed from this mind-set, when successful, a person may feel a sense of superiority, since success means that their fixed traits are better than other people's. Such a perspective, however, raises the question: If you're somebody when you're successful, what are you when you're unsuccessful? (32). Personal physical and psychological challenges can affect performance and achievement (Pecen et al. 2018, 1).

Contemporary Research on the Study and Teaching of Music

Social science research on the contemporary study and teaching of music constitute the third category of academic literature explored. To identify relevant studies systematically, searches of the Library of Congress and New York Public Library online catalogs and databases (RISM, RIPM, RILM) were conducted using the terms "piano teaching," "piano lesson," "piano

pedagogy," and "piano instruction." From resources cited in the initial studies and further searches on specific factors (e.g., passion), additional sources
were identified. This process was repeated several times. Additionally, publications on barriers and challenges confronted in pursuit of a career in music
were identified through the networking website researchgate.net.

The studies reviewed were organized into three broad categories: (1) the
development of musical talent and the process of becoming a musician;
(2) approaches and issues related to the teaching of music, especially individual piano studies; and (3) barriers and challenges to a career in music.
The research reviewed was primarily conducted in the United States or the
United Kingdom. Although usually focused on the musician as performer,
the student, or music educator in a school, selected studies provide insights,
structure, and context for the current study, specifically, deciding to become,
becoming, and being a piano teacher.

Developing the Talented Young Musician

Of particular relevance to the current study is the research of U.S. scholars
Sosniak and Subotnik and British psychologists Howe and Sloboda on developing the talented young musician, especially factors that contribute to musical growth. Although differing somewhat in research approach, each study
draws directly from the life experiences of musicians, including pianists.
Lending further support for the observations reported in these studies are
recent accounts of music study in the United States and research on Polish
pianists.

U.S. Studies of the Talented Young Musician. Under the auspices of the
University of Chicago, Department of Education, during the first half of
the 1980s, researchers investigated influences on developing young talent in piano, athletics, math, and neurology (Bloom 1985a). As part of the
project, Lauren Sosniak's study of twenty-one talented young U.S. pianists
examines (1) factors affecting musical development, (2) stages of learning,
and (3) characteristics of the piano teacher (1985a, 1985b, and 1990).[1] From
interviewees' recollections, Sosniak discerns that pianists' development
follows a typical pattern, which she divides into three broad periods, generally related to but not defined by the age of the learner: early, middle, and
later years of learning. As the age at which the experience occurs (e.g., first
experience with the piano or first formal teacher) varies widely, emphasis
is on the context and process of learning during each stage (e.g., amount of
experience with music and the piano) (1985a, 20–21).[2] Movement through
the stages is not always smooth and occurs at different rates with an enormous amount of prompting, guidance, structure, and support from parents
and teachers (1990, 157).

The study explains how factors, including family and teachers, contribute to the musical growth of the young pianists during each stage in the developmental process. Family encompasses social standing and occupation; the role of music in the home; parental commitment to music education; and the commitment of the family to developing the child's talent (Sosniak 1985a, 1985b, 1985c). Differences in the characteristics of the piano teachers, variation in the quality of teaching, and the changing student-teacher relationship associated with each stage in the young pianists' development are described (1985a, 1985b, 1988, and 1990). In addition to the factors identified in the general social science literatures, the study highlights the importance of early listening to music, a personal support system, and a conscious commitment to becoming a musician to musical development (1990, 149, 154, and 158–59; 1985a, 56; and 1985c, 502).

Renata Subotnik's studies of Juilliard students at the precollege and college levels focus on the development of talent within the educational setting, specifically the conservatory. Her research on the Juilliard Pre-College program delves into the question of how the program serves the children who have "been caught" by classical music, and want to think about music as their life and career (2000, 252). Among the issues that she explores through interviews with students (six), faculty (six), and alumni (six) is faculty beliefs about the source of musical talent (2000, 251). In her later study of the conservatory experience at Juilliard, which is generally considered to be the most prestigious music school in the United States if not the world, Subotnik explores the environment in which classical music students are trained to become professional artists (2004). Through interviews with thirty-four Juilliard faculty and staff, she considers such questions as the definition of elite talent, relationship between teacher and student, and role of curriculum in transforming talent.

Additionally, accounts describing Juilliard students, faculty, and administration elaborate themes identified in the social science research (Olmstead 1999, Kogan 1989, and Sand 2000).[3] Olmstead (1999) details the history of Juilliard, profiling its administrators and chronicling the school's changing philosophy from its founding through the late 1990s. In *Nothing but the Best: The Struggle for Perfection at the Juilliard School*, harpist and lawyer Judith Kogan draws on experiences from her student (ages eight to eighteen) and later years (age twenty-three) at Juilliard during the 1980s. Barbara Lourie Sand's biography of Dorothy Delay, one of the foremost violin teachers who taught at Juilliard, raises questions regarding the importance of music education beyond the teaching of genius. The historical and personal descriptions of professionally oriented music education in the United States provide additional perspectives on the factors extrapolated from the social science research.

British Studies of the Talented Young Musician. Howe and Sloboda's research on the musical backgrounds and influences on progress in learning musical instruments reports the perceptions of forty-two students (ages ten to eighteen) attending the Chethams School of Music.[4] Data were gathered through face-to-face interviews between September and November 1989.[5] This body of work considers influences on the early lives of young musicians, including family and musical background, teachers, and practicing; biographical precursors of musical excellence; and the role of talent versus hard work (Howe and Sloboda 1991a, 1991b; Sloboda 1990; and Sloboda and Howe 1991). Expanding the range of factors identified, the authors consider, for example, the contribution of early experiences listening to music to musical growth. While the findings are generally consistent with Sosniak's, they are sometimes more nuanced, for example, concluding that the significance of the first teacher may be more varied and less clear-cut than Sosniak reported (Sloboda and Howe 1991, 19).

Study of Polish Musicians. Complementing the findings of the U.S. and British research is Maria Manturzewska's longitudinal life span study of 165 Polish professional musicians (including thirty-two pianists), ages twenty-one to eighty-nine (1990). A subset of twenty-eight musicians was interviewed regarding their period of greatest achievement in teaching. Conducted between 1976 and 1980, the sociopolitical environment in Poland may have affected the experiences of these musicians. Nevertheless, because the study extends over the lifespan of a musician, considers teaching, and provides insight into musical education under the influence of the former Soviet Union, the research suggests additional issues to explore in the current study. While teaching experiences occurred at all stages, interviewees generally showed a greater interest in pedagogical issues between ages forty-five and fifty-five, with optimal teaching achievement reported between ages fifty-five and sixty-five. Former soloists and virtuosi begin to "let out" their students, are capable of identifying with their students' achievements and successes, and demonstrate a greater sense of social responsibility (128 and 136–37).

Contribution of Studies on Developing the Talented Young Musician. Taken together, research on the talented young musician underscores the contribution of certain factors to musical growth and development. While focused primarily on the development of the pianist as performer, this research identifies factors that may be relevant to the development of the pianist as teacher and piano teaching. Despite certain methodological limitations, especially reliance on small sample populations precluding generalizability, these studies (1) confirm the relevance of factors extrapolated from the career choice and achieving success literatures to the pursuit of a career in music, (2) identify other factors (e.g., listening to music, personal commitment, and a personal support system) associated with musical growth, and (3) elaborate on the musical context of the factors identified. How these studies contribute to our understanding of the pursuit of a career in music and the factors that play a role in deciding to teach piano are explored in chapter 4.

Studies on Music Teaching

The second category comprises contemporary social science research on teaching piano. The studies reviewed were generally situated in a school setting and focused on such issues as the decision to become a school music teacher (Madsen and Kelly 2002) or social problems confronted by the public school music teacher (Kelly 2016). While for the most part falling outside the purview of the current study, several studies reviewed addressed themes pertinent to the piano teacher and the one-on-one music lesson. As in the case of the research on the talented young musician, social science studies on contemporary teaching tend be conducted with small populations, limiting the generalizability of the findings. Moreover, this research often focuses on the student's perspective and music education in the United Kingdom. Nevertheless, the selected studies, which focus the music educator; tradition; pedagogical training; effective instrumental teaching; the individual music lesson; practicing; and promoting the general culture, confirm or identify additional factors to consider in exploring the contemporary teacher and teaching of piano.

The Music Educator. The influence of early teachers has been found to contribute not only to the decision to pursue a career in music, but, specifically, to the decision to become a music educator in a school setting. For example, Madsen and Kelly's study of education majors, enrolled at a large comprehensive music school located in the southeast United States, found that the decision to become a music educator is made early and primarily influenced by teachers and teacher-like music activities such as being a student conductor (2002, 330). Seventy-six percent of the interviewees decided to become a music teacher before entering a teacher preparatory program; the decision was remembered vividly, with school music teachers reported as the primary influence (323). Other major factors found to contribute to the decision to become a music educator include getting compliments from others, an awareness of one's performance ability, realizing the powerful effect music has on one's life, and not wanting to give up music. Moreover, once the subjects made the decision to teach, even if at an early age, they did not consider changing careers (330).

Tradition. Viewed through a social science lens, tradition is a complex concept, encompassing attitudes, principles, and techniques of teaching and playing associated with various pedagogical styles, particular pianists and their students, and national schools. Analyzing the philosophies, methods, and contributions to piano performance continues to provide subjects for dissertation research (see Soderlund 2006, Kofman 2001, and Rego 2012). Pianist and author, Joseph Rezits has observed that teaching philosophies and techniques of such "greats" as Leschetizky, Deppe, Clementi, Czerny, Schnabel, Liszt, and Lhevinne have been well-documented. Charts and pianist family trees have been constructed to trace the influence of particular teachers and "schools." For example, the lineage of Leschetizky can be traced back to Beethoven and Czerny and forward along one branch to Schnabel and Curcio and a second branch to Vengerova. Rezits poses the question whether any method or system—influence of a particular teacher or "school" of piano teaching—is strong enough and defined enough to survive not only one generation but others as well (1979, 16).

Among pedagogical traditions within piano teaching is the maestro model or the "break down and build up approach." British educational psychologist Roland S. Persson explores the so-called maestro model by considering the common experience of eminent performers who withdrew from the pressures of concert life and turned to teaching, despite having little or no training as teachers (1994 and 1996). The maestro may be exceedingly knowledgeable in his/her field of performance but, as a teacher, knows little about the learning process and the dynamics of the teacher-student relationship (1994, 79 and 1996, 34). The approach, which is product rather than person-oriented, has generated great artists but may negatively impact artistic development as a result of its characteristic harsh and insensitive treatment. Persson asserts that such negative effects could be avoided if a higher priority was given teacher training in musical performance at a higher level (1996, 33).

Pedagogical Training. Pedagogical training may be expected to contribute not only to the decision to teach piano but also the approach to teaching piano and qualities of a good teacher. Miller and Baker (2007) explore the career aspirations and notions of pedagogical training of conservatoire undergraduates through interviews with sixteen students from the School of Wind and Percussion, Royal Northern College of Music, United Kingdom. Two years of pedagogical training were mandatory at the time the article was written. The authors conclude that while students begin with a focus on performance and a limited intention to teach, pedagogical training serves as a catalyst for changes in career orientation (5). Additionally, they assert that the boundaries between performance and other spheres of musical study must be transcended to prepare students fully for a varied career in music (16). Similar findings were reported by Australian researchers, studying the effects of providing a unit of study to a combined cohort of second-year undergraduate music education, composition, and performance students (Bennett and Stanberg 2006). In the final survey, performance and composition students reported a positive change in their perception of the role of teaching in their future careers, while education students reflected a growing awareness of the benefits of working in partnership with performers (225).

Effective Instrumental Teaching. Through a survey of 134 (fourteen piano) instrumental teachers in music services in England, Mills and Smith (2003) seek to identify teachers' beliefs about effective instrumental teaching—the hallmarks—in schools and higher education. Overall, the qualities identified at the school and higher education levels differed. At the school level, teacher's enthusiasm and patience and the student's enjoyment of the lesson were considered to be more important than at the higher education level. At the higher education level, the focus fell on teacher's high expectations, ability to give career advice, and enabling the student to develop an individual voice. Teacher's knowledge and praise to students were consistent at both levels (10). Additionally, the authors debunk the anecdotal assertion that instrumental teachers simply teach as they were taught (22).

The Individual Music Lesson. Individual lessons are viewed as an "indispensable, intense, and intricate" part of instrumental and vocal learning (Gaunt 2008, 230). Within the arena of the lesson, the teacher-student relationship unfolds and develops. Several small scale studies explore the dynamics of this relationship from the perspective of the teacher or the student. From these studies a number of themes emerge, including (1) perspectives on the teacher-student relationship (e.g., issues of dependency versus self-sufficiency and the dynamics of power), (2) negotiating the appropriate relationship (e.g., socializing beyond the lesson), and (3) parental involvement in music lessons (Davidson et al. 1995/1996; Carey and Grant 2015; Gaunt 2008 and 2011; Presland 2005; and Macmillan 2004). Nevertheless, research on aspects of the individual lesson highlights differences of opinion among study participants. These differences further underscore the appropriateness of using this research to identify areas of inquiry to pursue in the current study (e.g., interviewees' perspectives on the teacher-student relationship) rather than conclusive answers.

Teacher-Student Relationship: Noting the absence of systematic studies, Gaunt's (2008) research of the perceptions of twenty British principal voice or instrumental teachers explores the different educational goals, sometimes in tension, pursued in the practice of the one-on-one lesson. The teaching process described is primarily teacher-led, with the transference of skills and tradition often paramount (215). The most common aim that emerged was to provide the student with a "general vocational toolbox," including technical, musical, and professional skills. Developing lifelong skills was emphasized by only two teachers. Nevertheless, nearly all participants wished for their students to take responsibility for their own learning, or to become autonomous learners. The study found the two aims to be in tension, posing a challenge for the teacher (238). Focusing on the transmission of skills emphasizes the role of teacher as holding the power and may contribute to the dependency of the student on the teacher. In contrast, stressing student independence, the role of teacher is "to get rid of your role" (221).

Appropriate Relationships: Different views on socializing with students were also found among participants in the studies reviewed. Gaunt reports variation in the extent to which her interviewees socialized with students outside the lesson or were involved in students' personal issues. Opinions ranged from actively seeking, to sometimes in response to an occasion, to avoidance (2008, 234–35). Students were also found to have different attitudes toward socializing with professors, ranging from acceptable (i.e., those who regarded telephoning, messaging, emailing, or text messaging their teachers as an important line of communication between lessons) to unacceptable (Presland 2005, 241).

Parental Involvement: Another area of differing opinions among study participants was on the question of parental involvement in lessons. Among the ten instrumental teachers surveyed as part of Macmillan's qualitative study of attitudes toward parental involvement, opinions were divided equally (2004). Half discouraged parental involvement but put forth reasons for doing so, including parents tend to interfere during lessons and parental attendance inhibits the development of an independent teacher-student relationship and makes it difficult for the student to take responsibility for their own practice. Half encouraged participation in lessons and practice, believing that practicing was more efficient when supervised and what was expected of practicing could be explained to the parent at the lesson (308). Nevertheless the author asserts that the crux of the matter seems to be training parents to help in a positive, noncritical way and building parents' confidence in their ability to make a difference in their children's development (308–9).

Davidson et al.'s study of 257 children between the ages of eight and eighteen years, who had received instruction on at least one musical instrument at a specialist music school, underscores the importance of parents, at least initially. The study considers the relationship of parents of children who persist and those who give up studying an instrument (1995/1996, 41). The authors conclude that musical relationships differed between the parents of persistent music learners and those of children who give up learning. Supporting the earlier findings of Sosniak (1985c) and Sloboda and Howe (1991), the study shows that initial motivation for the persistent learners was extrinsically provided by the parent but, with time, the children's motivation became increasingly intrinsic and self-sustaining. The inverse pattern emerged for the children who gave up: there was little extrinsic motivation initially and then great amounts of external input at the point at which the child's own intrinsic motivation became almost nonexistent (Davidson et al. 1995/1996, 44).

Practicing. Contemporary social science research also considers the age-old question: What is the optimum amount of time that a student should devote to practicing? Like the historical pedagogical texts, these studies do not provide a definitive answer to the question. That is, the answers given are opinions and beliefs; solid evidence is lacking (Howe and Sloboda, 1991b, 62). Studies exploring the relationship between sheer level of practicing and performance differ in their conclusions. For example, Ericsson et al. (1990) find the sheer amount of practicing to be fairly strongly correlated with the level of performance in adult musicians, while Howe and Sloboda (1991b, 62) suggest a fairly weak or nonexistent relationship among relatively successful child musicians. In and of itself, practicing may not explain excellence, but it is an indicator of hard work and diligence and a fundamental element of music training.

Promoting the General Culture. Contemporary research on the study of piano teaching also considers the role of music education and piano lessons beyond the training of future professionals, fulfilling the purpose of the general cultural education of society. Given this broader purpose for music study, the first question one might consider is why—that is, what factors affect the decision to study a musical instrument? MacKenzie's 1991 study of primary school children (forty-eight students between ages seven and eleven) in Great Britain found that almost one pupil in five reported that starting to play a musical instrument was mainly attributable to the encouragement of the teacher (1991, 19). As to young people's musical engagement once they leave school, Stephanie Pitts (2012) used retrospective accounts of the formal musical education of 100 adults in the United Kingdom and Italy to investigate how teachers and parents can inspire and nurture musical learning beyond formal education (4–6). Among the responses, she found many illustrations of lifelong benefits of musical education for enriching leisure and continuing musical development in adulthood (163). Although focused on music education in schools, these studies underscore the importance of music education and the role of the music teacher in promoting culture in society.

Challenges and Barriers

The extant literature points to a variety of challenges and barriers within the music profession that affect the pursuit of a career in music. For the most part, these studies were conducted outside the United States (e.g., United Kingdom, Australia, the Netherlands, and Finland). Differences in sociocultural context, political support for the arts, and educational systems, notwithstanding, the research highlights problems and issues that cross national boundaries, as they are intrinsic to the music profession. Moreover, although the personal barriers and challenges identified are usually associated with a performance career (e.g., performance anxiety), they suggest categories of challenges to explore—physical and psychological impediments to a career in music.

The State of the Profession. According to *Webster's* dictionary, a musician is a composer; conductor; or performer of music, especially an instrumentalist, and a pianist is a person who plays the piano, especially a skilled or professional performer on the piano.[6] The emphasis is clearly on performing, with no mention of teacher or teaching. The definition is not far from the early career expectations of the music student. Yet, the reality for most contemporary musicians in the United States, as well as other countries and even historically, is that music is a protean career—careers in which multiple roles are undertaken (Bennett 2016, 9).[7]

> Most music students intend to pursue a career in performance, conducting or composition; however, academics and students are aware of the low probability of achieving such a career. Although performance is a fundamental part of a musician's life, for many this engagement will be primarily through teaching, ensemble direction, technology and management. The reality is that musicians sustain their careers within an increasingly complex competitive cultural environment. (Bennett 2016, 11)

Although performance continues to define the profession, the research underscores the need for contemporary musicians to undertake multiple roles. In *Understanding the Classical Music Profession*, Dawn Bennett (2016) investigates the career of classically trained musicians, including how they spend their time and the skills required to develop and sustain their careers (5). One hundred fifty-nine musicians from Australia, the United Kingdom, Europe, Asia, and the United States, ranging in age from eighteen to over sixty-five, completed the survey or attended interviews on questions of work, education, and training (102). The study found that musicians tend to have at least two different music industry roles, reflecting the multifaceted nature of careers in music (161). Focusing on the classical music profession in the United States, Robert Freeman asserts that the current crisis is, in part, because of the continuing production of music degrees—now more than 30,000 collegiate degrees each year in a field where there have never been many jobs but where there are now fewer each year (2014, xvii). Ignoring the law of supply and demand, the number of music degrees awarded has increased while orchestras have gone bankrupt, reduced salaries, or become a chamber orchestra—reducing performance positions (xvii and xix–xx).

In short, the literature underscores the difficulty of supporting a music career solely by performing and the need for musicians to engage in more than one type of employment. Among Bennett's participants, for example, 8 percent reported working solely in performance. The most common role reported was teaching, not including classroom teaching. Over 80 percent of the musicians reported teaching, as compared to 70 percent reporting performance (Bennett 2016, 103 and 161). The attractions of teaching noted were regular income, regular hours, and a level of artistic and administrative control (108). While teaching music is not the only option, it is the path frequently chosen.

Personal Factors. The literature identifies a range of physical and psychological challenges that may impinge on a pianist's performance career. Physical problems include injury and playing-related pain—muscle-tendon injuries, joint issues, nerve compression disorders, and so on (Pecen et al. 2018, 7–8; and Kenny and Ackermann 2015). Performance anxiety and developing ways to offset it—positive and negative—are recurring themes (Sadler and Miller 2010; Kenny 2011; Kenny et al. 2014; Kenny and Ackermann 2015; Buma et al. 2015; and Pecen et al. 2018). Common performance-related problems in the early years also include isolation, comparing oneself to peers, and competitive environments. Other problems are of a more clinical nature—depression, panic disorder, eating disorders, thoughts of suicide, and addiction to alcohol and drugs (Pecen et al. 2018, 7).

Specific to the decision to teach is adjusting to the reality of teaching, especially given the emphasis of the profession on performance. Bennett observes that musicians' roles change throughout their careers as they adapt their practice to reflect personal circumstances (2016, 120). Reflecting on her own transition from the pursuit of a soloist career to piano teacher, Huhtanen's study of Finnish pianists is anecdotal, preliminary, and focused on performing as the primary role with its subtitle, *Facing reality as an ex-promising pianist* (Huhtanen 2004, 23 and Bennett 2016, 89). Nevertheless, her categorization of piano teachers as "realists" or "dreamers" presents two different perspectives on the decision to teach piano. The realist, as defined by Huhtanen, accepts teaching as a part of their musical identity; the "dreamer" drifts into teaching, using it to make a living but still holding onto the dream of being a soloist (23). The former embraces teaching as part of one's identify as a musician, while the latter considers it to be a temporary adjustment while waiting to achieve the ultimate definition of musician—performer. Despite the limitations of this study, it suggests an aspect of the decision to teach piano to explore with contemporary U.S. teachers.

Sustaining a Career in Music. The challenges posed by the music profession; physical injuries; and psychological issues, including performance anxiety may contribute to the decision to teach. The same factor may affect teaching as well as performance—the availability of teaching opportunities may fluctuate with demand or psychological factors such as depression may make it difficult to develop effective teacher-student relationships. Additionally, changes in the music profession have created the need for new skills (e.g., networking and public relations) (Pecen et al. 2018, 6). Such skills may not only be relevant to performance but teaching as well. For example, networking and creating websites have not only become important aspects of securing performance opportunities but are also necessary vehicles for attracting private students. The ultimate challenge is sustaining a career in music and one's identity as a musician.

CONTRIBUTING FACTORS AND ARENAS OF MUSIC EDUCATION: DECIDING, BECOMING, AND BEING A PIANO TEACHER

The factors identified from the social science literature, in conjunction with the historical memoirs and pedagogical treatises, provide a starting point from which to explore systematically each of the three topics addressed in this study—deciding to become, becoming, and being a piano teacher. The set of factors to be used in the analysis of each topic is laid out here. While the one-on-one piano lesson is fundamental to the teaching of piano, the literatures reviewed revealed a broader definition of music education, extending beyond the lesson and encompassing the promotion of the general culture. The contribution of the factors is actualized within these three educational arenas.

Deciding to Teach Piano: Contributing Factors

From the literatures on career choice, achieving success, and the study and teaching of music, factors that may affect the decision to teach piano were extrapolated. Because the literatures do not focus, specifically, on one-on-one piano teaching, the factors identified are considered to be areas of inquiry. Table 3.1 presents a general description of each factor.

In the next chapter, selected contemporary studies on developing the talented young musician are reviewed to ascertain what is known and not known about the contribution of these factors to the decision to pursue a career in music.

Table 3.1   Potential Contributing Factors to the Decision to Teach Piano

Factor	General Definition
Family	Family of origin—birth family—and family of destination—created in adulthood.
Education	Music education (e.g., teachers, the lesson, and activities beyond the instrument) to prepare the piano student.

(Continued)

Table 3.1   Potential Contributing Factors to the Decision to Teach Piano (*Continued*)

Factor	General Definition
Adolescent Employment	After school activity, undertaken to earn money but not related to the career track.
Community Labor Market Conditions	Job market and opportunities for employment.
Talent	Born with a special gift denied to the rest of us.
Hard Work and Diligence	Application of toil and training.
Passion	(1) Self-directed—interest for its own sake and (2) purpose—intent to contribute to the well-being of others.
Perseverance	Quiet determination to stick to a course once decided and tendency not to abandon tasks in the face of obstacles.
Listening to Music	Early opportunity to experience intensive positive emotional or aesthetic states in response to music.
Personal Commitment to Music	Intrinsic motivation for musical activities and long-term commitment to continuous learning.
Personal Support System	Resources and emotional support from parents, teachers, and friends.
Challenges and Barriers	Societal (e.g., racism and sexism) and personal (e.g., physical and psychological) challenges and barriers affecting pursuit of a career.

Becoming a Piano Teacher: Developing an Approach to Piano Teaching

Contemporary academic research on the study and teaching of piano, especially social science studies of piano teaching, situate the discussion of becoming a piano teacher within a social science context. Fundamental to becoming a piano teacher is developing a teaching approach. The term "approach" is used to indicate a broader conceptualization of piano teaching that extends beyond the transfer of keyboard skills and theory—methods—(Uszler et al. 1995, 113) and encompasses music education beyond the lesson, the promotion of the general culture, and the development of the student as a musician and person. From the studies reviewed, three factors that may contribute to the development of an approach to teaching piano were identified: early teachers, tradition, and formal pedagogical training.

The contribution of each factor to a teaching approach may be positive and/or negative. For example, an early teacher may provide be a model of how to or how not to relate to students when teaching piano. Tradition may be reflected in an emphasis on technical skills but also recognition of a responsibility to promote the general culture. Pedagogical training may identify teaching resources and insight into how to approach students differently.

Being a Piano Teacher: Qualities of a Good Teacher

An array of qualities of a good piano teacher were identified in the literatures, including personality and temperament, motivation to teach, having a method or not, repertoire, knowing each student, recognizing the individuality of each student's playing, and beyond the instrument. The order of presentation does not reflect an assessment of the contribution of each quality, as the relative importance of each quality may vary according to the stage of a student's development. For example, what is deemed essential when teaching young children during the early stages (e.g., the personality of the teacher) may be considered less important during later stages, particularly relative to other qualities (e.g., recognizing the individuality of a student's playing). These qualities further underscore that teaching piano is more than passing on the skills necessary to play the instrument; it is about developing the student as a musician and a person.

The qualities extrapolated from the social science literature mirror those discussed in the historical literature, suggesting continuity in the perception of the qualities essential to the teaching of piano. For example, the importance of knowing each student was recognized in the early pedagogical literature. A particular quality may not be universally accepted, as educational cultures vary across countries and continents as well as time. Moreover, changes have occurred in what are considered to be the attributes of the good teacher and what are acceptable and unacceptable teaching practices and behaviors. Nevertheless, the qualities identified provide a structure for the discussion of the qualities of a contemporary U.S. piano teacher.

Arenas of Music Education: The Lesson, Beyond the Lesson, and Promoting the General Culture

From the social science research, in conjunction with the historical literatures, emerges a conceptualization of music education and piano teaching that encompasses three arenas—the lesson (i.e., philosophy and practice), beyond the lesson (i.e., education goals, activities, and responsibilities of the piano teacher outside the lesson), and promoting the general culture (role and contribution of the piano teacher, piano lesson, and music to society). The one-on-one lesson is the primary setting for piano study. Historically and today, however, music education and the interaction between teacher and student continue beyond the walls and hour of the lesson. The memory of attending a concert by a great pianist with a beloved teacher may contribute to a love of music. The decision to teach may be affected by experiences beyond the lesson. The development of a teaching approach and qualities of good teacher are actualized within each arena. The personality and temperament of the teacher—patience—and activities engaged in beyond the instrument—arranging recitals, encouraging the study of composers, or taking students to concerts—are demonstrated within and beyond the lesson. Teaching average students may reflect recognition of the responsibility to promote the general culture.

SUMMARY AND CONCLUSION: ESTABLISHING THE SOCIAL SCIENCE CONTEXT

To situate the current study within a social science context, this chapter considered selected studies from the career choice, achieving success, and the study and teaching of music literatures. General factors that may contribute to the decision to teach piano were extrapolated from studies on career choice (e.g., family, education, adolescent employment experiences, and community labor market conditions) and achieving success (e.g., talent, hard work, perseverance, and passion). Contemporary U.S. and British social science research on developing the talented young musician corroborate the contribution of the general factors and also identify additional factors (e.g., listening to music, personal commitment, and personal support system) affecting musical growth and development. Social science studies on teaching music highlight factors that may play a role in becoming a piano teacher and developing an approach to piano teaching (e.g., early teachers, tradition, and formal pedagogical training). These studies also describe qualities of a good teacher, underscoring that the responsibility of the piano teacher extends beyond the instrument, lesson, and individual student to the general culture.

For each of the topics explored in this study, the factors identified from the social science and historical literatures provide the structure and context for the analysis of interviewees' experiences and observations. Before proceeding to the current research, selected studies on developing the talented young musicians and teaching music are explored in chapter 4. Ascertaining from this literature what is known and not known about the contribution of the identified factors to the three topics—deciding to become, becoming, and being a piano teacher—offers a starting point for the study of the contemporary U.S. piano teacher.

NOTES

1. Sosniak also interviewed the parents of sixteen of the twenty-one pianists (1985a, 19).
2. Stages reflect the amount of experience with music and a piano; psychological perceptions of the activity of music making and future of the activity; and nature of the pianist's interaction with parents, teachers, the instrument, and the world of music.

The periods refer to qualitatively different sets of learning experiences. Age is noted where appropriate (Sosniak 1985a, 20–21).

3. Located in New York City, Juilliard is viewed by many as the ultimate training school for the performing arts (Olmstead 1999, 1). Founded in 1905, to rival or improve on the conservatories of Europe, the Institute of Musical Art became the pre-eminent conservatory in the United States because of its distinguished faculty, high standards, and a core curriculum. In 1969, Juilliard moved from the edge of Columbia University to Lincoln Center (Kogan 1989, 3–5). (For details on Juilliard's history, see Olmstead 1999 and Kogan 1989.)

4. The Chethams School of Music is a special school for the musically gifted located in Manchester, England (Sloboda and Howe 1991, 5).

5. Sloboda and Howe interviewed a subsample of twenty parents either through face-to-face interviews or by telephone between September 1989 and January 1990 (1991, 6).

6. *Merriam Webster Dictionary.* https://www.merriam-webster.com/dictionary/pianist.

7. Protean careers are also commonly described as "portfolio," "multiple," or "composite" careers. Protean careerists self-manage their careers and adapt their practice as necessary to meet personal and professional needs (Bennett 2016, 9).

Chapter 4

The Extant Literature

What Is Known and Not Known about the Contemporary Piano Teacher

Contemporary U.S. and British social science research on the study and teaching of piano provides insight into the pursuit of a career in music, including the contribution of the factors identified in the previous chapters. Drawing on these studies, this chapter explores what is known and not known about the roles that the factors, extrapolated from the extant literature, may play in deciding to become, becoming, and being a piano teacher. Focused primarily on the musician as performer and music educator in schools, less is known about the development of the piano teacher and teaching within the context of the one-on-one piano lesson. Identifying the gaps in our knowledge of the contemporary piano teacher, piano teaching, and the arenas of music education—the lesson, beyond the lesson, and promoting the general culture—highlights areas of inquiry and questions to be probed. The gaps identified and described in this chapter provide a starting point for the current study.

DECIDING TO BECOME A PIANO TEACHER: POTENTIAL CONTRIBUTING FACTORS AND GAPS IN THE LITERATURE

Using the matrix of factors, presented in Table 3.1, to explore the literature on the talented young musician provides a structured approach for examining the decision to teach piano. The gaps in the literature raise issues and questions to consider to better understand the decision and the decision process.

Factors Affecting Choice: The Literature on Developing the Talented Young Music

That the factors identified may affect the choice of a musical career is evident from the literature on developing the talented young musician, especially the research of Sosniak (1985a and b), Sloboda and Howe (1991), and Howe and Sloboda (1991a). These studies describe the role that each factor may play in the pursuit of a career in music. The factors explored include family, education, adolescent employment, community labor market conditions, talent, hard work, passion, perseverance, listening to music, personal commitment to music, personal support system, and challenges and barriers.

Family

Focusing on the young musician, the literature explores the contribution of the family of origin, especially the characteristics and activities of parents to encourage and support early musical development. Exploring general family characteristics (i.e., social standing and parental occupation) reveals the diverse backgrounds of the young pianists studied. The choice of a career as a pianist, however, is not simply a matter of being born into a musical family, which perhaps occurs less frequently than one might expect. What appears to be of paramount importance, penetrating the diversity, is valuing music in the home, commitment to music education, viewing the musical child as special, and continued adjustment to the changing role of the family as the child's musical development progresses.

Social Standing and Occupation. Although family social standing and parental occupations varied among the young pianists interviewed in the U.S., British, and Polish studies, a higher percentage reported professional and white-collar than blue-collar backgrounds. Sosniak's twenty-one respondents came from professional (35 percent), white-collar (45 percent), and blue-collar families (20 percent) (1985a, 21).[1] The majority of the forty-two students in Sloboda and Howe's study came from higher socioeconomic sectors, although father's occupation varied—professionals (sixteen, e.g., teacher, doctor), senior managers (sixteen, e.g., company director proprietor), office workers (seven, e.g., clerk, technician), and manual workers (four, e.g., mechanic, fitter) (1991, 6). The musicians in Manturzewska's study were from the intelligentsia and craftsman families (50 and 28 percent, respectively); few were children of farmers and blue-collar workers (4 and 9 percent, respectively) (1990, 119).

Perhaps most notable, however, is how few of the young musicians in the U.S. and British studies were from professional musical families. Among Sosniak's interviewees four came from families with musical backgrounds. In two families, the parents were members of a professional symphony orchestra, not pianists, who supplemented their incomes by giving lessons in the home. In two families, the discussion of music was abundant, although not of the same high quality (1985a, 23). Howe and Sloboda report that the parents of 6 percent of the interviewees were professional musicians or music teachers and 14 percent were regular amateur musicians; 36 percent were not interested in music or restricted their involvement to passive listening (1991a, 42–43). In contrast, Polish musicians were more likely not only to come from families with some musical tradition (93 percent) but also to follow in the footsteps of a parent (father—nearly 50 percent and mother—25 percent) (Manturzewska 1990, 119).

Music Valued. Creating a family environment where music was valued appears to have been more important than having a parent who was a musician. Almost from birth, music was a natural part of the lives of Sosniak's interviewees. During the early learning years, they heard recordings and live performances regularly and naturally, and a piano was present in fifteen of the twenty-one pianists' homes (1985a, 24–25). Music was not only pervasive but highly valued—important, beautiful, and worthwhile (43). Similarly, Howe and Sloboda report that the majority of interviewees' parents had experienced some active participation in music and the early home environments of a "substantial number" of the subjects were strongly influenced by parental musical interests. Additionally, older siblings playing an instrument created an awareness of music, the possibility of learning to play, a model to copy, and an atmosphere in which playing and practicing were seen as normal events of everyday life. In a number of instances the child was not aware that a family background in which music played a role was in any sense unusual: "Music as an element of home life was simply taken for granted" (1991a, 43–44).

Commitment to Music Education and Treating the Child as Special. Additionally, parental commitment to musical education whether from the perspective that all children should be educated in music or the belief that the particular child possessed a quality others did not—gift for music—permeated the child's experience. Imparting that belief to the child was another way in which the family could exert influence (Howe and Sloboda 1991a, 46). Sosniak reports a "striking consistency" in the pianists' statements of being special or the best. "Special" meant being best in the neighborhood or better than a sibling at the same age; a small number accomplished something extraordinary—winning an important youth competition before age nine (1985a, 39). The perceived specialness seems important, perhaps critical, in the pianist's development for its effects—increasing the pianist's motivation to study and practice and parental involvement in the process (40). Similarly, Howe and Sloboda observe that what matters and can be influential, in itself, is the very belief that a particular child has inherited certain attributes—a gift—that others do not possess (1991a, 46).

Changing Role of the Family. Among the primary conditions for musical growth identified by Sloboda were resources for extended engagement with music, including time, economic support, and social support (1990, 175–76). In Sosniak's study, parents played an active role in the education of the young pianists during the early and middle stages (1985a, and 54–58). During the early years, a parent might sit in on lessons to learn how to help the child and monitor at least the quantity if not quality of practicing (34–35). In the middle years, families made extensive investments of time, money, and lifestyle direction to help the child become a good musician (Sosniak 1985a, 54–58; and 1985b, 415–18). Howe and Sloboda report nearly all the parents in their study provided the vital elements of time, transport, money, organization, and motivation; weekly lessons and daily practice were viewed as the norm (1991a, 51). As the motivation, commitment, and the resource needs of the young pianist change over time, so does the role of the family. As the student progresses musically, demands for resources increase; for example, buying a better piano, driving farther, or even moving the entire family to enable the child to study with a better teacher (Sosniak 1985a, 54–58). During the later stage, the parental role devolves to one of being supportive—primarily financially (66).

Education

The development of a young musician is a long-term process, not always smooth, with an enormous amount of prompting, guidance, structure, and support from parents and teachers (Sosniak 1990, 150 and 157). Essential to this process are the teacher and one-on-one piano lesson, although the roles change at each stage in the process (Sosniak 1985a, 29–33, 47–59, and 61–63). Moreover, the musical education of the pianist extends beyond the lesson and beyond the study of the piano, per se, whether in the conservatory or in the private lesson.

The Teacher. The characteristics of the teacher and the nature of the teacher-student relationship evolve over time. In the early years, the teacher's personality plays an important role. As the student progresses, the importance of the teacher's personality, relative to musical experience, changes.

Pianists' emotional response to first teachers is well acknowledged in the literature (Sosniak 1985c, 498; and Sloboda and Howe 1991). Often a nice and patient woman from the neighborhood, known to the parents but not a very fine musician or expert music teacher, the portrait is similar to that presented in the children's literature. While the quality of the teaching varied, students responded to the teacher's warmth and affection (Sosniak 1985a, 29–33; and 1985b, 411–15). Sosniak observes that over and over the pianists made reference to the impact of teachers for whom they felt love, admiration, and respect and from whom they felt dedication to music making and to their student's development (1985c, 498–99). Although similarly observing that having a warm and friendly teacher is beneficial, if not invariably essential, for the young learner, Sloboda and Howe conclude that the significance of the early teachers may be more varied and less clear cut (1991, 19). Additionally, early teachers were found to have an influence on the decision to become a music educator (Madsen and Kelly 2002, 323).

During the middle and later years, emphasis shifts to the expertise of the teacher and developing the independence of the young pianist. Second teachers were of a higher quality and rated higher for musical abilities (Sosniak 1985b, 415–19 and 1988, 81–82; and Sloboda and Howe 1991, 19). While still warm, the students valued expertise equally; the relationship was based on reciprocal respect between teacher and student and extended beyond the weekly lesson to competitions and recitals (Sosniak 1985b, 418–19). In later years, the student was usually taught by a master teacher from the respected faculty of a professional school of music and part of the inner circle of professional musicians (Sosniak 1985a, 59; 1985b, 420–24; and 1990, 156). With the help of expert teachers and like-minded peers in similar pursuit of excellence in the field, interviewees began identifying and developing personal concerns and ways of working; finding and solving their own problems; and looking to satisfy themselves rather than their teacher (Sosniak 1990, 157).

The Lesson. The format and content of the lesson also change over time. For Sosniak's young pianists, instruction during the early years of learning was informal; usually weekly but the length varying with the child's age; designed to teach some technique (e.g., scales and exercises) and some music; but filled with smiles, positive reinforcements, and rewards (1985a, 33; and 1985b, 411). To help the child, some parents attended lessons and teachers might keep notebooks to outline practice schedules and record accomplishments (1985b, 415). During the second stage, weekly lessons involved solving problems, usually identified by the teacher, and time was spent on details, technical skills, vocabulary, and looking for and correcting flaws (1985b, 416; and 1985a, 48–49). Fingering, phrasing, sound quality, the shape of the hand, articulation, and other technical aspects of piano playing—the requisites identified in chapter 2—were discussed in detail (1985a, 49). During the third stage, lessons were irregular—two hours every three weeks, and a large amount of work was assigned. The student began to take responsibility for his or her own development, becoming more independent in their lessons by listening to but not necessarily agreeing with or following the teacher (1985a, 61–66).

Beyond the Instrument and the Lesson. Music education and the study of piano extend beyond learning the notes of the composition, technical skills to play the instrument, or how to perform of a particular piece of music. The early pedagogues recognized the importance of understanding the social and cultural context of a musical composition and life of its composer. Music education may also include practical aspects of pursuing a career in music. Although focused on education within the conservatory, the Juilliard studies illustrate the broadening of the content of music education and suggest ways to enrich the private lesson.

Beginning in 1984 with the presidency of Joseph Polisi, the Juilliard curriculum was extended beyond individual lessons and other performance sessions (Olmstead 1999, 272). Ensembles or lessons with other students; courses on ear training and music history; liberal arts classes and electives focused on the humanities; and seminars on negotiating a successful musical career became part of the curriculum. Philosophically, a broad education enhances the interpretive abilities of the performer. On the practical level, Subotnik asserts that the most practical creative skill that a Juilliard student implements as part of their career is teaching, noting that teachers are paying more attention than in the past to having students think about how they might help another student solve some musical problem (2004, 148–52).

Adolescent Employment

Adolescent employment, as generally described in the career choice literature, entails an after-school activity, undertaken to earn money, and not related to the career track. In contrast, performances of various kinds are an important part of the pianist's education during the middle years of learning. Class recitals become routine. Youth competitions are opportunities to play before large and musically sophisticated audiences, perhaps earning the privilege to play with a full orchestra (Sosniak 1985a, 51). Pianists also play solo recitals for school programs, community organizations, women's groups, and the like, even receiving pay for some. Missing from the literature, however, is a discussion of teaching experiences, as early employment.

Community Labor Market Conditions

Community labor conditions generally play an important role in shaping occupational choice and attainment, particularly at the beginning of the career trajectory (Johnson and Mortimer 2002, 58–59). Opportunities may vary between and within communities, within a profession, and over time. Biographies of early composers and musicians provide historical examples of the challenges of a music career. Some composers had difficulty earning a living in music (e.g., Wolfgang Amadeus Mozart, Franz Schubert, Robert Schumann); others did not need to make a living (e.g., Felix Mendelssohn); and still others worked at other professions—American Charles Ives (1879–1954) was a lifetime insurance executive (Freeman 2014, 110).

The employment situation for musicians also varies by country and within countries over time. For example, the Bolshoi never knew financial difficulties under Stalin, who set their high salaries, conferred their decorations, and personally presented their Stalin Prizes. After his death, the government's attitude changed and the high salaries vanished, pensions decreased, and the years required to receive a pension increased (Vishnevskaya 1984, 125–26).

In the United States, the performing and teaching opportunities for musicians have fluctuated. As Freeman reports, while the number of music degrees awarded has increased, orchestras have gone bankrupt, reduced salaries, or become chamber orchestras—reducing performance positions and ignoring the law of supply and demand (2014, xvii and xix–xx). Not only in the United States but also in other countries, musicians, including pianists, undertake multiple roles within the music profession (e.g., Bennett 2016, 119). Teaching is one of, if not the predominant, role. Yet teaching, even in the major conservatories has been subject to economic downturns. In 1932, the Juilliard faculty voted to accept salary reductions of 10 percent for those receiving $25 or more per hour and 5 percent for those receiving between $10 and $25 per hour. As a result, the income of one of the school's most renowned teachers, Rosina Lhevinne, was decreased from $4,900 to $4,410. The New England Conservatory reduced faculty salaries by 10 percent in 1932 and another 25 percent in 1934 (Olmstead 1999, 96 and 115).

Talent

The attribution of talent distinguishes an individual as "different" in a particular field (e.g., sports, mathematics, science, etc.) because of an innate gift. According to what has been referred to as the "folk psychology of talent," few people become expert musical performers because few people have the necessary talent. Such beliefs are evident in the structures and rhetoric of the music conservatoire and the people involved in the schools (Sloboda 1996, 108). A closer scrutiny of musical talent suggests a complex interrelationship between talent and hard work, rather than a simple dichotomy between those who "have it" and those who do not or the "naturals" and "strivers."

In her study of the Juilliard Pre-College program, Subotnik identifies variables that faculty associate with the source of musical talent, ranging from those considered to be almost entirely innate to the almost totally trainable. The innate include musicality (a personal quality of communication which shows intense love of music and a drive to express it) and musical intelligence (high understanding of concepts being taught). The teachable include aesthetic sense (question of what makes music beautiful) and technique (central focus of individual lessons and master classes), which is most trainable. Physique, the most important physical attribute being sense of touch, and coordination can be addressed though training (2000, 260–61). The analysis suggests areas of musical growth that can be achieved through education and training.

The question of talent is relevant to the discussion of piano teachers, as an often heard comment is "those who can't, teach." Such comments suggest that those who perform are talented and those who teach are not. In fact, many music graduates who teach believe they have failed and that teaching is a second-rate profession (Durrant 1992). Yet, it has also been observed that child prodigies and concert musicians may fall short as teachers (Persson 1994 and 1996). Therefore, perhaps the most appropriate observation regarding musical talent for purposes of the current study is this: the formidable artist and formidable pedagogue may be attributes of the same individual but they describe different roles as well as different skills in different contexts (Persson 1994, 89).

Hard Work/Diligence

Growth requires work, as suggested by the studies of genius (Howe 2004, 116), blurring the line between "naturals" and "strivers." Moreover, research has documented cases of a major adolescent decline in the performance and progress of child prodigies (Sloboda 1990, 168). Fundamental to music training, practicing perhaps best demonstrates hard work and diligence in music, with studies of talented young musician substantiating the increase in hours spent practicing as the student progresses (Sosniak 1985a, 34, 63, and 65; and Howe and Sloboda 1991b, 57). Nevertheless, contemporary studies of the relationship between level practicing and performance, as the historical pedagogical literature, do not provide a definitive answer to the question: What is the optimum amount of time that children should devote to practicing? (Howe and Sloboda 1991b, 62; Sloboda and Howe 1991, 17; and Ericsson et al. 1990).

The relative contribution of talent and hard work/diligence to musical achievement continues to be debated. Sloboda argues that both precocity— "you have to start excellent"—and diligence—"if you work hard enough and long enough at anything you become excellent at it"—fail as explanations of musical excellence (Sloboda 1990, 167). Rather, he posits:

> For musical growth then, it would seem necessary that the person concerned likes music, is interested in it, and wants to engage in it for its own sake. Only then will practice make perfect. (169)

This observation points to the importance of "passion" to the pursuit of a music career.

Passion

What is it that motivates musicians to spend hours studying and practicing? Canadian and Australian researchers answer—passion. Neither their courage nor their sacrifices are mentioned, when professional musicians are asked how they managed to practice for the thousands of hours required over many years without giving up. What they talk about is their passion for music (Bonneville-Roussy et al. 2011, 123). Similarly, when asked about personal attributes, the musicians surveyed in Bennett's study placed passion at the core of their practice. Passion, they said, drives their determination to succeed (2016, 119).

Definitions of passion vary, but it may be characterized as a strong inclination to an activity that is loved, considered important, and to which a significant amount of time and energy is devoted (Bonneville-Roussy et al. 2011, 124). Duckworth asks: What do I like to think about? What do I really care about? What matters most to me? How do I enjoy spending my time? Passion is defined to include interest, which is self-directed, and purpose, which is directed toward the well-being of others (2016, 100, 114–15, and 143). That performing involves interest is evident—one is interested in the music itself. To the extent one also seeks to communicate to the audience, performing involves purpose—contributing to the well-being of others. Because of the nature of teaching, purpose may weigh heavier than interest, at least relatively to performing. The teacher, especially in the context of the one-on-one relationship, is necessarily concerned with the other.

Perseverance

Drawing from the achieving success literature, perseverance is defined as the quiet determination to stick to a course once decided and the tendency not to abandon tasks in the face of obstacles (Duckworth 2016, 77). Violinist and teacher Dorothy Delay observed: One of my friends who taught used to say that determination and drive were the most important (qualities to look for in a student). He thought the important thing was to keep going, not get too excited, just keep going—I think he had something there (Sand 2000, 69). Daily practice requires perseverance. Perseverance is also demanded of the parent. As observed by Howe and Sloboda—the unspoken theme is one of quiet and dogged perseverance in the undramatic process of helping the child get the work done (1991a, 51).

Listening to Music

Listening to music was identified as an influence on the decision to pursue a career in music, although less consistently than other factors. Sosniak observes that the young pianists listened to music almost from the time they were born, and learned to identify the names of well-known composers, musicians, or musical pieces without anyone being conscious of the process of education (1990, 154). From the early opportunity to experience intense positive emotional or aesthetic states in response to music, the intrinsic motivation for musical activity may arise (Sloboda 1990, 167, 170–71, and 176).

Personal Commitment to Music

The literature on developing the talented young musicians highlights the importance of making a personal commitment to music (Sloboda 1990, 176; and Sosniak 1985a, 56). Sloboda identifies intrinsic motivation for musical activities as one of the main conditions for musical growth (1990, 176). Among children who continued to study an instrument, parents extrinsically provided the initial motivation but, with time the child's motivation became increasingly intrinsic and self-sustaining; in contrast, those who gave up had little extrinsic support initially and then greater input at the point when the child's motivation because almost nonexistent (Davidson et al. 1995/1996, 44). A conscious commitment to becoming a musician, with a tendency to value everything else less and let other things slide, was observed among Sosniak's study participants (1985a, 56; and 1985c, 502).

Support System: Parent, Teacher, Friends, and Community

The development of talent does not take place in a vacuum but is a tribute to the support of many people and communities (Sosniak 1990, 149 and 158–59; and Greenspan et al. 2004, 121). For each young pianist in Sosniak's study, the race was long but the help of parents, teachers, and the larger community apparently prevented the pianist from getting so distracted that he/she lost the chance to excel (1990, 161). For much of the time it took to develop talent, parents and teachers created activities and opportunities because the pianists were too young to create them. Parents supplied the resources and encouragement that allowed students to take advantage of the opportunities teachers made available (159). Although a personal support system is a composite of factors, it is included in the current study as a discreet factor because of the evidence of its importance to the successful pursuit of a music career.

Challenges and Barriers

The development of the talented young pianist is not without its barriers and challenges. Responding to conditions within the profession, a pianist may engage in at least two different careers. On a more personal level, as in any family, young pianists may confront the death of a parent, alcoholism, and conflict. Sosniak notes that unfortunately for a few of the pianists interviewed, one of the early rewards of practicing was to escape from the noise and fighting in the home or their loneliness (1985a, 40). Physical and psychological issues may impede career progress and success, affecting motivation and perseverance. While subjective and sometimes controversial, Kogan's observations about student life at Juilliard point to challenges in the educational process—the initial audition, pressures and agonies of daily practice, juries, competitions, and the relationship between teachers and students. An overly assertive parent can adversely affect the success of the child (1989, 64–68, 75–83, and 85–121).

Gaps in the Literature: The Decision to Teach Piano

The literature on developing the talented young musician provides insight into factors affecting the pursuit of a career in music. Focusing primarily on the musician as performer and the preprofessional years, these studies offer little evidence of how the identified factors may contribute to a career teaching piano. Nevertheless, both from the perspective of what is known about early musical growth and not known about later musical development, the research suggests issues to be explored in the current study. For example, family of origin may contribute to the early development of pianists, generally, but family of destination may precipitate the decision to teach piano (e.g., marriage, children, or family needs).

Other factors, while relevant to both performing and teaching, may play different roles. As described in the literature, participating in recitals, youth concerts, and community programs provides career-relevant experiences for the performer. Not addressed is experience teaching neighborhood children, which can be not only a source of income but an impetus to continue teaching. Conditions in the music profession may precipitate the decision to teach piano, but availability of teaching opportunities may affect decisions about where and which students to teach. Reflecting differences in the demands of performing and teaching raises the question, what constitutes talent and hard work and what is the relationship between the two in the context of teaching? How may passion, perseverance, and challenges be defined differently?

BECOMING A PIANO TEACHER: POTENTIAL CONTRIBUTING FACTORS

Research on music teaching provides the social science context for exploring becoming a piano teacher, specifically the development of an approach to piano teaching. While the selected studies concentrate primarily on music education in the classroom, factors considered are relevant to the structure and content of teaching piano within the one-on-one piano lesson. In this section, these factors are explored individually and within the arenas of the lesson, beyond the lesson, and promoting the general culture. Gaps in the research raise questions for further study.

Factors: Developing an Approach to Piano Teaching

From contemporary studies of music teaching, early teachers, tradition, and formal pedagogical training were identified as factors that may contribute to becoming a piano teacher, specifically the development of teaching approaches. As previously noted, the word approach is used to encompass aspects of teaching beyond "the how" of playing the instrument.

Early Teachers

That early teachers can play an important role in the development of a young pianist and the decision to become a music educator is well-documented in the literature, as reported earlier (Sosniak 1985a, 1985b, 1985c; Sloboda and Howe 1991; Howe and Sloboda 1991b; Madsen and Kelly 2002; and Bennett and Stanberg 2006). Moreover, the research also debunks as myth the belief that instrumental teachers simply teach as they were taught (Mills and Smith 2003, 22). Early piano studies are likely to contribute not only to performance but perspectives on teaching piano. During the middle and later years of musical growth, the role of teacher and the teacher-student relationship change—expertise becomes important (Sosniak 1985a, 59; 1985b, 418–19 and 420–24; and 1988, 81–82; and Sloboda and Howe 1991, 19). Considering musical development as a process, later teachers may be expected to contribute to a pianist's becoming a teacher and developing a teaching approach.

Tradition

The concept of tradition in the context of piano performance and teaching is complex, referring to a pedagogical style, particular pianists and their students, and national schools. Because of the influence on U.S. piano pedagogy of such notable teachers as the Lhevinnes, Vengerova, and Schnabel-Curcio, the contribution of tradition to teaching approaches is fertile ground for exploration. The underlying question considered is: To what extent does tradition, in its various meanings, contribute to contemporary piano teaching in the United States?

Exploring contemporary piano teaching in the context of tradition highlights both continuity and change. A general teaching tradition that has crossed geographic and temporal boundaries is the "maestro" model or "breakdown and build up approach" (Persson 1994 and 1996). Subotnik concludes that most high-quality teachers say they do not subscribe to the "break down and build up approach." Citing a Juilliard studio teacher, she also posits the continuity of the tradition: "It's possible that people are (employing the maestro model), but are not willing to share that about themselves" (2004, 146).

During the nineteenth century, "Schools" of "pianism" emerged, evidencing certain national characteristics, although the world of piano was international (Soderlund, 2006, 419 and 453). Because of the breadth of its influence on twentieth-century piano teaching in the United States and with approximately half the interviewees in the current study having studied in the former Soviet Union or with Russian émigrés in the United States, or both, a brief discussion of Russian or Soviet tradition is necessary to provide context for references in later chapters. Conservatories were established in St. Petersburg and Moscow in 1862 and 1866, respectively, and later in other large cities (Gelfand 1986–1987, 39; Barnes 2007, xv; and Kofman 2001, 97–104). The noted Juilliard professor Rosina Lhevinne, who graduated from the Moscow Conservatory and emigrated from Russia in 1919, describes her experience:

> As students in Russia, we were taught from the earliest age to strive for perfect technique, in other words, "a complete command of the instrument." But *technique was never a goal in itself*; rather *it was only a means* to express the ideas of the composer. From the outset it was instilled in us that music is one of the arts that requires a middleman to present it to the public, and that the performer has the tremendous responsibility of remaining true to the composer's ideas. This basic principle dominated the whole of our musical lives, both as teachers and performers. (Lhevinne 1972, Introduction, v)

After the Revolution of 1917 changes were made to the syllabus and curriculum and a new system of music education was formed when the Soviets took control over all spheres of the economy and culture during the early 1930s (Gelfand 1986–1987, 39). Later émigrés among the interviewees studied under the Soviet system.

Across the Soviet Union a subsidized system of music schools emerged; the curriculum was prescribed by the government; the private music teacher practically disappeared; and continuation of music education required passing rigorous exams (Kofman 2001, 100–101; Rego 2012, 90–92; and Gelfand, 1986–1987). The base of music education was The Children's Music School, where students (ages seven through fourteen) attended classes after school, including two lessons a week on a chosen instrument, solfeggio, theory of music, and the basics of music literature. The undergraduate music college was a four-year program, the diploma being the equivalent of a U.S. bachelor's degree. Leningrad, Moscow, and a few republics established special professional schools to prepare students for direct entrance into the conservatory (Gelfand 1986–1987, 39–40). The conservatory was a five-year program and the education was free (40–42). In addition to professional courses, students took five years of courses in the history of the Communist Party of the U.S.S.R., Political Economy, Philosophy, and Aesthetics (44). Artists taught under this system excelled in technique and methods (Hechinger 1968, 144).

Formal Pedagogical Training

While all pianists have experience with the one-on-one piano lesson, not all are exposed to formal pedagogical training. For this reason, a distinction is made between education and pedagogical training. The social science literature points to pedagogical training as a catalyst for change in career orientation from performance to teaching (Miller and Baker 2007, 5).

Nationality, age of the teacher, type of educational institution, and where or when piano studies were pursued may explain differences in the role and extent to which teachers of piano formally study pedagogy. Pedagogy was one of four areas of qualification, in addition to solo, chamber, and accompaniment, usually completed by U.S. piano teachers trained in the former Soviet Union. A search of the 2018–2019 Juilliard website for Music Graduate Studies identified two two-credit courses in piano pedagogy—Piano Pedagogy and the Art of Teaching in the Piano Studio (Juilliard 2018–2019). The former is described as a practical approach to teaching at different levels (e.g., the psychology of learning and teaching, study and evaluation of teaching repertoire and materials, use of technology in teaching, and approaches to the learning and teaching of keyboard skills and musical literacy). The latter focuses on the skills necessary to be effective private studio teachers (e.g., exploring learning styles, teaching strategies, assessment strategies, resources, and methods and approaches to cultivate a creative learning environment) and teaching a limited number of private lessons.

Arenas: Developing an Approach to Teaching Piano

Broadening the definition of music education and piano teaching to encompass not only the lesson but beyond the lesson and promoting the generally culture requires the teacher to expand his or her knowledge of music beyond the teaching of the instrument. Early teachers, tradition, and formal pedagogical training may provide examples, advice, and information pertinent to developing and implementing an approach to teaching within each of the three arenas.

The Lesson

As the primary setting for piano study, the one-on-one lesson is necessarily a crucial component of any approach to teaching piano. Although the extant literature may focus on voice or other instruments, the observations on aspects of the lesson highlight areas to be explored, including the teacher-student relationship (e.g., the tension between student dependency on the teacher and aspirations of facilitating student autonomy) (Gaunt 2008, 238), expectations of the effects of practicing (Ericsson et al. 1990 and Howe and Sloboda 1991b, 62), and parental participation in the lesson (Macmillan 2004, 308). The requisites to piano teaching, identified from the historical literature, are also integral to an approach to piano teaching. Deciding how to address fingering, pedaling, or selecting the appropriate piece is a challenge for the piano teacher. The model of an early teacher, tradition, and pedagogical training may offer options to the contemporary teacher.

Beyond the Lesson

The historical and contemporary literatures on piano study consider the role of the piano teacher beyond the lesson. Activities may include encouraging students to learn about the composer whose work they are studying or listening to music, taking students to concerts, and socializing through a variety of activities (e.g., Rezits 1995, 39; Gaunt 2008, 234–35; and Presland 2005, 241). What is available and viewed as appropriate varies among individual teachers, broader sociocultural environments, and over time.

Promoting the General Culture

Early pedagogues recognized a responsibility to teach not only the genius but also the more average student as a means to raise the culture of the entire society. Similarly, the contemporary studies of MacKenzie (1991) and Pitts (2012) underscore the role of music teaching and education in fostering a lifelong interest in music. The importance of music and the arts to contemporary U.S. society, including the role of educational institutions in this process, is reflected in the words of the sixth president of Juilliard, Joseph Polisi.

> The concept that the arts can enhance the quality of life of our citizenry through its positive force must be re-introduced to the collective American psyche. This process of understanding and appreciating the arts can only be realized through education—in our primary and secondary schools, in our institutions of higher learning, and through our performing-arts institutions. (Polisi 2016, 35)

Awareness of the importance of music and the arts, generally, is being actualized through community programs in music that have emerged across the country.

Gaps in the Literature: Becoming a Piano Teacher

Contemporary research on music teaching, in conjunction with the historical literature, highlights the contribution of early teachers, tradition, and formal pedagogical training to the development of a teaching approach. Nevertheless, because available research usually focuses on music teaching in school, is written from the student's perspective, and does not specifically address one-on-one private piano teaching, gaps exist in our understanding of how these factors may contribute to contemporary U.S. piano teaching in the arenas of the one-on-one lesson and beyond. The unanswered questions include: How and to what extent are experiences of early teachers and traditions incorporated into contemporary piano teaching? What role does pedagogical training play in the development of an approach to teaching piano? Are there other factors that contribute to the development of the teaching approach of today's piano teacher?

BEING A PIANO TEACHER: QUALITIES OF A GOOD TEACHER

Having become a piano teacher raises the question, what does it mean to be a piano teacher? The historical and social science literatures identify and describe a range of qualities of a good piano teacher. The qualities identified illustrate both continuity and change in the teaching of piano.

Qualities of a Good Teacher

Personality and temperament; motivation to teach; having a method or not; repertoire; knowing each student; recognizing the individuality of each student's playing; and beyond the instrument are consistently identified as qualities of the good piano teacher. While the categories of qualities remain constant, the emphasis on and description of a particular quality may vary with time and location. Accordingly, contemporary studies of piano teaching are explored to ascertain what these qualities mean today.

Personality and Temperament

The personality traits most frequently identified as hallmarks of effective teaching by the interviewees in Mills and Smith's study of English music service teachers included "is enthusiastic," teacher's knowledge and accomplishment, praises, inspires, and is patient (2003, 25). Nevertheless, as discussed earlier in this chapter, the relative importance of the personality of the teacher varies with the age and/or stage of development of the student.

Enthusiasm and warmth, for example, may be particularly important for young students but less so for older or more musically advanced students.

Not only positive but negative attributes and changing attitudes on what is appropriate behavior can also be identified from the research. Although the maestro model has been a long-standing tradition in piano teaching, students who lack self-assurance and independence may fare badly. Artistic development may be negatively affected because of the harsh and insensitive treatment that characterizes the approach (Persson 1994, 79 and 1996, 33). While acknowledging that some students are prepared to undergo whatever necessary to learn what they need to advance, Subotnik asserts that no student needs to be subjected to the browbeating of the maestro model (2004, 145–46).

Motivation to Teach

As a quality of a good piano teacher, motivation is defined to include a drive toward music, the ability to motivate students to learn, and the motivation/ commitment to teach. Among the factors of paramount importance to the musical careers of the Polish musicians, interviewed in Manturzewska's study, was musical motivation (drive toward music) (1990, 132 and 124–25). Additionally, the study suggests that the professional situation of the pianist may affect the motivation to teach. Participants generally began to show an interest in teaching later in their careers (usually between forty-five and fifty-five), as they sought safer, less stressful ways of functioning as a musician (136). The optimum age of teaching fell between fifty-five and sixty-five, when previous soloists and virtuosi were capable of identifying with the achievements and successes of their students (136–37). That teachers can motivate the pursuit of music is evident from the research on developing the young musician and studies of piano teaching (Sosniak 1985c, 498; Sloboda and Howe 1991; and Madsen and Kelly 2002, 330); however, beyond anecdotal evidence, for example Schnabel encouraging Curcio to teach (Ashley 1993, 11), the effect of teachers motivating students to teach is less evident.

Among the themes that pervade the anecdotal accounts of the early pedagogues are commitment and the desire/even felt obligation to pass on the tradition. Nevertheless, not all great pianists want to, can, or do teach. Moreover, music teachers do not make their pupils famous but the reverse— teachers owe their reputations to their successful students, and even the greatest pedagogues are usually known only within the music world (Sand 2000, 41). Accordingly, making a commitment to teach raises a number of questions about the difference between the performer and teacher, or at least differences in motivation to perform and to teach, even if embodied in the same person. Transmitting their knowledge and skills to the next generation may be perceived as a way of fulfilling a debt of gratitude to their professors

(Gaunt 2008, 221). The importance of passion to the performance career is acknowledged in the literature. Perhaps the source of the passion and commitment to teach is the desire to pass on the tradition—beyond any personal indebtedness.

Having a Method or Not

Among historical pedagogues and contemporary teachers, opinions vary widely regarding the need for a precise and systematic method for teaching piano. Some claim to have no method, while others are quite precise. Certain requisites of piano study—fingering, pedaling, sound/tone, daily practice, artistic image—are to be mastered to produce beautiful music. Nevertheless, how each teacher teaches these requisites may differ-. Being able to teach has more to do with one's desire to transfer knowledge than knowledge (Brown, 2009, p. 37, citing Menahem Pressler).

Repertoire

The vehicle through which tradition, technique, and love of music are transferred from teacher to student is the music itself. As the student develops, more importance is placed on the teacher's knowledge and musical expertise (Sosniak 1985b, 418–19; and 1988, 81–82; and Sloboda and Howe, 1991, 19). Participants in the Mills and Smith study identified wide repertoire among the hallmarks of good teaching at the higher education level (2003, 9). Teachers may use their personal repertoire differently in teaching. Internationally renowned classical pianist and professor Russell Sherman describes two types of teachers: those who assign pieces with which they are most familiar and those who don't, but all teachers are likely to recommend certain favorite composers and pieces deemed useful to the growing-up stages of the student (1997, 76).

Knowing Each Student

Historically, the importance of knowing each student musically and psychologically—his/her personality and interest, difficulties in playing, what each student needs and when—and tailoring the demands of one's teaching approach to each student's need is a recurring theme. As a teacher, renowned violinist and pedagogue Dorothy Delay paid attention to the non-genius as well as the genius. "I found myself being interested in how certain talents can be developed because I always had the desire to believe that environment was more important than heredity" (Sand 2000, 54). Delay was committed to the individual rather than imposing her own ideas. She might stand a problem on its head, turn it inside out, break it into tiny bits, and lay out ten different possibilities, but the final choice of a solution is left to the student. "Do it my way" or "Do it this way" were simply not in her lexicon (66). Sherman asserts that curriculum requirements for each student should be differentiated according to individual needs and goals:

> If one student requires more counterpoint and the other more solfege, why feed the same portions to disproportionate needs? Why not tailor a curriculum which could respond to and compensate for personal strengths and weaknesses? (1997, 66)

Knowing the needs and goals of the individual student and tailoring one's teaching is identified in the contemporary social science literature as a valuable part of the one-on-one experience and a hallmark of effective teaching (Carey and Grant 2015, 7–8; and Mills and Smith 2003, 9). Subotnik observes that studio teachers at Juilliard tended to view each student as a puzzle to be analyzed and developed and, consequently, many strategies were employed, particularly when the performance styles of student and teacher were not compatible (2004, 146–47). The opportunity to adapt the teaching approach to the needs of the individual student is a vital part of what makes the one-on-one lesson valuable, as was observed by both students and teachers in the Carey and Grant study (2015, 7). From the teacher's perspective, priorities may include treating each student as an individual, reacting to students' changing needs, and providing the right learning environment. For students, the value is to cater to their needs (8).

Recognizing the Individuality of Each Student's Playing

Among the hallmarks of effective teaching identified at the higher education level was "the development of individual voice" (Mills and Smith 2003, 9). Stated as a question, do all the students of a teacher sound alike or is it possible to identify the expression of a student's own artistic individuality? Liszt, Curcio, and Pressler are said to have grasped the importance of cultivating the individuality of the student. Dorothy Delay was committed to the individual (Sand 2000, 66). Within the parameters of the composer's meaning, there is room for interpretation. One of the criticisms of the Russian/Soviet school is the failure to foster originality and stimulate creative influences and the lack of spark of creative imagination—principally because attention is given to the development of the technical side (Hechinger 1968, 144–45).

Individuality of playing would seem to go hand in hand with the development of independence. What is important is freeing the students from their teachers and making the students their own teachers (Sosniak 1988, 84). As Sherman observes, the goal is independence and the goal of every teacher should be the cultivation of the student's independence (1997, 62). Autonomous learning requires the development of skills including self-confidence, the breadth of experience through different teachers and learning environments, and the ability to think "outside the box" (beyond an established way of doing things) (Gaunt 2008, 221). Of her teacher, Dorothy Delay, violinist Nadja Salerno-Sonnenberg observes: "She was teaching me to teach myself—and that's why she is a great teacher" (Sand 2000, 214).

Beyond the Instrument

Within the lesson, teaching piano extends beyond conveying the skills necessary to play the instrument. Beyond the instrument may signify teaching about the composer of the piece being learned, including its historical background, and having the student engage in related activities—listening to music outside the context of the lesson. The teacher may even have to be a psychologist. Beyond the desire to pass on music traditions and skills to the next generation is the realization of the powerful effect music has on one's life (Madsen and Kelly 2002, 330).

Arenas: Being a Piano Teacher

From the literatures, especially the contemporary research on the study of music, what is known about the qualities of the "good teacher" in practice? How do the desirable qualities play out in the arenas of the lesson, beyond the lesson, and promoting the general culture?

The Lesson

The historical and contemporary social science studies identify qualities of good piano teaching. The student memoirs portray the personalities and teaching approaches of selected pedagogues, while the pedagogues, themselves, describe desirable teaching qualities. The studies of music teaching identify hallmarks of good teaching (Mills and Smith 2003), although the importance of a particular quality varies with different stages of musical growth (Sosniak 1985a and 1988).

Beyond the Lesson

The memoirs of the students of the historical pedagogues are filled with examples of musical education beyond the individual one-on-one lesson. Leschetizky's classes, for example, included singers, actors, painters, as well as other students (Newcomb 1921, 33). Sosniak describes how teachers extended the teacher-student relationship beyond the lesson, including prodding students to participate in public musical activities, arranging recitals, negotiating auditions with important musicians, writing letters for summer camps, and even driving students to special events (1985b, 418–19). Recent studies report differing views among teachers as to what constitutes appropriate interaction with students outside the lesson ranging from actively seeking to avoidance (Gaunt 2008, 234). Similarly, students' opinions were also found to vary in what they believed to acceptable and unacceptable socializing with professors (Presland, 2005, 241). Whatever the specific activity, music education takes place beyond the lesson.

Promoting the General Culture

The responsibility to pass down the love of music and the traditions associated with the study of piano extends beyond the individual piano student to different populations in the larger community and society, in general. The writings of the historical pedagogues and contemporary scholars reflect their cognizance of this responsibility. Neuhaus speaks of creating culture, which is the soil on which talent prospers and flourishes (1973, 171)—a high level of musical culture worthy of our people and of the great times in which we live (203). Considering the contribution of music education beyond training future professional musicians, contemporary studies provide evidence of the lifelong benefits of musical education for enriching leisure and continuing musical development in adulthood (Pitts 2012, 163), underscoring the importance of such education to society, in general.

Gaps in the Literature: Qualities of a Good Teacher

While the identified qualities of a good piano teacher have generally remained constant, what constitutes a particular quality and acceptable behavior may vary over time and place. For example, is it or when is it appropriate to yell at a student? Because the extant research generally does not focus on the pianist as teacher within the context of the private lesson and is usually written from the perspective of the student, gaps exist with regard to contemporary views on the desirable qualities. Further study of how to motivate a student to become a piano teacher and the transmission of the qualities of a good teacher is needed. While contemporary studies help to identify qualities, the richness of personal experience can be lost in the quantitative presentation, underscoring the need for qualitative research. Accordingly, in the current study, each quality is considered to be a concept to be explored in its contemporary context.

SUMMARY AND CONCLUSION: POINT
OF DEPARTURE FOR THE STUDY OF
CONTEMPORARY PIANO TEACHING

The historical and social science literatures present, at best, an incomplete picture of the piano teacher and teaching. Providing evidence of the relevance of the identified factors, for example family and early teachers, to musical growth, the research on developing the talented young musician provides the backdrop for exploring the early years of the pianist—teacher and/or performer. In exploring the later years of musical growth, these studies generally fail to address, specifically, the contribution of factors to deciding to become, becoming, and being a piano teacher. While highlighting the contribution of early teachers and pedagogical training to music education within the school, the social science research generally does not consider approaches to piano teaching within the one-on-one lesson. The questions and issues left unanswered by the white-collar literature provide the point of departure for the current study of the contemporary piano teacher and teaching, laid out in chapter 5.

NOTE

1. Although the studies use different terminology and categorizations to describe parental status and occupations, the family backgrounds of the participants are similar.

Chapter 5

This Study

Having established the limitations of the extant research, this chapter lays out the qualitative approach used to develop a more complete portrait of the piano teacher and teaching. The first section of the chapter presents the factors, extrapolated from the historical and social science literatures, adapted to elicit information on deciding to become, becoming, and being a contemporary U.S. piano teacher. Grounded in the social science research tradition that views those who have experienced a situation as meaningful informants regarding that situation (Stolz 1985, xiv–xv), the second section explains the process employed to obtain firsthand information about U.S. piano teachers and teaching, today. The interviewee—a piano teacher with ten or more years of experience—is viewed as the expert regarding his/her experiences as a pianist and teacher. Exploring interviewees' observations and experiences, using the factors extrapolated from the literatures, should highlight common themes and patterns—the role of social science research—enhancing our understanding of the contemporary piano teacher and teaching.

DECIDING TO BECOME, BECOMING, AND BEING A PIANO TEACHER: FACTORS AND QUESTIONS

The overriding purpose of the current research is to develop a portrait of the U.S. piano teacher and teaching, situated within its historical and social science contexts. Given that the extant research confirms the relevance of the factors, extrapolated from the historical and social science research, to the pursuit of a career in music, the identified factors are used to explore systematically the process of deciding to become, becoming, and being a contemporary piano teacher. In this section a matrix of factors and questions focusing on the piano teacher and teaching piano is developed for each topic and presented in Tables 5.1 through 5.3.

Topic 1: Deciding to Become a Piano Teacher: Defining the Factors

Drawing from the social science literatures on career choice, achieving success, and developing the talented musician, factors that may affect the decision to teach piano were identified. These factors provide a structure and direction for the investigation of the pursuit of a career teaching piano. During the early years, young pianists are likely to be similarly affected by the identified factors (see chapter 4). Nevertheless, because of the emphasis on the developmental years of the musician as performer, the extant literature offers little insight into the choices and preparation of the musician as teacher. To explore the decision to teach piano, the developmental history of the piano teacher is defined to include later stages in the career of the pianist and the identified factors are refocused to elicit information on the piano teacher and teaching.

Extending the Developmental History of the Pianist as Piano Teacher

For the most part, studies of young musicians focus on the years of musical growth and development leading to a professional career in music (see chapters 3 and 4). For example, the developmental history of the pianist, as described in Sosniak's study of the talented young musician, encompasses three stages—early, middle, and later years (1985a, 20). Yet, as illustrated by Manturzewska's study of Polish pianists, the decision to teach piano may occur at any point in a pianist's career (1990). Accordingly, the current study extends the developmental history of the piano teacher through two additional stages—advanced education (graduate school and professional training) and the professional musician (the mature pianist). During the fourth stage, education and training include courses in piano pedagogy and experiences teaching. The fifth stage takes into account those pianists who decide to teach later in a professional career in music. As in the earlier research, the stages are related to but not defined by age; rather, they reflect experiences with music; level of education; and interactions with parents, teachers, the instrument, and the world of music. Age is referenced, as appropriate, when relevant to the analysis.

Although the factors identified as contributing to the decision to teach piano may remain constant, the relevance and role played by a particular factor may vary if this decision is made earlier or later in the career of the pianist. Extending the stages in the developmental history of the piano teacher from the early through mature years affords the opportunity to consider this possibility. Moreover, experiences at later stages in the development of the pianist, for example, courses in piano pedagogy or experience teaching, may further the decision to teach, especially becoming and being a piano teacher. Even if the decision to teach piano occurs within the middle and later stages of the young musician's musical development, the process of becoming a mature piano teacher continues.

Factors Contributing to the Decision to Teach Piano

Factors extrapolated from the literatures on career choice, achieving success, and developing the talented young musician are used to explore the early developmental years of the pianist, as teacher, and the decision to teach piano across the stages of the developmental history of the piano teacher. Given that almost thirty years have passed since the earlier studies on developing the talented young musician were conducted and to situate the current study within the extant literature, the identified factors are used to explore the early musical growth and development of the contemporary piano teacher. As the identified factors are relevant to career choice, generally, they are used to explore the decision to teach piano. The contribution of a particular factor to the development of a young pianist's interest in music during the early years and the decision to teach piano may differ. For example, early music education focuses primarily on first teachers, while education related to the decision to teach piano extends through graduate school.

Accordingly, as presented in Table 5.1, each factor is defined somewhat differently in column 2—early years: interest in music, and column 3—decision to teach piano. Specifically, in column 2, the factors are defined to elicit information on the early experiences of the young pianist and development of an interest in music and the piano. Given the age of interviewees during this stage of their musical development, two factors—adolescent employment and community labor market conditions—were considered not applicable. Column 3 defines each factor, as it will be used to explore the decision to teach piano.

Taken together, chapters 6 and 7 describe the contribution of each factor to the decision to teach piano over the developmental history of the piano teacher, as defined in this study.

Table 5.1 Factors Contributing to Interest in Music and the Decision to Teach Piano

	Definitions	
Factor	*Early Years: Interest in Music*	*Decision to Teach Piano*
Family	Family of origin—birth family.	Family of origin—birth family—and family of destination—created in adulthood.
Education	Music education (early teachers, the lesson, and activities beyond the instrument) to prepare a piano student.	Music education (early and later teachers, college, and graduate training) to prepare to teach piano.
Adolescent Employment	N/A	Early experiences teaching piano.
Community Labor Market Conditions	N/A	Job market and opportunities for employment in the music profession and piano teaching.
Talent	Special gift for music, self-identified: for example: "I was a child prodigy" or "My teacher recognized that I was talented."	Special gift, to teach piano, self-identified: for example: "I discovered I was good at it (teaching)."
Hard Work/ Diligence	Training as a performer (practicing).	Training as a performer (practicing) and teacher (planning and preparing for each lesson).
Passion	(1) Self-directed—interest in music for its own sake.	(1) Self-directed—interest in music for its own sake—and (2) purpose—intent to contribute to the well-being of others (drive to share the love, knowledge, and traditions of music).
Perseverance	Quiet determination to stick to a course once decided and tendency not to abandon tasks in the face of obstacles to pursuing music.	Quiet determination to stick to a course once decided and tendency not to abandon tasks in the face of obstacles to pursuing music and piano teaching.
Listening to Music	Early opportunity to experience intensive positive emotional or aesthetic states in response to music.	Sharing the experience of music.
Personal Commitment to Music	Intrinsic motivation for musical activities and long term commitment to continuous learning.	Intrinsic motivation to teach piano and long term commitment to continuous learning.
Personal Support System	Resources and emotional support from parents, teachers, and friends.	Resources and emotional support directed toward teaching piano.
Challenges and Barriers	Societal (racism and sexism) and personal (physical and psychological) challenges and barriers affecting pursuit of music.	Societal, professional (music profession and piano teaching), and personal (physical and psychological) challenges and barriers affecting pursuit of music and piano teaching.

Topic 2: Becoming a Piano Teacher: Potential Contributing Factors

From the historical and social science literatures, three factors—early teachers, tradition, and formal pedagogical training—stand out as contributing to becoming a piano teacher. Specifically, these factors may affect, positively or negatively, the development of an approach to teaching piano. For purposes of this study, approach includes, but it is not limited to teaching keyboard skills—methods. Using the broader term—approach—piano teaching is considered in three arenas—the lesson, beyond the lesson, and promoting the general culture, which were also identified from these literatures.

Factors Contributing to Contemporary Approaches to Teaching Piano

Early teachers, tradition, and formal pedagogical training were consistently identified in the social science literatures as factors that contribute to the development of an approach to teaching piano. While considering questions about piano teaching, because of the emphasis of these studies on music education within the classroom, gaps exist in our understanding of how the three factors may affect the development of an approach to one-on-one piano teaching. Moreover, the role and relative importance of the contribution of each factor may vary with time, geographic boundaries, and the teaching approach of an individual pianist. Table 5.2 lays out questions to be explored to elicit information on how each factor and the three factors, taken together, affect the development of contemporary approaches to teaching piano within the one-on-one piano lesson.

Table 5.2   Factors Contributing to the Development of an Approach to Teaching Piano: Questions

Factors	Questions
Role of teachers	
Early teachers	How and to what extent do the teaching practices of early teachers, positively or negatively, contribute to the teaching approaches of contemporary piano teachers?
Tradition	
	The definition of tradition is self-identified, for example, "My teacher taught in the true Russian style." How does tradition, in its various meanings, contribute to contemporary piano teaching? How are traditions incorporated, changed, modified, or even rejected in the context of U.S. society and culture?
Pedagogical training	
Formal	How may formal pedagogical training contribute to the development of contemporary approaches to teaching piano?

The importance of these factors notwithstanding, other factors may play a role in the development of contemporary approaches to one-on-one piano teaching. Accordingly, chapter 8 not only expres the factors, extrapolated from the literatures, but also sets out to identify additional contributing factors.

Arenas of Piano Study and Developing an
Approach to Teaching Piano

While the primary arena in which piano study and teaching occur is the lesson, two other arenas are evidenced in the historical and social science literatures— beyond the lesson, and promoting the general culture. The contributions of early teachers, tradition, and formal pedagogical training are reflected in the approach to teaching piano within these three arenas. As a pianist's approach to teaching, in practice, is usually a composite of factors that interact within each arena, isolating the specific contribution of a particular factor may be difficult. Such difficulties, notwithstanding, considering the role of each factor and the interaction among factors is essential to the analysis of the development of contemporary piano teaching approaches and furthering of our understanding of continuity and change in piano teaching. Accordingly, the contribution of individual factors and the confluence of factors to the development of teaching approaches actualized within each arena are explored in chapter 8.

Topic 3: Being a Piano Teacher: Qualities and Practice

The third topic to be explored in this study is being a contemporary U.S. piano teacher, specifically, qualities of a good teacher and contemporary piano teaching, in practice. An examination of the historical and social science literatures reveals an inventory of qualities of a "good teacher" of piano. While identified as a characteristic of a "good teacher," each quality is also a concept to be explored within the context of contemporary piano teaching, as the definition of a particular quality and, especially, how it is implemented and observed in practice may vary with the time period and geographic location in which the piano teaching occurs. The extant literatures provide little insight into being a contemporary teacher of piano, in practice, given the emphasis on the musician as performer and music educator within the school.

Qualities of a Good Piano Teacher

The qualities, extrapolated from the literatures and interviews, provide a framework for constructing or perhaps reconstructing the image of the contemporary piano teacher. Given the historical and cultural differences in perspectives on teaching, generally; teaching music; and teaching piano, specifically, two questions underlie the current exploration of the qualities

Table 5.3   Qualities of a Good Piano Teacher: Questions

Qualities	Questions
Personality and temperament	What are the desirable personality traits of a contemporary piano teacher? Do the characteristics vary with the student's age or other situational variables?
Motivation to teach	Motivation includes (1) a drive toward music, (2) the ability to motivate students to learn, and (3) the motivation/commitment to teach. How is each aspect of motivation reflected in the experiences of contemporary piano teachers?
Having a method, or not	Is having a method perceived to be necessary to contemporary piano teaching? What is entailed in teaching keyboard skills, by way of example?
Repertoire	Is having a wide repertoire essential to effective piano teaching? Is there a difference between knowing how to play and knowing how to teach a particular composition?
Knowing each student	For the contemporary piano teacher, what constitutes knowing each student?
Recognizing the individuality of each student's playing	Is developing a student's individual voice viewed as an important quality? If so, what does developing a student's individual voice—as a pianist—entail?
Beyond the instrument	Does the role of contemporary piano teacher extend beyond the transfer of skills necessary to play the instrument? If so, how?

of a "good teacher" of piano: Do the qualities identified from the literature inform contemporary approaches to piano teaching in the United States and, if so, how? The specific questions to be explored, pertinent to each quality, are presented in Table 5.3.

The qualities of a good teacher, as defined within contemporary piano teaching, are described in chapter 9. Drawing on original research, chapter 10 explores being a contemporary piano teacher, including how the identified qualities are reflected in practice, within each of the three arenas—the lesson, beyond the lesson, and promoting the general culture.

Framing the Current Study

The factors identified from the literatures provide the starting point for the current study of the contemporary teacher and teaching of piano, specifically, deciding to become, becoming, and being a piano teacher. The factors and questions presented in Tables 5.1 through 5.3 help to frame the research presented in Part II of this book. Interviews with a selected population of piano teachers provide the firsthand information about contemporary piano teachers and teaching in the United States. The interviews probe the questions, presented in the tables, and additional questions on being a contemporary piano teacher not addressed in the extant literature. The next section lays out the qualitative approach used in this study, including the identification and selection of interviewees, interview process, and limitations.

CURRENT STUDY: METHODOLOGICAL APPROACH

To obtain firsthand and current information on (1) deciding to become (2) becoming (i.e., factors contributing to the development of an approach to teaching piano), and (3) being (i.e., the qualities of a good piano teacher and contemporary piano teaching in practice) a contemporary piano teacher, this study is grounded in the social science research tradition that views those who have experienced a situation as meaningful informants regarding that situation (Stolz 1985, xiv–xv). The interviewee—a piano teacher—is considered to be the expert regarding his/her experience. Using a similar approach to study talented young musicians, Howe and Sloboda underscore the importance of the qualitative results of their investigation—observations in which children describe their experiences and perceptions of key aspects of their early musical education (e.g., family background and listening to music), which may have played crucial roles in their early musical progress (1991a, 41).

The process by which a pianist decides, prepares for, and then pursues a career teaching piano is unique to the individual. The teaching experience, including the formulation of one's teaching approach and the development of relationships with students within the piano lesson, is very personal. The richness and complexity of the individual stories can be lost in the generality of the quantitative data, although both quantitative and qualitative data are complementary and necessary (Howe and Sloboda 1991a, 40–41). The qualitative information presented in the current study is key to the fuller understanding of what actually happens in the course of becoming a musician, in this instance a piano teacher. The proposed approach should begin to address gaps in the extant literature and suggest areas of inquiry for further qualitative and quantitative research not only with respect to teaching piano but also the teaching of other instruments, voice, and even conducting.

Identification and Selection of the Interviewees

The objective of the identification and selection of study participants was to find piano teachers with diverse backgrounds and experiences, who could speak to their personal development and professional life as a piano teacher. The primary consideration in the selection of interviewees was that he/she was currently teaching piano and had experience teaching piano in the United States; nationality and country of music education and training were not restricted to the United States. Considering the number of U.S. piano teachers in the northeast, alone, and the purpose of the current study—to obtain information on "good piano teaching"—random sampling was not considered.

Rather, the interviewees were judgmentally selected using the following criteria: gender, age, educational training, national origin, and country of piano study and training. Variation was also sought in the types of students taught (e.g., children, precollege, university, or adult) and types of institutional affiliations (e.g., conservatory—precollege, college, and graduate programs; liberal arts college [department or school]—undergraduate and graduate levels; schools of music—children, precollege, and adult; and nonaffiliated independent private teachers). It should be noted that interviewees were often teaching in more than one setting and working with students of different ages. Not considered as a selection criterion was the pedagogical "lineage" of the interviewee; nor, did the author deliberately seek to find contemporary teachers who had been trained by noted pedagogues or their students.

The initial group of interviewees was comprised of individuals currently teaching at different types of educational institutions in Washington, D.C., and New York City. The first interviewees selected were identified through the institution where I was studying piano. The faculty is diverse with respect to gender, age, and country of piano study and training. With the assistance of the piano administrator, we identified a pool of potential interviewees using the selection criteria. An email from the administrator was sent to the identified faculty members, after which the author followed up via an email requesting an interview. This email provided more detailed information on the project, including underscoring that participation was voluntary and anonymous.

Using the institutional criteria, additional interviewees were identified through music program administrators at recognized New York City institutions of higher education in music. The administrator usually provided the researcher with the names of potential interviewees, considering the selection criteria and notified the faculty member about the project by email. The request for an interview was then made directly by the researcher, primarily via email or telephone. Additionally, through a snowball technique—asking interviewees or other contacts to recommend potential interviewees—still other study participants were identified in Washington, D.C.; New York; Pittsburgh, Pennsylvania; and Baton Rouge, Louisiana. These interviewees were contacted directly by the researcher, as referred.

Interviewees

Twenty current piano teachers from different geographic locations and with different institutional affiliations were interviewed. At the time of the interview, all study participants were full-time musicians and teaching piano, giving one-on-one lessons. Generally, study participants had considered what is entailed in the teaching of piano, and, therefore, were well-prepared to reflect on their experiences. The twenty interviews included fifteen in person; one in person and in writing; two by telephone; and two in writing. The interviews conducted by phone and in writing contributed to the geographic diversity of the interview population. Whatever the means used to obtain the information, interviews were guided by the semi-structured data collection schedule described here. From the analysis and synthesis of their observations emerged common themes and patterns.

Description of the Interviewee Population

In accordance with the selection criteria—gender, age, educational training, national origin, and country of piano study and training—the background characteristics of the participants in the study are diverse. While pedagogical lineage was not a criterion, several interviewees were students of well-known piano pedagogues and traditions. Interviewees had extensive experience teaching different types of piano students in different institutional settings over the course of a teaching career.

Personal Sketch. Of the twenty interviewees, seven were male and thirteen were female. The age range spanned sixty years—thirty to over ninety years of age. Fifteen were over the age of forty, four of whom were over seventy years of age. Five were between the ages of thirty-one and forty. Country of birth included the U.S. mainland (10); U.S. Puerto Rico (1); the former Soviet Union, including Russia (3), Lithuania (1), and Georgia (1); Poland (1); South Korea (1); Australia (1); and Canada (1). During the early years interviewees began piano study in the country of origin. In the middle and later years interviewees might continue piano studies in the country of origin or in other countries, sometimes more than one country. Although interviewees received their music education and piano studies in different countries with different educational systems, all pursued formal advanced studies, sometimes in more than one country—fourteen in the United States; four in the former Soviet Union; three in Austria; and one each in Lithuania, Israel, the Netherlands, Ukraine, and Great Britain. Interviewees had usually completed advanced degrees, either a master's degree or doctorate. Table B.1 in appendix B provides more detailed background information by interviewee.

Lineage: An Unintended Consideration. Reference has been made to the "lineage" of piano teachers dating back to the early pedagogues. The selection criteria did not include nor did the author deliberately seek to find contemporary teachers who had been trained by famous pedagogues. Unexpectedly, a number of interviewees reported having studied with a pedagogue or the student of a pedagogue discussed in the literature reviewed in the first two chapters. Examples of lineages included those of Leschetizky (through his students Vengerova and Schnabel to Curcio), Neuhaus (and his student Vera Gornostaeva), Josef Lhevinne (through his student Adele Marcus), and Rosina Lhevinne. Additionally, three interviewees studied with other interviewees, who were students of Vengerova, Marcus, and Neuhaus, thus continuing the line. Determining whether any method or system—influence of a particular teacher or "school" of piano teaching—is strong enough and defined enough to survive not only one generation but others as well, as noted by Rezits (1979, 16), is difficult. Nevertheless, an interviewee's observations regarding the influence of a piano pedagogical lineage on his/her teaching approach, although anecdotal, show both continuity and change in the profession.

Teaching Experience. The stage in the musical lifespan age at which interviewees began teaching piano varied, with ages ranging from twelve to over forty years old. More than half of the interviewees began teaching during high school or college, between approximately fifteen and twenty-one years of age. All but three were teaching piano by graduate school. Interviewees, who began teaching after having established a performance career, had given master classes but commenced one-on-one teaching as a mature pianist. Whatever the age at which an interviewee began teaching piano, at the time of the interview his/her experience teaching was extensive.

Given the focus of this study on "good piano teaching," having experience teaching piano was considered in the selection process. As shown in Figure 5.1, the length of teaching experience ranged from twelve to seventy-eight years.

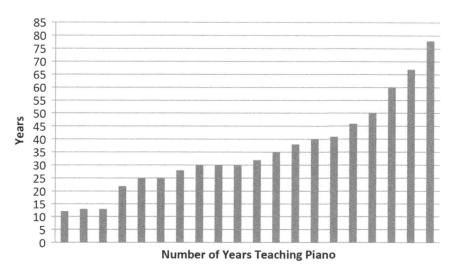

Figure 5.1   Range of Experience: Number of Years Interviewees Reported Teaching Piano

Seventeen interviewees had taught for more than twenty years, including seven who had taught for forty or more years.

The number of years taught, by interviewee, can be found in appendix B, Table B.1.

Types of Students and Teaching Settings

Interviewees usually taught a broad spectrum of students from children to adults, with ages ranging from four or five years old to well into their eighties or older. At the time of the interview, an interviewee might be working with a specific population, especially if the primary teaching venue was a university or conservatory. Within a conservatory, an interviewee might teach students from a precollege division, in addition to undergraduate and graduate students. Across a career teaching piano, even those associated with a university usually had experience teaching children and teenagers of different levels and abilities and adult students. Additionally, not only did each interviewee typically teach a diverse student population but was teaching in more than one institutional setting—a music school, college, or university, and also in a personal studio or the student's home. Within the various settings and with different types of students, the one-on-one piano lesson is essential to the learning process.

Criteria and Expertise

Following the selection criteria, the personal and professional backgrounds of interviewees for this study were diverse. They taught different types of students and in different institutional settings. What they have in common is a breadth of experience. Given the years of teaching piano, individually and collectively, the interview population has a vast expertise in the topics to be explored in this study—deciding to become, becoming, and being a piano teacher in the United States, today.

The Interview Process

From November 2014 through January 2019, intensive interviews using a semi-structured data collection schedule were conducted. Information gleaned from the interviews is the primary source of the evidence presented in chapters six through ten. The approach used was similar to that employed in a number of the qualitative academic studies on piano study and teaching, cited in chapter 3. In advance of the interview, each participant was sent a description of the project and the schedule of questions to be used to facilitate the process, enhance the quality of the responses, and limit the length of time required for the interview. The interview was usually conducted in-person

(15), although telephone interviews (2) and written responses to the questions (three written only and one in addition to the in-person interview) were used to expand the participant pool. Each interview ran about an hour to an hour and a half, although several ran longer.

Participation in the study was voluntary and, as agreed in advance, anonymous. To maintain anonymity, each interviewee was assigned a unique identification number. References to interviewees, cited for purposes of illustration in Part II, are by identification number (e.g., I#). Additionally, the teachers of interviewees are not mentioned by name but by a letter (e.g., C), because descriptions and characterizations are solely the opinion of the interviewee; others might hold different opinions.

The interviews were used to collect information on the identified factors and qualities, presented in Tables 5.1 through 5.3. The stages of the developmental history of the piano teacher, as defined in this study—early, middle, late, advanced education, and professional musician—were also considered. A semi-structures data collection instrument was developed to guide the interviews and provide consistency in the information collected from each interviewee. Through open-ended questions, interviewees were given the opportunity to express additional opinions and suggest other areas of inquiry.

Specific issues explored with interviewees included the following:

Background: The Early Years

1. Motivation to pursue the study of piano: first experiences of music, first desire to play the piano, and decision to commit to music.
2. Role of early teachers, positive and negative, in developing an interest in music and the piano.
3. Role of later teachers, positive and negative, in developing an interest in music and the piano.
4. Role of family, positive and negative, in developing an interest in music and the piano.
5. Other influences on desire, decision to pursue music.

Topic 1: Deciding to Become a Piano Teacher

6. Decision to pursue the piano, especially teaching piano as a career—when, how, and why.
7. Early teachers—influence on the decision to teach piano, challenges and obstacles, and steps to overcome any obstacles.
8. Later teachers and other individuals contributing to the decision to teach piano, challenges and obstacles, and steps to overcome any obstacles.

9. Other factors contributing to the decision to teach piano, challenges and obstacles, and steps to overcome any obstacles.

Topic 2 Becoming a Piano Teacher

10. Process of becoming a piano teacher, including (a) formal training pursued and (b) formal and informal influences.
11. Developing an approach to teaching piano—actions taken to develop an approach and contributing factors (e.g., early and later teachers, tradition, and formal and informal pedagogical training).
12. Additional factors contributing to the interviewee's approach to teaching.
13. How "factors," identified from literature and by interviewees as contributing to a teaching approach, are incorporated, in practice—focusing on the lesson, activities outside the lesson, and other considerations (probes).
14. Challenges, obstacles, and steps to overcome any obstacles affecting the development of an approach to teaching piano.

Topic 3: Being a Piano Teacher

15. Qualities of a good teacher—open-ended questions—in contemporary piano teaching.
16. Being a piano teacher—approach in practice.
17. Being a piano teacher—implementing a teaching approach—responsibility of the teacher (the lesson, beyond the lesson, and promoting the general culture), relationship between teacher and student in the lesson, expectations of the student, applying one's approach to different types of students, and the role of the parent.
18. Advice to students.
19. Teaching versus performing—conflicting or complementary careers?
20. Challenges, rewards, and steps to overcome any obstacles to being a piano teacher.
21. Advice to future teachers.

Limitations

The study does not purport to address all aspects of the questions why individuals decide to teach piano, how they become a piano teacher, and how they pursue a career as a piano teacher. Because interviewees were selected judgmentally, the analysis of responses is limited to interviewees' observations. Examples of statements of interviewees are included for purposes of illustration. Although the study is not generalizable to the total population of piano teachers, the responses do provide insight into quality piano teaching in the United States, today. Despite its limitations, by drawing on the experiences of current experienced piano teachers, this study should enhance our understanding of the contemporary U.S. piano teacher and piano teaching.

SUMMARY AND CONCLUSION: THE CURRENT STUDY

As described in this chapter, the factors extrapolated from the historical and social science literatures provide the point of departure for the current study. Adapted and refined to focus on the piano teacher and teaching of piano, the factors and questions structure the exploration of the three topics addressed in Part II—deciding to become, becoming, and being a piano teacher. The twenty pianists and piano teachers interviewed are the primary source of firsthand evidence. The musical journey of each interviewee was and continues to be unique. Differences notwithstanding, the analysis and synthesis of interviewees' experiences and observations, taken together, highlight patterns and common themes.

While not generalizable to the universe of piano teachers, given the interviewees' vast experience as pianists and teachers, their observations provide insight into the early years of the young pianist; diverse paths taken to become a piano teacher; factors contributing to contemporary piano teaching approaches; qualities of a good teacher; and the contemporary piano teacher and piano teaching, in practice, including the relationship between teaching and performing. In Part II, chapters 6 through 10 follow the interviewees from their early years and emerging interest in and love of music, through the process of deciding to become and becoming to being a piano teacher. Taken together, the chapters create a portrait of the piano teacher and teaching, situated within its historical and social science contexts.

Part II

A STUDY OF THE CONTEMPORARY U.S. PIANO TEACHER

In this part of the book, the factors and qualities extrapolated from the historical and social science literatures, adapted to the study of piano teaching, frame the analysis of and synthesis of interviewees' experiences in pursuit of a career teaching piano—deciding to become, becoming, and being a piano teacher. Considering factors associated with the decision to pursue a career, especially music, chapters 6 and 7, respectively, focus on the contribution of each factor to interviewees' music growth during the early years and the decision to teach piano. Chapter 6 considers the development of interviewees' interest and love of music, generally mirroring the findings of the literature on developing the talented young musician. Analyzing interviewees' decisions to teach piano in chapter 7, the factors are organized into four categories—precipitating, motivating, sustaining, and supporting and/or confounding. Examining the process of becoming a piano teacher, chapter 8 explores the contribution of teachers, tradition, pedagogical training, and other factors to the development of an approach to teaching. Chapters 9 and 10 present interviewees' observations and experiences as contemporary piano teachers, including the demands and vicissitudes of the music and piano teaching professions and qualities of a good teacher (9) and teaching piano, in practice (10). The final chapter, by way of conclusion, offers a portrait of the contemporary U.S. piano teacher.

Part II.

A STUDY OF THE CONTEXT OF NEW
U.S. PIANO TEACHER

Chapter 6

The Early Years

Developing an Interest in Music and the Piano

The journey to becoming and being a piano teacher begins in childhood. For some pianists, first experiences teaching piano may occur early in life, but, generally, an interest and love of music and the piano would seem necessary to precede the decision to teach. Although the families, educational experiences, and challenges of the young pianists described in earlier studies varied, common themes as to the factors that contribute to musical growth and development emerge (e.g., Sosniak 1985a, 24–45; and Howe and Sloboda 1991a, 42–49). Because of the limitations of these studies—generally focused on the pianist as performer and conducted about thirty years ago—and to situate the current study within this literature, the first section of this chapter explores how the identified factors helped to shape interviewees' early musical growth and development. The second section describes challenges and barriers affecting their pursuit of music. By exploring interviewees' early experiences with music and the piano, this chapter sets the stage for the discussion of the decision to teach piano, presented in chapter 7.

DEVELOPING AN INTEREST IN MUSIC AND THE PIANO: FACTORS

Although experiences during these early years differed, a combination of personal and environmental factors contributed to each interviewee's nascent interest in music and development as a musician. Typically the journey began with the first exposure to music, with the love of music and, specifically, the piano—the passion—emerging between ages four and six, or even earlier. The presentation of factors in this chapter follows the development of interviewees' interest in music and the piano—listening to music, passion, recognizing talent, family, education, perseverance, hard work, personal commitment, and personal support system. As the analysis shows, the contribution of each factor is complex, varying with the stages of musical development and often interacting with other factors, making it difficult to isolate the contribution of a particular factor or categorize the factors by contributing role. Nevertheless, taken together, the identified factors provide the backdrop for the decision to teach piano.

Listening to Music

Recalling being drawn to music as a very young child, interviewees' first exposure often occurred in the home, listening to a parent or older sibling play an instrument or recordings of a variety of types of music.

> Music was always there. The impact of the music was all around, even before my birth. (I9)[1]

For some, the first experiences of music came from outside the home—listening to a neighbor or friend play an instrument, or attending a concert. Sosniak's young pianists had similarly reported listening to music almost from the time they were born, learning to identify composers, musicians, or musical pieces without being conscious of the educational process (1990, 154).

Perhaps hearing rather than listening, passive rather than active, might better characterize the earliest exposure to music because of the age of the child. In any case, participants in the current study vividly described childhood memories of pleasurable experiences, often as young as age four, that influenced their love of music. The experience of listening was similar, wherever the music was heard for the first time.

Asia:

> We lived in a neighborhood outside downtown Seoul, Korea. One day I heard music. I could not see the instrument being played. It was a piano. The woman who lived in the house was a piano teacher. I used to climb on the trash can and sit and listen to the music coming over the wall in front of her house. I was fascinated by the sound. I had a good ear and was able to sing melodies I heard. (I6)

Former Soviet Union:

> My first conscious memories of the piano are linked to "Cliburn, U.S., America"—as one phrase. In 1958, Van Cliburn came to Tbilisi. My mom took me in a pouch to the open dress rehearsal. (I9)

> From a very early age, I listened to my mother's playing; she was a pianist who graduated from the Kiev Conservatory. I remember very well all the pieces she

played for me. It was mainly Chopin, but she also sang and played popular arias from operas and operettas (both the female and male roles). (I14)

Australia:

I lived on a farm in a village in Australia, with no piano. The village was musical—singers. A woman who was a personal friend of the family was my inspiration. (I1)

U.S. Mainland:

I went to classical concerts with my grandparents and father's family. Recordings had a huge influence. I had a strong innate interest in music. I also listened to other types of music, to what my sister listened to. I had a ton of pop cassettes: Madonna, Indigo Girls, and the Bangles. (I19)

Puerto Rico:

Next door to us lived a pianist. She and her daughter practiced the piano. I heard them practicing. (I11)

Sloboda underscores the importance to musical growth of the early opportunity to experience intense positive emotional or aesthetic states in response to music (1990, 167, 170–71, and 176). For interviewees, such experiences were often the impetus to pursue music, specifically the piano. Whether hearers or listeners as children, they did not remain passive in their relationship with the piano but sought to create their own music, usually before the age of six. Gender, nationality, and family background differed. What was constant was the desire to make music, to do (imitate?) what they heard—to play the piano.

I wanted to play that thing. We did not have a piano and my parents had no plans to buy one. It was not a necessity of life. I begged. I don't know why but I was given the choice of either going to kindergarten or taking piano lessons. I chose piano lessons. (I6)

We had a piano. I played with the neighbor's youngest daughter and would try to pick up by ear what she was playing. The neighbor, a pianist, asked my mother who was trying to play the Grieg *Piano Concerto*. The woman said: "Send the boy to me." I started piano lessons six months before I turned five. (I11)

After hearing Cliburn play the Tchaikovsky *Piano Concerto*, I thought I could bang it out on the piano—imitating him in three-quarter time. When Neuhaus came, I asked him to "teach me to play the Tchaikovsky better." He helped with my hands, playing along with the scenario. (I9)

My grandparents had a wonderful Knabe piano with deep tone and beautiful cabinetry. I loved hearing my father play it and I wanted to play that piano as well. I eventually did and my grandparents loved to hear me play. (I16)

At age four, I came home from seeing the *Wizard of Oz* and played the music. (I20)

Additionally, an early teacher might emphasize listening to music as an integral part of the piano lesson. Teachers might also provide the opportunity to listen to music outside the confines of the lesson. These early experiences communicated the importance of listening to the study of music.

Listening to music was an integral part of being her pupil. When she played Rachmaninoff's *Moment Musical* in E minor, I remember how incredibly her left hand moved, the immense power of her sound, and the clarity and intensity. (I14)

From early listening emerged an interviewee's interest in and passion for music, often focused specifically on the desire to play the piano.

Passion

Whether an interviewee grew up in the United States or abroad, was a boy or a girl, when asked when and how the desire to play the piano was first felt, the response was similar. Even before knowing that he/she had talent, interviewees described feeling a passion for the piano, usually by age four, six, or younger.

Female:

I always knew, about age 6. (I1)

I wanted to play that thing. I asked my parents. They said no. (I6)

I knew when I was six years old. It was natural. I was not interested in anything else. (I12)

I had no other thought. My mother started to teach me at age two—singing, not piano. I was always with music. (I14)

Someone gave me a toy piano; I was about 4 years old. (I15)

My dad showed me chopsticks and other small songs. It is his influence that was my motivation. (I16)

I loved playing and improvising from a very young age. (I18)

Male:

I can't remember a time when I did not have the desire to play, three or four years old. There was music in the house. (I8)

Since I was four years old, I had the desire to play the piano. (I11)

At age four. (I20)

Since I was 4 years old. It was a given. My mom played, not professionally, but she took lessons. I liked it. (I7)

That is not to say that all interviewees experienced a passion for music early in life. Beginning lessons and early exposure to music might be prompted by a parent's unfulfilled desire—fulfilling a parent's dream—to study the piano. I took lessons because she (mother) wanted me to; it was not that I did not enjoy it, but it was expected (I2). Or, a child might consider playing music—the piano or in a school orchestra—as just something children did. Playing the piano was the normal pursuit of a kid; I started to feel a connection to music (I10). The intrinsic motivation for musical activity—wanting to be engaged in music for its own sake—has been found to be a condition of musical growth (Sloboda 1990, 176). Whether the passion is experienced in childhood or later, self-motivation to follow the desire for music and the piano emerged.

I only became self-motivated in college. (I2)

I did not come to the realization that I wanted to commit myself to music until high school. (I10)

At some point, each interviewee became self-motivated in the pursuit of music.

Following the passion was not always smooth. Family dynamics or finances might present obstacles, e.g., insufficient resources to buy a piano or pay for lessons. A "poor" teacher might be a source of discouragement. Nevertheless, perhaps it is the passion and self-motivation that explain interviewees' perseverance, overcoming challenges and obstacles early in life, to pursue an interest in and love of music. After commenting on her difficulties with early inadequate teachers, an interviewee observed: "My experience is that there can be talent without passion, but it is passion that is unique" (I1).

Recognizing Talent

The belief that one is "special" or "the best"—possessing a quality others do not—marked the development of pianists reported in earlier studies, whether as an influence exerted by the family (Sosniak 1985a, 39) or the very belief itself (Howe and Sloboda 1991a, 46). Among interviewees, awareness of talent seemed to emerge after and independent of experiencing the passion for music. As discussed in chapter 5, the ascription of "talented" to any interviewee is self-identified, focusing on general musical ability and playing the piano during the early stages of musical development. Such statements as "I was a child prodigy" (e.g., I12 and I20) or "My teacher saw I had talent" (I19) indicate an early self-awareness of talent as a pianist.

The literature further underscores that during the early stage, what may be most important for the future pianist is the recognition of talent by family and teachers (Sosniak 1985b, 414–15). Similarly interviewees' recognition of talent often seemed to depend, to some extent, on external affirmation, including acknowledgment from teachers, the "state," friends, and even passersby, as well as accolades after winning a completion.

My first serious teacher was in Dallas; I was a special student at the university (age 12). It was apparent that I was a pianist. I would get up to practice at 4:30 AM. Life changed. I was not just a kid—I was an artist. I got my vocation. I was not just playing piano, but I was an ambassador to a world of culture. I had a duty to represent European culture and art. (I8)

There was all the attention. At school I received a lot of attention. I was asked to play for guest artists, for example Isaac Stern. In the Soviet Union, as Lithuania was, if you stood out there were benefits: better credentials, better living conditions, and eventually better salaries. The government protected these people. (I12)

My mother's friend (first teacher) took me to try out pianos in a Brooklyn Department Store. Someone brought a chair around and a group of people followed us from piano to piano. The man wanted me to play on a radio broadcast the next week—the store sponsored a radio program. On the program, I played a Clementi *Sonatina*. The store had a picture of me in its window. (I15)

I prepared the Beethoven *Sonata*, Opus 10 No 3 for the scholarship competition. I was awarded the grand prize. The affirmation helped me to decide to pursue the career. (I3)

Nevertheless, not all interviewees knew they were "good" until later.

I was never driven, treated as a prodigy. I did not know that I was good until I came here (mainland U.S.). (I11)

Talent, alone, does not explain the pursuit of a career in music. Moreover, the development of talent is a long-term process (Sosniak 1990, 149–50). At this stage in the pianist's life history, other factors—family, education, and a personal support system—contributed to his or her musical growth.

Family

Family played an important role during the early stage of interviewees' musical development, especially by creating an environment where music was valued. Interviewees typically shared a love of music with one or both parents, a sibling, or other relative—aunt, uncle, or grandparent. A parent or family member supported the interviewee's interest in music, including a commitment to music education and providing the necessary resources for piano study. Nevertheless, families also presented challenges with potentially negative consequences.

Occupational Diversity

Similar to the family backgrounds of the participants in the earlier studies (Sosniak 1985a, 21; Howe and Sloboda 1991a, 42–43; and Sloboda and Howe 1991, 6), interviewees' parents were usually not professional musicians but engaged in a variety of occupations. Parental occupations, usually the father's, included engineer, doctor, dentist, tailor, computer scientist, electrician, artist, businessman, farmer, biochemist, hygienist, English teacher, and housewife. Five female interviewees reported being born into a family of professional musicians. Among the five, three reported having one parent, a mother, who was a professional musician, including an opera singer, a pianist, and a piano teacher. Two interviewees reported that both parents were professional musicians—a pianist (mother) and a famous tenor (father) and a pianist (mother) and a violinist (father). Four of these five interviewees, who emigrated from the former Soviet Union, were similar in family background to the Polish musicians studied (Manturzewska 1990, 119); the fifth, whose mother was a piano teacher, emigrated from Canada. Additionally, one father, a former U.S. Marine, studied music under the GI Bill in order to be able to pass on music to his children. Three fathers were described as "amateur musicians" and three mothers "played the piano."

Music Valued

Whether parents were professional musicians, amateurs, or simply music lovers, music was not only present but a valued and vital part of the home life of the talented young musicians, again similar to the literature (Sosniak 1985a, 24–25 and 43; and Howe and Sloboda 1991a, 43–44). Interviewees' recollections underscore the importance of a family environment that stimulated and supported an interest in and passion for music.

> My parents were musical. The bond was music. My father and mother liked and had books about music, art, and ballet. They encouraged my interests in music and art. (I1)

My father brought home a piano to teach his three sons. He was a Marine and had studied music under the GI Bill. He wanted to pass music on to his three kids. (I3)

Watching my father play and his joy when playing! It is his influence that was my motivation. (I16)

I grew up in a house where music was played—on the stereo and my dad played piano, guitar, and cello. I loved it at an early age. (I17)

I was surrounded by music. Playing music played a massive role in my life. My father was a serious amateur musician. (I19)

My dad was a dentist and my mother, a hygienist. However, my father played guitar his whole life. He could play anything by ear but couldn't read a note! My mother studied piano and taught me to read notes when I was under 4. I have no memory of learning to read notes. (I13)

My parents did not have a music education, but loved to sing. (I6)

A sibling might play an instrument, providing an example, or not.

My brother was a violinist. I could hear him practicing. (I12)

My older brother is a violinist. (I4)

My brother and I would play piano together. (I3)

My sister played the piano. (I19)

My brother, who was 7 years older, was forced to play the piano. When I was three I told him he had made a mistake. He became a psychiatrist. (I20)

Extended family members—aunts, uncles, and grandparents—as professional or amateur musicians—often contributed to the musical atmosphere interviewees experienced.

It was the world I lived in. On my mother's side of the family, six people were musicians—my grandmother, her two sisters, my mother, her sister, and a cousin. I was number seven. My grandmother knew Neuhaus. He was like a grandfather and would come and rock my cradle and take me to the apartment. He would play the *Grand Gallup* of Liszt and *Berceuse* by Chopin for me. (I9)

I came from a very musical family on my mother's side. My grandfather was an opera lover. My uncle played the violin. My aunt took voice lessons. (I11)

My grandmother (mom's mother), born in 1898, used to sneak out of the house at night to sing on the radio! She had a gorgeous voice. (I13)

My grandmother was an organist. My aunt was a piano teacher. It runs in the family. (I2)

Parents and relatives provided opportunities for the young musician to experience a variety of musical activities during childhood and early teenage years. Music might be performed live—by parents, siblings, relatives, or family friends. Concerts and live performances offered exposure to famous musicians. Or, when live music was not readily accessible, recordings were a source of musical enjoyment, providing the chance to listen.

> My father's grandparents used to play duets together. I went to classical concerts with my grandparents and father's family. I remember hearing Beethoven's 9th Symphony with the Cleveland Orchestra and Boulez conducting. My maternal grandmother, who died when I was two years old, was an inspirational mythical character for me. (I18)

> Because we lived outside the city, we did not go to live concerts. I listened to records—what my father listened to—jazz. (I3)

> My brother is my lead fan. For my high school graduation, he transferred all my father's records to CDs. It was the greatest gift when I went away to college. (I6)

Treating the Child as Special

One or both parents recognized an interviewee's talent and supported the musical development of the child, demonstrating a commitment to music education. Support was manifested in a variety of ways. Being born into a musical family, the pursuit of a career in music might be assumed:

> Since my childhood, it was always understood that I would be a musician. (I14)

> It was the world I lived in. (I9)

To play an active role in the development of the young pianist, parents did not, however, need to be musicians.

> My family played a huge role; they were instrumental in my development. My father was a computer scientist. My mom was a biochemist. They came to the United States from Taiwan in 1970, as graduate students at Cornell. They were intellectual, free thinking, but had no musical training. (I10)

Other interviewees reported fulfilling the dream of a parent—particularly a mother, although in recalling their experiences, none complained:

> My experience was parent-led. My mother was a piano teacher. I took lessons because she wanted me to. It was not that I did not enjoy it, but it was expected. (I2)

> Mother always wanted to play. She started taking lessons, but her studies were interrupted by the war. My mother's dream was fulfilled in us. (I5)

> My mother pushed me. (I8)

Resources

Family was usually the source of the concrete resources necessary to support musical development. Often parents, but sometimes friends or other family members, identified first teachers.

> My mother was in favor of my being a musician and did everything to advance my piano study. She took me to the Institute (Brooklyn). I went there from age 4 through 18—Monday through Friday, sometimes Saturday and Sunday. (I20)

> After two years, my father found a different teacher for me and my brother. I stayed with her up to my sophomore year of high school. She was absolutely nurturing, warm, and friendly; had a good sense of humor; and made me feel good about my ability. (I3)

Among the parents who were not musicians or not from musical families, support might include participating in lessons.

> My mom sat and took notes during my lessons; she took videos. (I10)

> At the beginning my parents did not know what to do with a musical child. That changed when I was 14. My mother sat in on my lessons. She enjoyed it and learned a great deal. My parents became educated. (I17)

Or, parents might show support by simply listening to the developing pianist.

> My father would listen to me play. I have a lovely memory of him as a quiet listener. He would sit in on my lessons and listen. It was my responsibility to take it seriously. (I6)

Although the interest and drive to study piano was personal, because of the young age at which studies typically begin, parental support was necessary to the development of the child. Nevertheless, at this stage, teachers also played a critical role. Moreover, other relatives; friends; neighbors; social workers; the government, in the case of those who studied in the former Soviet Union; and even strangers might be part of a personal support system.

Education

In this chapter musical educational experiences focus primarily on early teachers, prior to high school. A first teacher might be a parent or nonfamily member. Recollections of first teachers and early lessons are often intertwined. Memories of a first teacher varied, often positive but sometimes mirroring the negative images presented in the children's literature and movies. A teacher might be the kind and friendly older woman, described in studies of developing young musicians. Others were strict disciplinarians, who imposed punishment using the pencil, special tools, scolding, criticism, or abusive teaching techniques. Sometimes the decision to continue to study piano was despite the teacher. Early teachers might be a role model, but more often an inspiring first teacher was the exception rather than the rule.

First Teacher: A Parent

The first teacher of five interviewees (Russian, Georgian, Canadian, and U.S. (two), three female and two male students) was a parent—four mothers and one father. The parents were not all professional musicians. Memories were good, although typical parent/child tensions were also described. These children began their musical studies early.

My mother was an opera singer. She started to teach me at age 2—singing not piano. (I14)

My mom was my first teacher. At age 4 or 5, my mom started to take care of my music. I am not sure how I learned to read notes. My preparatory period was fast. I debuted at age 8, playing the Bach *G Minor Concerto* with an orchestra. I made my solo debut at age 9, playing Bach, Mozart, and Schumann's *Kinderszenen*. (I9)

I studied with my mom (a professional piano teacher) for less than a year. (I2)

My mother was my first teacher. I played by ear for a while; started regular lessons about age five. I gave my first concert at about age six years. I have good memories. My mother had an impact, although haphazard: love of music and singing, rather than how to hold my hands. She had her own approach, which was not a particularly pedagogical method. She never used methods. (I8)

The experience with my father, who was my teacher for about two years, was positive. (I3)

Parent-child dynamics were not absent from these experiences. As recalled by the interviewees, the young pianists, especially the boys, exhibited typical childlike behavior. Despite bumps in the road, these interactions had a positive influence on the musical life of the child.

Because it was parent and son, there were definitely discipline problems. I practiced studiously when my mother was in the house, but when she left I would read until I heard the car back in the driveway. I was precocious, but lacked discipline and pedagogic regularity. (I8)

And, the parent was not always patient with his own child.

> My first formal lesson was negative. My father was trying to teach me to read music. I was so young (4 ½) that, conceptually, I did not know the difference between a line and a space. He was Italian and did not have a lot of patience. He got mad, gave up, and left the room. My mom did know music, but she knew the difference between a line and a space and she had patience. I got the concept. She brought my dad back into the room and we started over. Everything was good. You could say my mom gave me my first lesson. (I3)

Whether a professional or amateur musician, these parents seemed to know when it was time to bring in an outside teacher.

First Teacher: Nonfamily Member

The first teacher, who was not family members, was often a kindly family friend or neighbor, as described in the research (Sosniak 1985a, 29–34 and 1985b, 411–15; and Sloboda and Howe 1991, 19). Similarly, the quality and approach to teaching varied, as Howe and Sloboda observed (1991b, 55–56). Patterns and progressions of teachers varied. First teachers might be for a short period or become a long-term relationship, more like a parent, particularly in situations of personal challenge. Images of the kindly older woman were found among first teachers described by U.S.-born interviewees.

> My mother's girlfriend played a little and started to teach me, but she did not know much. She was nice. Her boyfriend, a jazz pianist, told my mother to find me another teacher. (I15)

> My first piano teacher in the States was in second grade. She was an old woman, who was strict but not mean. She had a lot of high achieving students and, therefore, had high expectations. She gave me music that I had no business playing, but I learned it. (I2)

> My first teacher was the woman next door. I started piano lessons 6 weeks before I turned five. I could not read at that time. At first I had 10 to 15 minute lessons; a half hour when I was 6 years old and in the first grade; and by 7, I had an hour lesson. (I11)

A male first teacher, who was not a parent was rarer.

> I had a good teacher at the local music school. A gentlemanly man in his 30s, he taught at the piano school and church. (I10)

In the former Soviet Union and countries within its sphere of influence, piano study occurred in an institutional setting. Interviewees described positive experiences memories of their early teachers.

(K) taught me from age 5. I had regular lessons. I was lucky. She was a fantastic woman—"too good for the world." Aside from her outstanding pedagogical talents, she was exceptionally warm and kind. Pupils adored her. At about 11 years old, I also started playing for her husband, a renowned pianist, but I never stopped being her pupil until her untimely death. (I14)

My first teacher was about imagination. She would tell me a story while working on little pieces—a story about a garden and flowers. (I12)

I am still in touch with my first teacher in Poland. She comes to my concerts when I am in Poland. Her style was strict; she was an academic teacher. I played tons of Bach. She was an extremely warm person. I have the best memories. There was a mother connection. She was nice and kind, but demanding. (I7)

The portraits of the first teachers, even the negative ones, were typically not as drastic as those portrayed in the novels and adult nonfiction. Nevertheless, some were perceived to be too strict, especially for a child. Corporal punishment might be applied and sometimes took the form of a tool (e.g., the dreaded pencil). Others might be characterized as inattentive and even psychologically abusive.

My first teacher was very strict, too strict for children. She was not a child pedagogue, but an excellent musician, pianistically. I studied scales, Hanon, solfege, dictation. . . . We covered a lot of repertoire. She had a pencil—she would say keep your fingers curved. I had to count aloud, clap, read quickly; so, I learned. To teach children you have to have more pedagogical knack than she did. (I11)

My first teacher was horrible. She had a tool that looked like a pencil. She would hit you on the knuckles. Then I took lessons with the nuns. They used a ruler; it was harder than the tool. (I1)

My first piano teacher in the States was in second grade. She was an old woman who was strict, but not mean. She had a lot of high achieving students; therefore she had high expectations. She gave me music that I had no business playing, but I learned it. (I2)

She was on the phone a lot with her daughter during my lesson. I didn't like that. I think she was a nice enough person. My mother met her at church. (I16)

At times I did not practice; it was obvious. She did not have a ruler or a pencil— no tool—but her verbal remarks had a bite. If I did not practice, she would sit down at the piano and play the piece to demonstrate how it went. (I3)

Such approaches would generally be considered unacceptable today.

Like the family member, the time spent with the nonfamily early teacher was typically short. The impetus might be to find a more challenging teacher outside the family and neighborhood.

> First teacher—I do not remember. I had her for one year; she was also a kindergarten teacher. She was nice. I liked it. After one year, my parents wanted someone better. I went to L School, where my sister was taking lessons. I studied with her teacher for 3 or 4 years, until about age 8. I was young, enthusiastic, but not really practicing. At about age 7, I learned a Bach Invention. It changed me—I was surprised, happy, and became much more dedicated. On her recommendation I went to study with (O). (I19)

> I had 16 teachers and they start to blend together as their styles and personalities do as well. All were nice people. As an adult I could better evaluate their ability to teach and their credentials. Overall far too many were lacking in enough classical training or proper degrees. (I16)

Family circumstances and the search for the "right teacher" might precipitate a change in piano teachers, similar to participants in other studies (Sloboda and Howe 1991, 19). Finding that teacher might be a challenge.

> We moved a lot and as a result I had nine teachers, ten counting my mom. I studied with some teachers for only a year and with my mom for less than a year. (I2)

> Then we moved. I tried another teacher, but it did not work because I could not go to the lessons by myself. (I6)

> I had some lessons with teachers my mother sent me to, but none satisfied her or me. A local teacher in Arizona was a college professor at Mississippi. I was not serious, not about the piano. He had little impact. (I8)

An interviewee might also continue to study with a first teacher through their teens. Such teachers often took on the role of a parent, remaining a constant in the life of the student, sometimes because of the loss of the child's parents or other circumstances within the family. Other interviewees found such a teacher, after several attempts, continuing to study with them for years.

> Between ages 5 and 18, I worked with my first teacher. At age 12 we emigrated from Russia to Israel (part of the great migration in 1972). She went with us and I attended the academy in Tel Aviv. She became my second mother. (The interviewee's mother died of cancer; her grandparents were killed in the Holocaust.) (I12)

My first teacher was like a second mother. She knew your life. She had suffered oppression under Stalin. I stayed close with her until her death when I was about 36. (I5)

My first serious teacher was in Dallas. My relationship with him was like father/son. He had an old European approach. He was not just a mentor. It was a relationship of respect. I revered and learned from him; I owed him allegiance and respect, a model of the world. Born Kiev, he was Russian, trained at the Paris Conservatory, but did not have a typical Parisian approach. He was concrete, not a methods teacher, and strict about scales and arpeggios. I started practicing, studying with him. I worked with him through high school, until I went to the conservatory and even after. (I8)

He was like a father figure to me. (I17)

As Sloboda and Howe observed, the significance of the early teachers seems to be more varied and less clear cut (1991, 19). Not all first teachers were kindly, patient, and an inspiration to continue piano study or pursue piano teaching. Yet, interviewees persevered in their studies.

Perseverance

What constitutes perseverance evolves through the stages in the development of the pianist. The literature suggests that the emphasis during the early years is on the child enjoying playing. Not all interviewees practiced diligently at this stage. Nevertheless, several described persevering in their piano studies despite being inadequately prepared musically because of the dispositions of their teachers. The young pianists were self-motivated at an early age and did not abandon the task in spite of such obstacles—they persevered.

I have few positive memories of my early piano teachers. Their teaching was destructively negative. They were exhausted and cranky and they hit students. I had good years with the nuns, but they were cranky. But, that did not stop me. (I1)

It is hard to know how I felt and evaluated teachers at age 8. I did what she asked and progressed because I WANTED to get better in spite of teacher's inadequate skills that time and experience have shown me. (I16)

During the early years, a child's continued desire to play the piano, especially meeting the demands of practicing and preparing for a lesson despite poor teachers, may be considered an indicator of perseverance.

At this stage, perseverance is not only a characteristic of the child but also the parent in support of the development of a career in music, particularly in the process of getting the job done (Howe and Sloboda 1991a, 51). Doing so might mean ensuring that the child had access to opportunities and studied with the "best" teacher, for example:

> My mother pushed me. (U) did not take students younger than college age, but my mother wrote to his wife. He set up an audition to humiliate me and teach my mother a lesson, but the result was the opposite. I won him over. He brought in other faculty and hugged me. (I8)

Hand in hand with perseverance is hard work.

Hard Work and Diligence

Hard work and diligence as a performer may be defined in terms of practicing. For the child, the early period is usually a time when music, the piano, is experienced as fun—years of play and exploration. Reports of hard work and diligence varied. Some interviewees practiced diligently:

> I was very disciplined, curious. Once I learned to read music, I learned quickly. It was like a blind person having vision. I went through a lot of music, as much as I could. (I6)

Others did not practice but enjoyed playing.

> My first teacher never thought I would become anyone because I was talented, but lazy. (I7)

> I have strong memories around improvising, playing by ear, and not practicing, although I was playing concerts. (I8)

> I had a hard time practicing. I liked to play. For many lessons I was not well-prepared. I had a half hour lesson. I floated for a few years. (I3)

Although it is not possible to generalize by gender, it appears that girls were usually more likely to be disciplined about practicing during the early years. Boys were more likely to report liking to play the piano but less likely to be disciplined about practicing.

Family may contribute to the young pianist's recognition of the importance of hard work. As Bloom observes in the University of Chicago study of developing talented young people, it is in the home environment that the work ethic and the importance of the individual doing one's best is developed. In each group studied (pianists, sculptors, mathematicians, neurologists, Olympic swimmers, and tennis players), parents strongly encouraged their children in a particularly highly approved talent (1985b, 508). An interviewee's parent may play a supportive role by participating in the piano lesson and practice time. Nevertheless, as important as parental support is to the development of the young musician, the research underscores the importance of the student making a personal commitment to music and sustaining that commitment over time (Sosniak 1985a, 56 and 1985c, 502; Sloboda 1990, 176; and Davidson et al. 1995/1996, 44).

Personal Commitment to Music

The age at which the decision to commit oneself to music is made varies with the individual. When asked when and how they knew they wanted to commit themselves to music, interviewees usually identified a specific age, between six and eighteen, and circumstances. All recalled making the commitment to music prior to attending college. Nevertheless, the process described by those who made the decision early—age twelve or younger—and those who made the decision later—ages thirteen and eighteen—was different.

Those who made the commitment prior to age thirteen described a "natural" non-deliberative process:

I always knew—age 6. (I1)

The basic answer is I knew I wanted to be a musician about the time I knew I had brown eyes, as long as I was self aware. (I8)

Since my childhood it was always understood that I would be a musician. (I14)

At three years old, I remember ringing a bell and playing. (I9)

At age 6—since childhood I played as a child prodigy. In the Soviet Union if you were unique, it helped. It brought you bigger attention. I was sent to Moscow to perform at the Kremlin for Khrushchev. In Saint Petersburg I played in big halls since childhood. (I12)

Early. (I15)

Not any moment. I knew I wanted to after I played the Bach Invention—to be a musician in some serious capacity but not necessarily a professional musician. My interest never waned after that. (I19)

I decided, but I did not think about it. From age four, I knew would go into music. (I20)

Exposure to a special teacher or experiences with musical settings might contribute to the decision process.

I knew—when I met K. I knew it, when she said she could teach me to play at a higher level and could help prepare me to audition for the conservatory. (I10)

I knew early on that I wanted to commit my life to music, maybe ten years old. (I11)

Those who made the decision later, although still young, seemed to engage in a deliberative decision-making process, even weighing whether to study a different field. The process described suggests an awareness of the challenges involved in pursuing a career in music and the importance of developing the true and long-term commitment to continuous learning identified in the literature (e.g., Sosniak 1985a, 56 and 1985c, 502).

Generally, I decided to make music my life before I went to college. I was a music major in college. (I2)

I had a strong feeling growing. It was something I enjoyed. I knew I wanted to commit my life to music before I auditioned for D. University. (I3)

At about age 15: The question was what professional field to choose? I was not sure what I wanted to do, but there were only 4 professional schools—pedagogical, polytechnic (engineering), medical, and the conservatory. I was not good at math, and my mother, who was a teacher, said no to pedagogy. It came down to a choice between medical school and the conservatory. (I5)

It was when I applied to college. My parents did not encourage me to pursue a music career; they very strongly discouraged me. They encouraged me to explore other options; I was a good student. They wanted me to have a stable life and knew music was not. (I6)

At age 16 I knew that this was what I wanted to do. I became fanatical; it was like a religion. I felt the urge to play. I played constantly, studied, and submerged myself into piano music. I played 12 hours a day, without interference from anyone. (I7)

At 14, with the new teacher—after a few years I moved strongly into music. (I17)

At age 13—I loved art and was much better at it than music, but I thought it would be too isolating to be an artist, so I chose music with the commitment of finding a teacher who had success in training students to an advanced level. I told him at the beginning of my training that I wanted to go to music school. (I18)

One interviewee tried another career first, while also teaching piano, before making the commitment to a music career.

I never really knew that I wanted to commitment myself to music. It evolved. I had three jobs in marketing and outside sales, which I found unrewarding. Only teaching piano was personally fulfilling. I started teaching while I had those other jobs. It turned full time as much as that could happen in 1986, after being laid off from an in-house marketing job. (I16)

The decision to make a commitment to music, whether at six or eighteen, is an early life decision. Although the young pianist has been studying and even giving concerts, the commitment is usually made more on the basis of love of music than an analysis of what is entailed in pursuing a career in music, particularly the financial challenges of making a living. Perhaps it is the passion for music that distinguishes the young pianist and overrides the practical. The commitment to teaching piano is explored in chapter 7.

Personal Support System

Fulfilling a commitment to music, to the piano, involves not only a serious commitment to learning and practicing but an investment of financial resources. Music education—private lessons, volumes of music, and an instrument—costs money even in the early years of the study. Parents usually play a vital role in the developmental years of a young pianist, but they cannot/do not always do it alone. A twentieth-century mantra describing the raising a child was, "It takes a village"; so much more so to meet the demands of developing a talented young musician and not dissimilar from training an Olympic athlete. Parents and teachers are essential not only individually but as part of a support system that provides the resources to develop talent and establish conditions that later facilitate disciplined learning. Interviewees described how relatives, friends, peers, members of the community, and sometimes strangers also offered support, ranging from the practical to the emotional.

Concrete examples of support included providing a piano or money for the lessons that parents could not afford.

My uncle, who did not play, sent me an upright piano. We were poor and could not afford one. (I15)

My aunt paid for my piano lessons. (I11)

My father met a man who manufactured a brand of piano. He gave us a piano. It was about 1969 in South Korea. (I6)

Recognizing the talent of the child, support might be recommending a teacher or prodding the parent to find a teacher.

A social worker found a well-known teacher in the neighborhood. Later, she found another teacher and helped me get into the C. S. Music School, a school for the gifted. (I15)

The piano manufacturer also suggested that we look for a university student who could come to the house. Two students came. They were very nice. I can't say I learned a lot. (I6)

My grandfather played the accordion, violin, and harmonica. He pushed my
mother to get a piano teacher for me because he saw the talent. (I7)

Sharing music with other children might encourage the pursuit of music,
sparking interest in studying and making music.

I had a childhood friend. At age 4 I started the violin and piano at age 6. I played
both for about 10 years. I also wanted to learn with the other kids—I played
oboe, bassoon, and bass drum in the marching band, through the local public
high school. (I10)

The young pianist might be the spark for other children, sometimes sow-
ing the seeds for teaching in preteen or early teen years. Interviewees were
examples, even in their teens.

I originally taught gang members on the streets of Flatbush (age 12). (I15)

When I was 16, students appeared and wanted to study with me. (I20)

There were a lot of kids in the neighborhood who wanted to take piano lessons.
I was known as a star in the community. (I10)

Peer relationships tend to evolve, especially with other students of music,
during high school and college years, becoming more important than family
or even teachers as the young pianist develops.
    Community may also play a role in establishing the environment in which
the young pianist experiences music.

There was a woman who was a great friend of the family who was musical and
had a music club; the community was musical. (I1)

I was so into the musical scene—the Casals Festival in Puerto Rico; I went to
recitals; there were local musicians. The experiences helped me to decide this is
what I wanted to do, to be one of them. (I11)

Parents, teachers, friends, neighbors, peers, and the community may have
contributed to the development of an interviewee as a pianist, a musician. The
role of each component of the personal support system changes over time.
Parents establish opportunities and access to early teachers, the piano, and
musical experiences. As the young pianist develops, the parental role changes
to one of primarily providing the financial resources necessary to pursue
music education and opportunities. The emotional support and musical acumen of peers, colleagues, and friends become more important in later years,
changing from sharing fun to mutual professional development. As illustrated
by the story of the little girl in South Korea, who wanted to play the thing, the
role of the personal support system is complex.

A teacher took me on as a student, although we did not have a piano. My father, who was an artist, drew a keyboard on cardboard. It was probably two octaves. He drew pictures on the keyboard to identify the notes of the solfege system used in Korea. The teacher would let me practice during her break after my lesson. That was all the time I had to practice on a real piano. Then we moved. We still did not have a piano. My father met a man, who manufactured a brand of piano. He gave us a piano. (I6)

CHALLENGES AND BARRIERS

The path to a career in music is not always smooth. Sosniak notes that, unfortunately, one of the early rewards of practicing can be escape from the noise and fighting in the home or their loneliness (1985a, 40). During the early years, several interviewees experienced challenges, including family issues, poor teachers, leaving home to pursue music, and immigration to a new country by their teenage years.

The death of a parent, divorce, alcoholism, and undefined parental absence presented emotional challenges. Music offered solace and sometimes the piano teacher provided the needed emotional support.

My mother was an opera singer. From my first lessons I learned to sing. She passed away when I was nine, from cancer. (I12)

He was like a father figure to me, especially when my parents' marriage broke up. (I17)

My relationship with (U) was like father-son. (I8)

A teacher might bring tragedy into the life of a young student. Two interviewees lost a special teacher to suicide. Both students—one in the United States and another in Russia—were very young at the time of the incident. The actions of these teachers were clearly challenges that pervaded the memories of these students.

My teacher committed suicide at age 36, after a conference at the Town Hall. I wrote him a letter and sent it to him after the concert, but he never received it. He committed suicide. I knew—he gave me his books and changed the concert program to play *Toten Tanz*. (I15)

She was a fantastic woman—"too good for the world." She committed suicide at age 46. (I14)

Their choice impacted the student. Although the death of the teacher of another interviewee, while still in her teens, was natural causes, the suddenness was traumatic.

We were studying the first *Ballade* and had reached the coda when he went on a trip to Turkey. He said we would finish when he returned. Our lessons would last three hours He went into great details on each piece and would perform the piece at the end of the lesson. He died on stage in Istanbul. He stimulated me in love, life, and interest. I played the piece recently. It touches my heart; I had a spasm in my throat. I wonder whether I would play it differently if he had come back to teach me the coda. (I12)

Securing the necessary resources to pursue the study of music and the piano posed challenges and choices. Finding a teacher could mean leaving home to attend boarding school.

I left home at age 13; I attended the performing arts high school. (I1)

The financing of advanced music education in the United States could strain family resources. Interviewees who emigrated from the former Soviet Union underscored the contribution of government-supported education to their musical development.

The first year I did not understand, but then I started to understand that the difficulty teaching in the United States was not just the students' lack of the conservatory structure, but because not everyone can afford what we had in the USSR as background. (I9)

Even when a student had the opportunity to study in a precollege program in the United States, the logistics of that education might be a challenge.

I attended a conservatory pre-college for four years in the 1960s. Every pianist was automatically a performance major. I had to leave school four days a week and trek to the city from Long Island. (I13)

I got a scholarship to a conservatory but my parents would not let me travel from Brooklyn into Manhattan. I went to C. S. Music School. (I15)

Political pressures in the former Soviet Union led to emigration; moving to a new country (e.g., Israel or the United States) meant not only leaving home but adjusting to a new culture. Such changes and the necessary adjustments are difficult at any age but especially for a child no matter how resilient.

When I was 12, we emigrated from Russia to Israel (part of the great migration in 1972). Things were different. I was an unknown. It was not easy to transition. My mother had died; my father, who was a tailor, was broken and had two children. It was my mother's will that we move to Israel and my father was a big Zionist—he loved it. I had no language. My classmates thought I was a weirdo because I played the piano. My piano teacher, who had emigrated with us, helped me. I had a scholarship. The first one to two years were difficult—a new school, a new country—as it would be for any child. (I12)

Many eminent individuals report difficult childhood circumstances, which may propel the individual to seek refuge in controllable intellectual activities. Nevertheless, the question remains whether unhappy childhoods are a necessary ingredient for creativity (Subotnik et al. 2003, 230–31). Family members, teachers, and a personal support system were a source of support to meet these challenges. Ultimately, despite such challenges, each interviewee persevered in their study of music and the piano.

SUMMARY AND CONCLUSION: SETTING THE STAGE

During the early years, factors identified from social science literatures helped to shape each interviewee's growth and development as a musician. While each story is personal, interviewees' experiences were generally consistent with those described in the studies of the talented young musician, situating the current study within the extant literature and creating a picture of these teachers as young pianists. From their first exposure to live or recorded performances emerged a love of music and the piano, which aroused the passion to play the piano. Personal factors—listening, passion, talent, perseverance, hard work, and personal commitment—begin to develop during this stage. Environmental factors—family, education, and a personal support system—provide the necessary resources, although at times presenting challenges. Parents, most not being professional musicians, did not always know how to deal with a talented young musician although usually at least one parent was supportive. Experiences with the first piano teacher were mixed, ranging from wonderful to horrid but frequently similar to those of most young piano students. Yet, with passion and perseverance, interviewees continued to pursue their love of music and the piano. Chapter 7 explores the contribution of these and two additional factors—adolescent employment and community labor market conditions—to the decision to teach piano.

NOTE

1. Interviewees are cited by way of illustration. As agreed to in advance, the anonymity has been maintained. Each interviewee was assigned a unique identification number, which is used to reference comments (e.g., (I1)).

Chapter 7

Deciding to Become a Piano Teacher

Confluence of Factors and Process

Why does a pianist decide to teach piano? Leschetizky observed that every pianist should have pupils, as people forget the artists who have only played, but pupils carry on the teacher's memory (Newcomb 1921, 91). While sage advice, the desire to establish a legacy does not fully explain the decision to teach piano. In this chapter, the underlying questions explored are: What factors contribute to the decision to teach piano, and how? The factors, extrapolated from the literatures, provide direction for this inquiry but not answers, given the emphasis of the research on the musician as performer and music educator in schools. Accordingly, this chapter draws primarily from interviewees' descriptions of when, how, and why each decided to teach piano. The first section explores these responses from the perspective of age and stages of musical development, as the age at which interviewees began teaching piano varied. In the next section, the identified factors are organized under four broad categories—precipitating, motivating, sustaining, and supporting and/or confounding—that characterize the contribution to the decision to teach piano. In addition to the general challenges discussed throughout the chapter (e.g., economic necessity), other personal challenges sometimes precipitated or adversely affected an interviewee's teaching piano. Taken together, interviewees' experiences describe a confluence of factors affecting the decision to teach piano.

DECISION TO TEACH PIANO: WHEN?

Each interviewee was able to recall and describe his or her early experiences teaching piano. As shown in Table 7.1, the stage at which interviewees

Table 7.1 The Decision to Teach Piano: When

Stage	Developmental Years[a]			Advanced Education	Professional Musician
	Middle years	Later years		Graduate school and professional training	Mature pianist
		Precollege	College		
Number of interviewees	1	8	7	1	3

[a]For purposes of this study, the developmental years include the (1) middle years, defined as under age thirteen and (2) later years, defined as age fourteen to twenty-one, and/or precollege- and college-level education in a university, conservatory, or the equivalent.

reported beginning to teach extended through four stages in the developmental history of the piano teacher—middle and later developmental years, advanced education, and professional musician, although clustering in later developmental years.

The age at which interviewees began teaching piano ranged from twelve to over fifty years of age.

The youngest reported teaching experience was age twelve, at the request of neighborhood gang members and other children. At fifteen, the interviewee began teaching at the 92nd St. Y in New York and at the end of a year became a regular member of the faculty. Now more than ninety years old, the pianist continues to teach.

> I was 15 years old and in college. At 16, I was on international competition committees with well-known people. My students were winning competitions. (I15)

At the other end of the continuum were the pianists whose regular teaching began later, in conjunction with an active although sometimes waning performance career. Typically, those who began teaching later in their musical careers had given master classes but viewed teaching in the context of the individual private lesson as a different experience. Continuing to perform regularly, teaching might be irregular and more like coaching (e.g., for a performance) at first but eventually evolved into giving one-on-one lessons on a regular basis, usually in a university or conservatory and sometimes a private studio.

> Until I was over 50, I never looked for a job as a teacher. The University was my first job as a teacher. Before then, I had given master classes and occasionally coached a student. (I8)

> I began teaching in my mid-twenties and received a university teaching offer after finishing my bachelor's degree from the conservatory. My mother told me to finish my master's degree first, but when I finished, I mainly played for 5 or 6 years—performing solo concerts at the Kennedy Center and in Los Angeles and Puerto Rico. Then the concerts dried up. I took a steady job, a regular university position. (I11)

> I taught only when I came to the United States. I played in many universities. These were official recitals. Then I was asked to combine concerts with master classes. I started teaching that kind of class. (I14)

Typically, interviewees began teaching early in their life as a musician, during the later stage of musical development. For purposes of the current study, this stage is divided into precollege and college—as the factors precipitating the decision to teach differed. Those who decided to teach before and during college included male and female pianists who had studied within and outside the United States. The extent to which teaching piano was a conscious choice, however, seemingly differed. As described by those who began teaching precollege, the initial decision was usually happenstance.

> When I was 16, students appeared and wanted to study with me. (I20)

> I started teaching when I was a sophomore in high school. There were a lot of kids in the neighborhood who wanted to take piano lessons. (I10)

Those who began teaching in college described a more deliberate choice. The decision to teach might be precipitated by economic need, especially to support music studies, or as an educational requirement (e.g., part of a program of study), although the decision was not always perceived as defining a distinct path in a music career.

> I began teaching in my student years. I did so to make money. (I12)

> I decided to teach late in college. I was a piano major from the start, but added a pedagogy concentration later. (I2)

> Teaching was part of my training in precollege and the conservatory—pedagogical practice. You had to teach a little. (I5)

> The piano teaching came about while I was still in college, and just hasn't stopped, so I don't think there was ever a conscience decision to become a professional piano teacher. (I13)

While interviewees, who ranged from about age thirty to ninety-one, began teaching piano at different stages in their musical development, at the time of the interview, all had taught for at least ten years and the majority for much longer (see Figure 5.1). All were teaching students, one-on-one, in a private studio and/or institutional setting. Cumulatively, their knowledge of teaching piano totaled decades of experience, dating as far back as the late 1930s.

THE DECISION TO TEACH PIANO: FACTORS

Factors associated with interviewees' musical growth and development, as described in chapter 6, may also contribute to the decision to teach piano. In this section, the role played by these and two additional factors—adolescent employment and labor market conditions—is explored. To further the analysis of the decision to teach piano, the factors are organized into the following four broad categories:

- Precipitating (adolescent employment, community labor market conditions, and education);
- Motivating (passion, listening to music, and talent);
- Sustaining (personal commitment, perseverance, and hard work/diligence); and
- Supporting and/or confounding (family and personal support system).

This organizational scheme reflects the journey described by interviewees.

The categories and factors are constant, although how a particular factor contributes may vary with the stage at which the decision to teach piano is made. Precipitating factors create the need or provide the opportunity to teach piano. Although the decision may be associated with economic need, economic incentives, alone or in conjunction with educational requirements or opportunities, do not explain choosing to teach piano rather than another musical path. Motivating factors—passion and talent—provide further insight into the choice—why teaching and not business or a music librarian. Personal commitment, perseverance, and hard work/diligence help to sustain the decision to teach piano. While family and a personal support system usually play a supportive rather than primary role, these factors may present challenges having an adverse or at least confounding effect.

Precipitating Factors

Each interviewee's decision to teach piano was an individual choice. Yet, despite differences in personal, educational, social, cultural, and political situations, the choice was usually precipitated by one or more of three factors: (1) adolescent employment; (2) economic need for supplemental income—community labor market conditions; and/or (3) education, often pedagogical training. A factor may be associated with a particular stage or across stages in a pianist's life history. Moreover, more than one factor may precipitate an individual's decision.

Employment was explicitly associated with the decision to teach piano across stages—later developmental years, advanced education, and professional musician, although the relationship between opportunity and economic need varied among stages. Teaching piano to friends or classmates can provide adolescent employment. In conjunction with education, the need for supplemental income might be, but was not always, a consideration in deciding to teach piano during college or graduate school. The need for supplemental income was consistently given not only as a reason to begin but also continue to teach during one's career as a professional musician in the United States. Education (e.g., a teacher or conservatory, college, and graduate course in pedagogy) may precipitate but also support and sustain the decision.

Adolescent Employment

As presented in the career choice literature, work during adolescence usually refers to an after school activity, undertaken to earn money, and not related to the career track (Mortimer et al. 1996, 1406, and 1411–14; Mortimer and Johnson 1998; Shanahan et al. 2002, 112; and Johnson and Mortimer 2002, 54–58). In contrast, opportunities for the young pianist may involve career-related activities—recitals, concerts, or accompanying—for professional, if not financial, gain. The initial impetus to teach piano, especially when made during adolescence, was often not monetary. That is, the opportunity to teach occurred before the recognition of the economic benefits of teaching. The source of such opportunities might be by chance or at the request of a teacher. Yet, whatever the impetus, the young student/teacher did charge for lessons, and so, by definition, was a working professional musician; therefore, these early experiences teaching piano are categorized as adolescent employment.

First students were often other children from the neighborhood. Sometimes a child made the request of the young pianist and, at other times, it was a parent.

> I have been teaching since I was 12 and am now in my 90s. I originally taught gang members on the streets of Flatbush. They were jealous of me. Other kids from the neighborhood came. We lived in a two-room apartment behind a store. People could hear me play. They brought their children for lessons. I charged a quarter a lesson. (I15)

> At 16, I built up a clientele of piano students. They lived close by our apartment in the Bronx. Mostly, I had elementary-level students, although not all were beginners. (I20)

> I started teaching when I was a sophomore in high school. It was a nice job. I would come and give lessons in the parents' living room. (I10)

> I decided to teach at a very early age—about 18—after my epiphany about music. My first teaching was a girl in the neighborhood who knew I played the piano. She was 14 or 15 years old and wanted to take lessons. She had had a teacher. We played Mozart sonatas and talked about good literature. (I17)

Informally, a piano teacher might facilitate early teaching experiences, by asking the young pianist to teach a younger student or helping to find students. Such opportunities occurred in the United States and abroad. Interviewees recognized both the tangible and intangible rewards of teaching provided by such opportunities:

> My high school piano teacher went on tour one year and asked me to apprentice for him and to teach some of his students while he was away. I had some success and felt a great satisfaction in finding ways to help students progress. I knew I

would need a way to make money when I went to music school. Learning how to teach seemed to be both practical and satisfying. (I18)

I taught informally for my teacher during the summer. I began teaching her students when she was away. It was more like dabbling. (I19)

It was natural. I began in my student years. I did so to make money. Even with a full scholarship, I had to do so for financial and economic reasons. I had private students; my first teacher helped me to get them. (I12)

I taught kids as a side income. The old policy was 100 to 120 rubles per month. That was how I got started teaching. I taught seven beginners in a music school. It was difficult to teach beginners after all the chamber music repertoire; however, I was trained in pre-college so I knew how to teach the seven. (I5)

Early experiences teaching piano are part of the educational and career development of the young pianist. The career choice literature raises the concern that too much time spent working after school at a noncareer related job can be detrimental to academic achievement (Mortimer et al. 1996, 1406, and 1411–14). Nevertheless, although adolescent teaching may interfere with personal practicing time, such exposure can also be beneficial beyond the financial. In contrast to other fields, the contribution of adolescent career-relevant experience teaching piano to the career choice and personal and professional development of the young pianist, as a musician and person, may be more important than the money earned.

Not all interviewees who considered teaching during their precollege or college years chose to or continued to teach. Sometimes the reason was simply lack of confidence or perceived ability: I decided I was not ready (I6). I had no idea how to teach; I learned later (I1) I didn't know if I was doing it right (I11). Sometimes there was no economic need to providing the impetus. Still other young pianists were simply too busy playing and studying.

With my high school teacher I had several conversations about music as a career. She said I could teach. Teaching was not appealing to me in high school. I felt that way through college. I wanted just to play, to do concerts, and some competitions. (I3)

These same individuals made the choice to teach piano at a later stage in their musical development.

Need for Supplemental Employment: Community Labor Market Conditions

In the music profession, generally, as in other fields, successfully pursuing a career is, in part, dependent on the existence of a job market and employment opportunities. Accordingly, community labor market conditions play an important role in shaping occupational choice and attainment (Johnson and Mortimer 2002, 58). Traditionally, the pinnacle of success in a music career is the individual concert performer. Among today's musicians, Joshua Bell—violin; Yo-Yo Ma—cello; and Lang Lang—piano are international household names. Not all musicians, even great ones, reach this level of prominence. Moreover, performance opportunities are likely to vary over the career lifespan of a musician, a function not only of audience attention but the general economy. The need to pursue additional paths to sustain a career in music financially is not uncommon, and teaching is viewed as a more stable option (Bennett 2016, 108). Teaching piano offered interviewees financial support during advanced graduate studies and supplemental income to the mature professional, however successful their performance career.

Graduate Education: Private Students. Teaching during graduate school can provide financial assistance and the opportunity to consider whether teaching might become a part of a music career. An interviewee might take on private students or other teaching opportunities to support graduate studies.

> I had the opportunity to teach, while I was in graduate school. It gave me some money. The university had a system where you could teach students who were majoring in other instruments (e.g., a piano grad student could teach voice or guitar students). I liked teaching, but I was teaching friends and colleagues. It was interesting. It was not necessary to teach theory, just what they needed to do. It was my first experience teaching. (I3)

Structured opportunities to teach, as part of an undergraduate or graduate program in the United States and abroad, offered an initial opportunity to teach with financial benefits. A graduate program or assistantship may offer the occasion to teach. Such opportunities are discussed in the section on education.

Other interviewees, however, did not need or have the desire to teach during graduate school or even early in their performance careers.

> I liked teaching, but did not consider it as a career. I was performing a lot on a concert tour. (I1)

The decision came at a later stage.

> I taught privately. The apprenticeship was difficult. I had a studio in (City). Then I came to L School in 1997 or so. I had an audition. I loved it immediately. (I1)

Professional Musician. Interviewees, who began teaching as professional musicians/mature pianists, identified economics as the precipitating factor leading to the decision. Although similar in age to the Polish musicians in

Manturzewska's study (1990, 136–37), the situations described and underlying reasons given to explain the decision to teach were different. Interviewees underscored the economic need to provide a stable income not afforded by a performance career.

> I did not really teach until well into my 30s. When I first started teaching, it was very irregular, more like coaching. Mostly, it was a way to make extra money. At 50, the desire was to do it for a living and economic stability. I needed a fixed place for students to come. (I8)

> I was very busy playing and traveling. I taught only when I came to the United States. I was told that in America, even the greatest pianists either have a business or teach. Business, I was not good at it. I needed to earn money. (I14)

In contrast, the Polish study attributed increased pedagogical interest to personal factors—drop in energy, learning capacity, and artistic efficiency, usually accompanied by vacillating self-esteem, depression, and various psychosomatic symptoms (136). Perhaps national and societal variations, affecting the employment opportunities available to musicians, may explain the differences in the reasons for mature musicians to consider teaching. Such comparative research is, however, beyond the scope of the current study.

Teaching and Performing: Not an Either/Or Decision. The need for a U.S. pianist to pursue more than one path—a protean career—is a theme that is reiterated throughout succeeding chapters. For the participants in the current study, the decision to teach piano was not an either/or choice between performing and teaching. At whatever age the decision to teach piano was made, interviewees usually continued to perform as solo musicians. In addition to solo concerts, chamber music, collaborating with other instrumentalists, accompanying vocalists, and playing in popular settings—restaurants, bars, lounges—and even private homes and churches provide other opportunities to perform.

Nevertheless, the challenges of a performing career contributed to the decision to teach.

> When I got out of school and went back to (City), I had to make a living. I was just doing concerts. From time to time I taught a few students. Trying to concertize became harder and harder and there were all these students coming along. (I3)

Pursuing both teaching and performing can be mutually reinforcing. On the one hand, recognition of the benefits of teaching piano, in conjunction with a performance career, especially balancing performing in multiple venues, may contribute to the decision to teach.

The problem was trying to make money as an accompanist and cocktail work. The cocktail work involved too many hours of playing, about 12 hours a day. That really influenced my decision to teach—I could make money, practice, and not have to play all the time. (I3)

On the other hand, a reputation as a performer could open doors to teaching opportunities.

I had a successful Lincoln Center debut; the *Times* reviewed it. After that, people started to know me. They invited me to teach at M College of Music and M School of Music. (I14)

Changes in community labor market conditions affecting opportunities for performing and conditions of piano teaching may, however, further tip the balance toward teaching. Those who have been teaching may choose to expand their teaching career over time.

Teaching replaced the playing. I have not been playing for the last 5 years. Concertizing has dried up; even cocktail work has dried up in (City). (I3)

I do almost no performing now, just teaching. (I2)

For the most part, however, having made the decision to teach piano, given the greater economic stability of teaching but considering performing and teaching as part of a musical identity, interviewees usually continued to follow both paths, as will be discussed in chapters 9 and 10.

Education

In addition to a teacher having informally "given" an interviewee a student to teach, formal courses and assistantships were reported to have precipitated the decision to teach piano. The European tradition included the use of assistants to prepare students for a lesson with the master (Bomberger 2001, 129). Interviewees born and trained in Europe were usually exposed to and were required or expected to teach as part of a program of study.

I eventually knew I had to teach as part of career. In my last year at the conservatory, I had an assistantship with a teacher and had a few students. (I9)

Teaching was part of my training in pre-college and the conservatory—pedagogical practice. You had to teach a little. I got started teaching in music school—seven beginners. At the conservatory, I was teaching young adults for professional training in chamber and accompanying. (I5)

The tradition of assistantships was transplanted to the United States through teachers trained under that system and U.S.-born pianists, who studied in the

European tradition here or abroad. Interviewees reported how the experience contributed to the decision to teach piano.

> I studied with (C) in London on a Fulbright. She was remarkable. Because of illness she stopped performing and dedicated her energy to teaching. She did not yell. She was insistent. She could make students cry, especially the girls; she was rough on female students. When you came out of a lesson, you felt she had put you through the mill. She made me her assistant. She was intuitive—she sensed I was a good teacher. I taught the weaker students. (I17)

> I apprenticed with my high school piano teacher, which is where I had the experience of enjoying teaching. I then went to undergraduate school for music education, where I took piano pedagogy courses with students as part of the program. (I18)

As the Miller and Baker study found, exposure to pedagogical training may serve as a catalyst for changes in career orientation from performance to teaching (2007, 5).

> I went into college loving performing. I wanted to be a performer. I was a piano major from the start, but added a pedagogy concentration later. I spent two years learning how to teach piano. (I2)

Additionally, courses in pedagogy may support the decision to teach, providing information on methods and techniques. Those who were already teaching or began teaching later found that such courses could be useful when developing a teaching approach. How such courses did or did not contribute to interviewees' approaches to teaching piano is discussed in the next chapter.

Motivating Factors: Passion and Talent

While, the need to earn an income at any stage in the musical journey may precipitate the decision to teach piano economics is not sufficient to explain this choice. Teaching is not the only option available to the pianist to meet financial need. Business enterprises related or unrelated to music; writing textbooks, memoirs, or articles; playing piano in a restaurant, bar, or church, while perhaps not classical music is still music; accompanying; composing; or becoming a music librarian are alternative ways of earning additional income. Although each of these options requires talents in addition to those required of the performer, each can generate income. Education also does not explain the choice. Courses in pedagogy, for example, might lead a pianist to choose a path other than teaching. As pianists do pursue alternative options, it is important to go beyond the precipitating factors of economics and education and delve into the factors that may contribute to the particular choice of teaching piano.

A passion and talent to teach piano may contribute to the explanation of why teach piano rather than another musical path. A passion for music and, specifically, the motivation to share the love, knowledge, and traditions of music may be a driving force underlying both the initial decision to teach and continuing to do so. As for talent, the formidable artist and formidable pedagogue may be attributes of the same individual but describe different roles as well as different skills in different contexts (Persson 1994, 89).

Passion

Asked about personal attributes, musicians wholeheartedly placed passion at the core of their practice. Passion, they said, drives their determination to succeed (Bennett 2016, 119).

> The biggest challenge is that music is not an economically viable field to be in. It requires a lot of love and being good at it, but there are not a lot of jobs. I was warned, but I did not get it at age 16. I just loved music. I don't regret it. (I10)

Considering passion as defined in the achieving success literature (Duckworth 2016, 114–15 and 143), the passion to teach piano extends beyond self-interest, which is self-directed (i.e., interest in music for its own sake), to purpose, which is directed to the well-being of others. One teaches with the intention of contributing to the well-being of others.

> When one is a teacher, one does not think about oneself; the performer puts self first. (I10)

The passion to teach involves the realization of the powerful effect music has on one's life (Madsen and Kelly 2002, 330), as well as a strong desire to pass on music traditions and skills to the next generation. This passion is well articulated in the recorded reflections of well-known contemporary pianists and master teachers. The internationally recognized pianist and teacher, Leon Fleischer, for example, has observed:

> I love teaching. I come by that love very legitimately, because my teacher also loved teaching. I guess I just inherited some of that affection. (In Mach 1991b, 104)

Interviewees identified a passion to teach. For those who began teaching in their preteen and teen years, this passion was experienced early in life.

Although the word "passion," specifically, might not be used, what interviewees described was a feeling, experienced from listening to music and playing the piano, and a desire to pass on to students that feeling, as well as the knowledge.

> Studying music awakens how it feels to be alive. (I15)

> When I was 16, students appeared and wanted to study with me. I knew about music and playing the piano. (I20)

> Teaching allows you to pass on the tradition—it is a great thing, rewarding. (I12)

Interviewees who began teaching later ultimately experienced both the passion for music and teaching piano but might or might not have felt the passion to teach early in their music development. An interviewee might feel the passion to teach early in life but not begin teaching until later in his or her career.

> Teaching is part of my make up as a musician. I began teaching in my mid twenties. I did not teach when I was young, because I didn't know if I was doing it right. (I11)

Others, who began teaching and then stopped for a period, expressed a lack of confidence in their ability and passion to teach at the earlier point in time. Both the confidence and passion to teach developed later, underscoring the importance of both in sustaining the decision to teach.

> My first encounter with teaching was bad. Then at I University, I had a teaching assistantship. I had students who knew how to read music. Those who came to me were the best students at the university. They were inspiring—peers in the masters program and undergraduates. I loved teaching them. (I6)

> I started teaching at about 17 or 18 years old. I had no idea how to teach. I learned later. I could never look at my first experiences for examples. I had to discover for myself. (I1)

> I began teaching in my student years. I did so to make money. Later on I became fascinated about teaching. It was rewarding. (I12)

At whatever age a pianist begins teaching, sustaining and continuing to teach piano involves the desire to pass on the traditions and share the love of music. Interviewees described listening to music, often in the home, as an important part of the developmental process. Part of the tradition to pass on and incorporated into contemporary teaching is listening to music, live or recordings, as will be described in succeeding chapters. Communicating this passion and doing so in one's teaching involves skills and talents different from performing. Recognizing that one has the talent to teach, or not, is usually perquisite to making a personal commitment to teaching.

Talent

Born with a special gift denied to the rest of us, like the performer, the talent of a teacher needs to be recognized. While the talents associated with performing and teaching may be complementary, especially when teaching a student about performing, concert musicians may be exceedingly knowledgeable about performance but fall short as teachers (Persson 1994, 79). The attribution of "talented as a teacher" to any interviewee is self-identified. Self-assessments of interviewees' teaching abilities are reflected in such statements as: "I discovered I was good at it (teaching)." From the experience of teaching piano emerges the recognition that one has the ability, the talent, to teach.

> The realization came early to me that I had the ability to teach. Because of a difficult case, I decided I had the ability to teach. A mother approached me to teach her three children ages 14, 11, and 6. They spoke German. The youngest did not speak, but in a year and a half we had discussions and he played fantastically at the recital. (I7)

> I discovered that teaching piano was accessible; I enjoyed it; I was good at it; and I wanted to do it. (I2)

As with performance, external acknowledgment may contribute to the realization that one can teach, for example, getting compliments from others (Madsen and Kelly 2002, 330). Such reinforcement may help at whatever stage the pianist begins teaching—as a high school student or a mature musician.

> There were a lot of kids in the neighborhood who wanted to take piano lessons. I was known as a star in the community. (I10)

> I taught a class (group of students, taught one on one) on a temporary basis. It was my first teaching experience. After that period was finished, the students decided to stay with me. (I14)

Being aware that one is "not good at" teaching is also an aspect of acknowledging the importance of teaching and effect of poor teaching. "Being a poor teacher" may be a matter of time and experience rather than a permanent condition—lacking the talent to teach. Among the interviewees who turned to teaching in graduate school or later were individuals whose first attempts at teaching had not gone well but with experience and preparation each later chose to teach.

I did not have a grand vision of becoming a teacher. A mother insisted that I teach her children. I was a freshman in college. I had no idea how to teach. I taught them the easiest piece I knew. I decided I was not ready. I needed to work on my teaching skills. Then, at I University, I had a teaching assistantship. Five years later I was more mature. (I6)

Experience can lead to the realization that one is more effective teaching a particular type of student, which may be another aspect of being a responsible teacher.

Children are easier for me to teach. I get along better with children than adults. (I2)

I taught in one college and one university. I took a step back. I decided I could be most effective with younger level students, before they go to college. I had a home studio. That was how I decided where I could be most effective. (I6)

Talent and the passion to pass on the tradition of music and the piano provide the motivation to teach, but motivation is not sufficient to sustain the decision. From passion and the recognition that one has the ability to teach piano emerges a personal commitment to the piano teaching profession. A commitment to teach, with perseverance and hard work, helps to sustain the decision to teach piano.

Sustaining Factors: Commitment, Perseverance, and Hard Work

From the historical and social science literature a personal commitment to music, perseverance, and hard work/diligence were identified as factors that may contribute to the decision to teach piano. The analysis of interviewees' experiences suggest that carrying out this decision involves a commitment to the piano teaching profession and continuous learning, perseverance to overcome professional and personal challenges affecting the pursuit of this decision, and hard work to develop as a teacher and respond to the changing needs of students and the piano teaching profession. Beginning with the decision to teach piano, sustaining the decision continues through becoming and being a teacher.

Personal Commitment to the Piano Teaching Profession

Deciding to teach piano is a commitment. While a career in music and performance requires commitment, the commitment to teach differs. A commitment, as does the passion, to teach involves a sense of purpose—the intention to contribute to the well-being of others and the desire/need to impart traditions, knowledge, skill, and love of music. Responsibility lies at the core of the commitment to teach, as described by Fleisher:

> I think, in a sense, that teaching is one step beyond performing. Teaching entails more responsibility; there's a greater obligation in teaching than in being a very great and successful performer today. . . . if you're a teacher, and you pass on nonsense, then I think you commit a grave sin. Yes, in that sense being a teacher is far more serious and responsible because it's something that is passed on to the next generation, which itself will pass it on, and so forth. (In Mach 1991b, 104–5)

Interviewees recognized this responsibility, although acting on or out of this sense of responsibility sometimes occurred later in a career. Those who had demanding performing schedules might not have had time earlier in their careers to do both, simultaneously, beyond master classes and occasional lectures as part of a concert tour.

> I thought it was my duty to be a teacher. Until I was over 50, it was theoretical; I never looked for a job as a teacher. N University was my first job as a teacher. (I8)

Or, the recognition and commitment evolved.

> As I moved into my adult years, I saw the good part of teaching. You were creating, educating a new generation to appreciate music. A student might not become a professional musician, but teaching gives you feedback that what you do is helpful to the future. (I12)

> I do not feel as compelled as (his teacher), but teaching is a way to stay sharp, be involved in music, and communicate musical things with people. I'm also driven increasingly by some sense of trying to right what I see in the culture of the profession of teaching piano (e.g., very conservative—closed minded). (I19)

Essential to the commitment to teach is a commitment to continuous learning. The literature on the talented young pianist underscores the necessity of sustaining a commitment to continuous learning in the context of a performance career as a pianist (Sosniak 1985c, 477–506). Building an increasingly more intense commitment is a function of an accumulating history of experiences (502). So too as teachers, interviewees accumulated experiences that encouraged continuous learning to enhance and improve their approach to teaching piano.

> I learned to be a teacher through teaching. I keep learning. It is humbling. After 50 years of teaching, I feel like a beginner. (I1)

Now—I am learning every day—reading; listening; and, as a teacher, learning from my teaching. (I14)

I have grown and evolved as a teacher from just doing the job, through gaining experience, additional training and conventions, workshops, and involvement with professional organizations. (I16)

Sustaining the decision and commitment to teach piano also requires perseverance and hard work.

Perseverance

The perseverance required of the piano teacher begins with the decision but continues through the becoming and being of a teacher, as will be described in later chapters. Deciding to teach may indicate perseverance (i.e., sticking to the course and not abandoning tasks in the face of obstacles) in pursuit of a commitment to a career in music—not wanting to give up music (Madsen and Kelly 2002, 330), especially if teaching supplements/complements performance. A commitment to teaching piano may require perseverance in order to respond to and overcome a variety of challenges and obstacles—professional (e.g., preparing to teach), emotional (e.g., not feeling confident about one's teaching ability), or practical (e.g., identifying a pool of students to teach). Each interviewee, at whatever age he/she began teaching, had to determine how to teach.

Whatever the challenge or obstacle, each interviewee persevered to sustain the decision to teach. As described in earlier sections of this chapter, first encounters with piano teaching could be negative: my first encounter with teaching was bad (I6). Or, the young pianist might simply lack confidence as a teacher: I didn't know what I was doing (I3). Such negative experiences led to hesitation and often a hiatus in teaching. The effect of such challenges could be mitigated through experience and perseverance—learning over time what to do. Specifically, interviewees identified taking courses in piano pedagogy, reading literature on teaching piano, or attending conferences as steps taken to learn how to teach or teach better. Taking such actions, each persevered.

For those who came to the United States as experienced teachers, the decision to teach piano in a different country meant adapting their teaching approach to differences in parenting practices and approaches to general and music education.

In the United States, my formation as a teacher happened. It was a completely different experience than in Russia. At the Russian conservatory, all students have the same background. In the United States, students come from different places. I have to find a possible way to get to the heart, brain, or ear of each student. (I9)

I have had to change my techniques from Austria. I modified my teaching at L
School. (I1)

Perhaps the greatest practical challenge, whatever the age or stage at
which an interviewee begins to teach piano, is identifying and sustaining a
student population. While neighborhood children or parents of—sometimes
"appeared" before the decision and, in effect, precipitating or contributing to
the decision to teach, a cadre has to be maintained, which can require flexibility, adaptability, and ultimately perseverance. Different student populations,
changing student populations, and teaching students from different cultures
call for different ways to reach and encourage students to continue studying
piano. Maintaining a cadre of students involves balancing economic interests
and quality of teaching—considering not only of the number of students
that one can teach but can teach well—and responding to a changing music
teaching market. The need for perseverance to address and overcome such
challenges involves hard work; talent is not enough.

Hard Work/Diligence

Teaching piano well requires talent but also hard work, even for the "natural
teacher." Hard work and diligence as a performer may be defined in terms of
practicing. Preparing to become a piano teacher may involve not only practicing but taking courses, reading studies of piano teaching, and reviewing
methods books to develop an approach to teaching. Balancing the different
aspects of a musical career as well as family can be hard work. Balancing
economics and quality of teaching may include finding the appropriate mix
of teaching and other aspects of a musical career path—performing in any
venue—as well as a personal life.

You need balance. If you have 50 students, there is no room for performing. (I5)

Being both a performer and a teacher is a hard thing to do well. (I10)

Whether perceiving him/herself to be a "natural" teachers or not, an interviewee demonstrated hard work and diligence in preparing to teach piano and
sustain the decision to teach. The hard work continued through the process of
becoming and being a piano teacher.

Supporting and/or Confounding Factors

The decision to teach piano may be supported or confounded by other factors. Family and a personal support system may play a positive or negative
role—presenting support but also challenges to the decision. For example,

the need to support one's family of destination may contribute to economic demand, while family and a personal support system may provide access to students or opportunities to teach. Nevertheless, family and personal support system tend to play a more subordinate role to the factors considered earlier, in contrast to their contribution to early musical growth and development, as described in chapter 6.

Family

Family of origin generally played an important role during interviewees' early pursuit of music, but family of origin and of destination may confound the decision to teach. Interviewees' childhood experiences with music and the piano were similar in many respects to the young pianists described in the research on developing the talented young musician (see chapters 3 and 4). Family often provided not only a nurturing musical environment but also access to teachers who furthered an interviewee's musical development. Lack of family resources might promote the desirability of taking on students during adolescence and teenage years, as well as during college. Interviewees generally did not identify family of origin as a factor contributing to the decision to teach.

Family of destination may be supportive of the decision to teach, but family needs may create pressures that confound that decision as well as the demands of being a teacher. Economic need (i.e., the ability to earn a consistent income) to support one's family of destination may not only precipitate the decision to teach but also provide the incentive to continue to teach female interviewees were more likely than male interviewees to identify family concerns.

> Other challenges are the real life obstacles—family and children. (I10)

Teaching can provide the opportunity to continue one's musical career while raising a family.

> I was prepared in teaching, performing, and accompanying. I emigrated from Russia to the United States in 1996. I came here without any idea of a job, without the language, not driving, with two children and divorced. My little daughter was born in the United States. I joined L School in 1998. I have a home studio on the side and I accompany here widely. (I5)

A spouse may play a supportive role by providing a second income necessary to maintain the family, supplementing the teaching income.

> My second husband was a dentist/artist—always art; he taught art. We shared the household responsibilities. We raised four children. (I15)

Unless one can teach at the college level, the earnings do not keep pace with the cost of living. One needs a second income either from you or a spouse. (I16)

Further research is needed on the relationship of family to the decision to teaching piano, especially issues of gender. For example, does the desire to have a family affect the decision to teach piano differently by gender? Is a female pianist more likely than a male pianist to decide to teach piano out of the desire to have a family? That is, for women pianists, is family an additional precipitating factor, contributing to the decision to teach piano?

Personal Support System

Interviewees did not specifically identify a personal support system as a factor affecting the decision to teach. Nevertheless, friends, teachers, as well as parents were reported to have provided access to students, by way of recommendation. Or a friend, another pianist already teaching, may open the door to and opportunity to teach piano.

A friend asked me to replace her for a semester at M State College. I taught every Saturday for three months, as her replacement. It was out of necessity, because I was living in New York. (I7)

In doing so, the personal support system can offer encouragement and access to opportunities, thereby, helping to sustain the decision to teach.

CHALLENGES AND BARRIERS

Throughout this chapter, a variety of challenges affecting the decision to teach piano have been identified, including economic need, availability of opportunities to teach, family considerations, and confidence in one's ability to teach piano. Responding to some challenges may precipitate the decision to teach, for example, the need for a steady income to support oneself or one's family or a stable and consistent work schedule to achieve a work/life balance, especially when raising a family. Other challenges may adversely affect the pursuit of a career teaching piano, for example, the demands of developing a pool of students, establishing a location in which to teach—a private studio or affiliation with an institution, or lacking confidence in one's ability to teach. Confronting and adjusting to these challenges shape the music career of the contemporary U.S. piano teacher.

Health issues and personal problems may affect both the pianist's ability to perform and teach. Interviewees confronted and overcame physical and emotional challenges that affected the decision and timing of the decision to teach. Physical challenges, both as a result of "poor teaching" and other activities unrelated to the piano, may create obstacles, or at least the need for adjustment, to be able to work with students.

> The major challenge of my life is contracting focal right hand dystonia nearly 30 years ago. I only strategically play with students because the dystonia puts limits on me. (I16)

Or, the pianist may have to suspend teaching.

> I already had experience teaching in early years, but had physical problems and could not play for a few years. Because of the physical problems I taught math and science and was not as committed to a music career for quite some time. It did not stop me in the end, but it was more difficult to pursue. (I19)

Performance anxiety may affect a pianist's career path, including teaching. The stability of teaching may allow the anxious or reluctant performer to pursue performance opportunities, selectively.

> I learned how to perform with more ease, but never enough that I felt I could make a career out of being a classical pianist. I have, however played classical music for dancers at N School in Connecticut for decades. Much of the music is concert music, so it keeps me challenged. In this context, I do not have the same pressure of being perfect. (I18)

Leon Fleisher has written of the personal physical challenges that affected his music career. As did many of the interviewees he started his teaching career young, at the age of fifteen; his first student was the daughter of his mother's friend. He notes, however, that "Through all the ups and downs of my professional life, teaching is the one career that I've been able to sustain" (Fleisher and Midgette 2011, 212). Similarly, despite personal challenges, interviewees persevered in their decision and continued to teach. Given the general focus of the social science literature on performance anxiety and its failure, generally, to address physical and emotional issues associated with the music profession, as discussed in chapters 3 and 4, the effects of such challenges on the decision to teach piano needs further study.

Additionally, continuing changes in society and the music profession affect opportunities not only to perform but also to teach, presenting ongoing challenges to sustaining the decision to teach piano. Such changes may lead to a decrease, or at least fluctuations, in interest in studying piano and the corresponding demands for piano teachers. The effects of such challenges on the decision to teach piano might be explored by comparing pianists who choose not to teach, similar to the research on children who choose to and choose not to continue to study a musical instrument. The current study considers the effects of such challenges as part of the discussion of being a teacher of piano in chapters 9 and 10.

SUMMARY AND CONCLUSION: REFLECTIONS ON THE DECISION TO TEACH PIANO

In this chapter, the factors identified as contributing to the decision to teach piano are organized into four categories—precipitating, motivating, sustaining, and supporting and/or confounding. Despite differences in the stage and age at which interviewees began teaching piano; gender; and personal, social, and cultural contexts, the precipitating factors, which create the need or provide the opportunity to pursue a musical path in addition to performing, were similar—economic or educational. Teaching piano—as employment—was a precipitating factor throughout a music career—in adolescence, as an undergraduate or graduate student, or supplementing an active performance career—although the relationship between employment and economic need differed, particularly at the ends of the continuum. While piano teaching as adolescent employment was financially beneficial, the decision was usually characterized as a response to opportunity rather economic need, in contrast to the mature pianist seeking additional income. Nevertheless, attributing the decision to teach piano to economic need misses the contribution of other factors, specifically those shown to motivate—passion and talent; sustain—personal commitment, perseverance, and hard work/diligence; and support, although sometimes confounding—family and a personal support system.

Although the circumstances affecting each decision to teach piano varied, interviewees' experiences evidence a complexity and confluence of factors that more fully explain the initial decision to pursue a career teaching piano rather than other musical paths. The motivation to share the love of music, knowledge, and traditions is a driving force both in support of the decision to teach and continuing to do so. As for talent, the formidable artist and formidable pedagogue may be attributes of the same individual but they describe different roles as well as different skills in different contexts (Persson 1994, 89). Sustaining the decision to teach involves a commitment to the teaching profession—contributing to the well-being of others and passing on the traditions; perseverance—developing one's confidence and skills as a teacher; and hard work. In addition to economic need, interviewees also experienced a range of personal and professional issues (e.g., health issues and confidence in teaching ability) that affected their respective career in music and decision to teach piano. The identified factors continue to play a role throughout a career teaching piano, as will be developed in the succeeding chapters on becoming and being a piano teacher.

Considering Huhatanen's dichotomy of teachers who are "realists" and teachers who are "dreamers" (Huhtanen 2004, 22–23; and Bennett 2016, 89), interviewees tend to be "realists." Most are performers and teaching is one path in a protean career. Teaching is considered to be part of one's identity as a musician, not a temporary adjustment while waiting to achieve the ultimate definition of musician—performer. While economics may have precipitated the decision to teach piano, economics does not explain the motivation to be a "good piano teacher," or, for that matter, a "good teacher" in any field. Becoming a "good teacher" requires preparation, professionally and personally, issues to be explored in the next chapter.

Chapter 8

Becoming a Piano Teacher

*Developing an Approach—
Eclectic and Pragmatic*

The historical and social science literatures point to early teachers, tradition, and formal pedagogical training as factors that may contribute to becoming a piano teacher. The first section of this chapter focuses on the role played by these and additional factors, identified by interviewees, in developing contemporary approaches to teaching piano. By way of example and illustration, the second section explores interviewees' observations as to how these factors, individually and collaboratively, are reflected in their respective teaching approach in three arenas—the lesson, beyond the lesson, and promoting the general culture. Given the diversity of interviewees' national and musical education backgrounds and the differences in the age at which each began teaching, these personal experiences provide a wealth of insight into the contribution of the identified factors to the development of the contemporary piano teacher and piano teaching. These factors not only inform the transfer of skills necessary to play the instrument—methods—but also help to form the pianist, as teacher, by conveying the qualities of a good teacher, or not, and raising awareness that the responsibility of the piano teacher extends beyond the lesson and the individual student to society, in general.

FACTORS CONSIDERED IN DEVELOPING
AN APPROACH TO TEACHING PIANO

Even if a "natural" or "born teacher" and whatever the impetus or inspiration, teaching piano requires learning how to and some preparation. To explore the journey of becoming a piano teacher, each interviewee was asked to describe the process and training that he/she had pursued. In relating experiences at various stages in their musical development, interviewees corroborated the contribution of the factors extrapolated from the literatures—early teachers, traditions, and pedagogical training. Early teachers and pedagogical courses provided examples of good teaching and how to relate to students, or not, in addition to direction on teaching resources. Interviewees, associated with a particular "lineage" or school of piano study, described how tradition was reflected in aspects of their approach. Asked to identify other factors that had contributed to their teaching and might be relevant to other piano teachers, responses included later teachers, peers and colleagues, reading books on piano pedagogy and methods, and learning by doing (i.e., experiences teaching and working with students). The expanded list of factors structures the discussion of the development of interviewees' approaches to teaching piano.

The Role of Teachers

At any stage in the musical development process, a teacher may contribute to a pianist's teaching approach. In response to the question of how he had learned to teach, an interviewee replied: "A life of taking piano lessons and being observant about what happens, as I got older" (I19). The influence of a teacher or teachers might be positive or negative, sometimes serving as a role model of how to but at other times as an example of how not to teach piano. Citing a friend at the conservatory another interviewee suggested: "To be a good teacher, you have to have had one really good teacher and one really bad teacher" (I17). Whether or not this observation is true, what is evident from the interviews is that by not dwelling on the negative feelings, even experiences with "bad teachers" could not only be examples of how not to teach but also provide the impetus to do things differently. Moreover, even more than being a model of how to teach—what to do—teachers at any stage may exemplify how to be as a person, or not.

Early Teachers

An early teacher might not only inspire a dedication to music and the decision to teach piano, as described in the previous chapters but also contribute to an interviewee's approach to teaching piano by demonstrating exemplary practices (how) and qualities of a good teacher (who). A first teacher, who was kind and nice but not a very fine musician or expert music teacher, while not conveying model pedagogical practices, could personify how to relate to students. In contrast, those who enforced harsh discipline with a pencil, tool, or stern words served as a model of how not to treat students. Early teachers, who were kind, patient, and fine musicians, might not only be the source of "good memories" of early lessons but also promote learning by creating a nurturing environment.

(O) has a psychological understanding of how students learn. She is not traditional in her approach. Her approach is different. She uses images. I react against teachers who believe there is one correct way of doing things. (I19)

He was a gentlemanly man. He was soft spoken, knew what he was doing. In his private instruction, he was encouraging. He was a great first teacher. (I10)

At this stage in the development of the pianist, it may be difficult to disentangle the love of the teacher from the teaching approach. Nevertheless, several interviewees were able to identify specific fundamentals of teaching, learned from an early teacher, which not only contributed to but remained important components of their teaching approach. Such fundamentals ranged from the physical aspects of playing to basic piano technique and allowing students to select pieces to study.

As preparation to working with (H), I took lessons with her mother. She was concerned that the chair be the right height for the piano. My father thought she was crazy. But, the height of the chair is important for the position of the forearm—horizontal, not sloped. (I15)

She would tell me a story while working on little pieces—a story about a garden and flowers. I continue to use this approach. (I12)

(K) was my earliest teacher—she was one of the best. She taught me the basics that I use today in teaching. She encouraged students, even at an early age, to choose their own repertoire. Since then, with my students, I always ask them first what it is they want to play. (I14)

"Bad experiences" could also be learning opportunities, demonstrating what not to do. Such experiences took different forms—emotional, physical, and technical. A teacher's demands might be considered too strict (I11) or too challenging for children.

She had me in advanced music too early. The music itself was too challenging. I somehow did it. (I16)

In today's world of teaching, generally, corporal punishment or use of a pencil or tool to impose discipline is unacceptable, but other practices may also be physically or emotionally damaging to the piano student.

I firmly believe the exercises set me up later in life for right hand focal dystonia. (I16)

She made me feel badly about myself. She did not have a ruler or a pencil, no
tool, but her verbal remarks had a bite. (I3)

As in any field, one may still choose to emulate negative practices—"If I went
through it, they can; it's part of the process"—or, act differently. Interviewees
chose to not pass on unpleasant or destructive experiences.

My experiences with my early teachers were no use to my teaching; they were
not good examples of how to teach. Their teaching was destructively negative.
They were exhausted and cranky and they hit students. (I1)

I try to not make students feel badly but motivate them. (I3)

Learning difficulties or challenges may also provide insight into how to
teach, especially when teaching students confronting similar challenges.
Learning to read music, for example, is fundamental to playing the piano.
Interviewees, who had not been taught to read music in a timely manner,
recognized that this failure had hampered their musical development.

I had several teachers who did not know how to teach. I was not taught well. I
could not read music; I read by reading the finger numbers. I did receive decals.
A decal of an oriole is one I remember . . . and stars—gold and green. (I17)

Such personal experiences were used to inform their teaching approach.

Practicing was recalling, up to age 9. I did not learn to read music or to count. It
was visual. I would have the teachers play the piece and then I would reproduce
the sound. I learned from that experience. In teaching, I emphasize reading and
counting in the beginning, because not reading and counting is a hurdle that
makes it difficult to learn new pieces. (I6)

The contribution of early teachers to the growth and development of an
interviewee, as a person and teacher, varied. An early teacher might serve as
a role model, exemplifying how to relate to students or demonstrating how to
teach the fundamentals of playing the piano. An early teacher might also be
an example of how not to live as a piano teacher.

The teachers were horrible because it was hard life. It was hard to earn a living
and teaching was intense even for a bad teacher. They did not have reserves—
intellectually, emotionally, and physically. You can only teach so many students
each day. They needed to replenish. (I1)

Similar to the observations in the literature on developing the talented young pianist, while a contributing factor, the significance of the contribution of early teachers to the development of an interviewee's approach to piano teaching varies and is not clear cut.

Later Teachers

The experience of an exemplary teacher often occurred during the later stage—precollege, college, or graduate school—in the development of the young pianist. Not only is the student older and perhaps better able to evaluate the learning experience, but experiences with later teachers may be more relevant to teaching.

> Upon reflection, it becomes apparent to me that Vengerova's influence is very much alive and active in both the "art" and science" aspects of my teaching and I expect it lives on in the work of many others. (Abram 1996, 2)

The contribution of a later teacher may be complex, not only informing how to teach but also the qualities of a teacher.

While the social science literature emphasizes the importance of the personality of early teachers to musical growth and development (Sosniak 1985b, 411–12 and 1988, 81; and Sloboda and Howe 1991, 19), a later teacher, even famous pedagogues teaching at an advanced level, may be a parental figure.

> (C) was a maternal figure. She would have you to dinner, go to concerts with her students; she was active in her students' lives. She was a force of nature. I have three pictures of her in my studio. (I17)

> (M) lived through her students; she had no family—we were her family. (I11)

> It wasn't until years and years later that I realized Mrs. B. was the first positive female adult role model I had. She was really the most nurturing person who helped me find a way to love myself and to use self-motivation to learn. I decided to take an extra year to graduate so I could study with her one more year and do a full recital under her tutelage. Since that experience my learning style completely changed from being in a constant state of fear, to feeling very secure that I could find solutions to any challenge that would arise. (I18)

Nevertheless, later teachers were more likely to contribute to the musical and pedagogical aspects of an interviewee's teaching approach, both positively and negatively.

From later teachers often came knowledge of how and what to teach—what a student needed to learn.

I followed my teacher (A)—the repertoire, scales, arpeggios. It was what needed to be done. (I17)

I did not need to take pedagogy classes because of the people who were teaching me, for example Neuhaus. Once I started teaching, I used what I learned from my teachers and my own everyday experience. (I14)

Sometimes they imparted a model of the teacher-student relationship that became incorporated into the student's teaching approach.

(S) was remarkable and patient, although moody. He was a teacher, linguist, lawyer, and pianist. He understood the performer. (S) had a particular style: He really taught the individual—students are all different. He goes on their journey with them. He knew what pieces to choose for the student. He never brought you down. He was behind me. (I1)

At times, however, it was difficult to follow the approach of the exemplary teacher precisely.

I observed, taking the advice of (O). But her style is still very mysterious. You absorb through osmosis. I can't replicate her style, nor have I tried. I could not replicate her style if I tried. She skips the concrete, but her students get it and you get the results. (I19)

Neuhaus studied in Germany with Godowsky. He then created his own approach to teaching. During a lesson, a student was playing, but the lesson was shared by a large group. Lessons were open to writers, poets, and the "intelligentsia" (artists, writers, in contrast to workers and white collar workers). Twenty percent of the comments were directed toward the student playing and 80 percent toward everyone listening. (I14)

Moreover, aspects of personality might also be difficult to emulate.

I worked with (D) when I lived in Toronto for eight months. He is an amazing pedagogue, very effective. He transfers his knowledge by his presence and the way he plays along during the lesson. He plays a phrase and then hands it over; his teaching comes from a genuine part of himself. People flock to him. (I10)

Neuhaus talked about the arts, psychology, and the brain, for example. Students wrote down what he said; some students wrote a lot. The students, with his participation, put together his book on the art of piano playing. The book is more about the person than methods. (I14)

Negative experiences with later teachers may contribute to a teaching approach, by way of example of what not to do. Severe criticism even yelling, which was part of earlier traditions of piano teaching, might be experienced at this stage. One might even suggest that sometimes the "better" or "more promising" student was more likely to be subject to the anger or critical tongue of the teacher, because of that promise. Nevertheless, as greater value is placed on the expertise than personality of the teacher at this stage of musical development (Sosniak 1985b, 420–21, and 1988, 81–82; and Sloboda and Howe 1991, 19), perhaps an interviewee accepted "abusive behavior" to learn from the master teacher, although not incorporating such behavior into his/her own approach to teaching.

> During my sophomore year of high school, I began to study with (M). She had a formal approach. She was an older woman with a great reputation. She was a stern German woman; her sternness was part of a formality that demanded respect. She communicated that it was a privilege to study with her. She was connected to a top notch group of piano teachers in the (City) area. The lessons were not much fun; there was no laughing. What I remember was the atmosphere, the seriousness. My teaching style was not influenced by her style. (I3)

> My high school teacher was male, very strict, but incredibly intelligent. He was blind. At my first lesson I cried because he was so critical. At the time, I could not distinguish between criticism to help one improve and aggression that was meant to be hurtful. (Nevertheless) he taught me scale discipline, how to practice, and how to sit better. He was strict on what I had to do to go to music school. (I18)

> During the lesson he stomped his foot and yelled a lot. At the door, he would press my hands and say: The only reason I get upset is because I care. He believed in me. I would have jumped out the window for him. He put me under pressure. He said we had no time to lose if I am going to make you a pianist. He pushed hard; he pushed ahead with the repertoire. (I17)

When asked whether he yelled at his students, the interviewee replied: "No, I don't; I almost never do. Times have changed" (I17). Despite the challenges posed by short-tempered teachers, whatever the motivation, interviewees learned. Still, the use of severe criticism during the lesson was a practice they usually chose not to perpetuate.

At the graduate level, advanced students might still encounter difficulties and experience inadequate teaching.

> In the United States, I studied at Y University for my masters degree. My professor was mean, negative, and never positive. He was not a good teacher. He

gave me wrong advice on performance, e.g., *The Pathetique Sonata*. He said to start with the problem areas. I believe you need to start at the beginning of the piece, when you sit down at the piano. You have to teach the student how to perform, from A to Z; teach how to get to Z. (I1)

Moreover, interviewees' experiences with the same professor, further under-score the importance of matching the student and teacher, not only according to talent but personality and teaching and learning styles.

I worked with (M) on my doctorate. She was at the conservatory for 40 years. She was not a wonderful woman. I had recorded the 4th Ballade and she said: "You don't like Chopin do you dear?" The relationship was bad to nonexistent. She would cancel lessons. (I8)

I felt honored, lucky, excited to study with her (M). The first year involved adaptation. Her system was different. The conservatory was a performing school—there were demands and expectancies. During the first week, you had to have the conception of the work, not just bring the notes, and observe all the markings—it was demanding. I was expected to have a piece memorized by the second week. She cleaned up my pedaling. Little by little I learned to listen to myself in a more objective way. Every lesson was a performance—you would work hard and get nervous before the lesson. When (M) said you were good, you were terrific; you had to be really good for her to say you were. (I11)

Among interviewees who sought to study with a particular teacher, the road was not always smooth. The teacher-student relationship was not always a constant; experiences could differ at different points in time.

When I got married and then pregnant, she was upset—"all that work down the drain." I still wanted to study with (V) for technical work—so I went back. She was easier to work with. At first I thought she had accepted me, but it was because she was not trying to turn me into a concert pianist. (I15)

There were pieces that she did not know how to explain what she wanted. She got frustrated with herself and with you. During the year, things were ok, but when the time for juries came she would freak out about preparation. Later when I went back to her privately, it worked wonderfully. We spent 3 to 4 hours per lesson. Lessons were relaxed, no pressure. (I11)

Whether positive or negative, interviewees were generally affected by their personal experiences as students and tended to incorporate what they found helpful and effective into their own teaching approach.

Every single one of my teachers influenced my teaching in a way. I have flash-backs to each one when I'm teaching. Regarding the way I teach now—my last teacher had the strongest influence (I11). I am still working with him, although he is a performer, not strictly a teacher. I am trying to copy him. I sent one of my students to him and he noticed that his way was so similar to mine. (I7)

Mrs. B. influenced my teaching considerably, as did my high school teacher. I would say I have used a combination of both of their teaching styles for the most part. (I18)

My philosophy is based on my frustration with teachers and approaches I do not like. I especially hate the conservative approach—the student plays and the teacher points; it is not enough. (I19)

And, rejected what they did not like or did not find effective in the style of their teachers.

I studied in Vienna, Austria for 6 years, where I learned what I would not do as a teacher. I would never keep a student waiting for two hours, put them down. (I1)

My style was definitely influenced by all the teachers I had. Most lacked cur-riculum development for the progressing student. Therefore I use many different method books and supplemental books of different styles like jazz, sacred, bal-lads, classical, and a variety of sheet music. (I16)

Whether positive or negative, often both, personal experiences with later teachers contributed to the development of each interviewee's approach to teaching piano. They chose selectively from these experiences, not merely imitating a teacher and teaching as they were taught (e.g., Mills and Smith 2003, 22). Teachers at any stage, however, were only one contributing factor.

Peers and Colleagues

Within the educational setting, interviewees also learned from peers, while students, and colleagues, in later years. Some relationships continued over decades. For example, one interviewee noted that a classmate at the music and arts high school, who became a conductor, was a good friend and stu-dents with him at the conservatory, who became members of university music faculties, remained lifelong friends (I20). Another observed that other pianists, not just teachers but peers, had had the biggest effect on him in the conservatory (I8). Considering the teaching of piano as continuous learning, colleagues contribute as well: "I learn from other teachers" (I1).

Tradition

Although distinguishing between the contribution of an individual teacher and a tradition presents a challenge, certain philosophies and practices, passed on through a teacher, are more than a personal style. Trying to assess the influence of a teacher, school, or lineage on performance, raises questions of similarity in approach—the "common denominators." Do the students of X play the same piece in the same way? Can you recognize the teacher from the way the student plays? Or, A plays in the Russian style.

> It's generally accepted that Russian pianists are more emotional than, for example, Germans. Russian playing is more physical, as compared to the German and American—although American playing is a mix from different backgrounds. Mostly, Russians are more vocal, more emotional. (I14)

Nevertheless, there is considerable discussion as to what precisely is meant by "tradition." The purpose, here, is not to become caught up in debate but to explore through interviewees' experiences how tradition may contribute to contemporary piano teaching.

Russian/Soviet Educational Approach

Because a majority of the pianists interviewed were taught by Russian émigrés or studied in the former Soviet Union, references were often made to the "Russian" or "Soviet" school, although sometimes the distinction was blurred. As discussed in chapter 4, after the Revolution of 1917 and during the early 1930s, changes were made to the system of music education when the Soviets took control over all spheres of the economy and culture (Gelfand 1986–1987, 39). The early émigrés, with whom U.S. students studied piano, received their musical education prior to 1917, while the later émigrés studied under the Soviet system.

U.S.-born pianists interviewed described being taught in the "real Russian" not the "Soviet" tradition. Commenting on their experiences with three famous female pedagogues, two were émigrés and the third was the student of émigrés:

> (L) was a great teacher, carrying on the Russian tradition. (I20)

> (V) studied with Leschetizky and was a descendant of that tradition. She worked a lot with the wrist; it was very helpful. (I15)

> (M) was very much in the Russian tradition—the real one—Rachmaninoff and Josef Lhevinne, for example, not the modern tradition. (I11)

Interviewees, who were more recent émigrés, described a structured system of musical training, which was consistent across the Soviet Union—Moscow, Tbilisi, or Vilnius, for example (I14, I4, I5, I9, I12). Within all music schools, the curriculum was the same and all students were to be taught in the same way (I5).

> In the Soviet Union, when I was a child, each area of a city had a music school. "Private" lessons—as anything "private"—were forbidden. (Russia, I14)

> I went to music school. It was not only the quality of the teachers. All training was enhanced from the first grade—ear, solfege, music history, Scarlatti and Bach to the twentieth century. The three cycles repeated—elementary, middle school, and high school—but at a deeper and broader level. By the time one entered the conservatory, you had it all. (Tbilisi, Georgia, I9)

> The approach in Vilnius during the period was similar to the Russian—Soviet approach. I attended a special school for artists. The Lithuanians created schools similar to the Russian schools. (Lithuania, I12)

> I went to the music pre-college. It was a four-year program. Classes included blocks of music and other subjects—literature, history, and English. The music program included solo, chamber music, accompaniment, duet, and analysis-theory. I graduated in four years with all As (5s) and the state committee recommended that I attend the conservatory. Without their recommendation, I would have had to work for three years and teach, and then try on my own. (Russia, I5)

> As a result of the structured system, all students entering the conservatory have the same background (I9).

Interviewees described a structured program within the conservatory, which included qualifications in four areas—solo piano, chamber music, accompanying, and pedagogy (I4, I5, I7). To study music, a student also had to take and pass courses in political economy and politics (I9) and pass an exam in Scientific Communism to graduate (I5). State exams in piano studies took place in the presence of the whole faculty—ten world-class faculty members (I4). For solo piano, you had to give a solo performance and receive a 5, but even if you received a 5 you might not qualify; for chamber, you had to receive a 5 as a soloist of the chamber group; in accompanying, you could receive a B; and pedagogy, a required course of study, was last. Most qualified as teacher and accompanist (I5).

Within the structure, however, one interviewee observed that professors at the Moscow Conservatory, at least during the period of Neuhaus, had different styles of playing.

The idea of a Russian approach is on shaky grounds. It is more like a legend. For example, at the time of Neuhaus, there was a group of five to six stars teaching at the Moscow Conservatory. All were Russians because they were in Moscow. Each had a different approach to playing the piano. (I14)

Nevertheless, there were also restrictions, emanating from the state, regarding the music that could be taught and played.

In the Soviet Union, it was forbidden to play certain composers, e.g., Schoenberg and Hindemith. One day—S—and another student were playing a 4-hand piece by Stravinsky, which was forbidden. The director came into the room and asked the students why they were playing the piece. Neuhaus responded for the students—They have to know "what to neglect." (I14)

Characteristics of the Russian/Soviet School of Piano

Despite differences in pre-Revolution and Soviet-era music education, interviewees associated certain characteristics of playing and teaching with the "Russian School"—imagination, "sound and tone," and technical virtuosity. These characteristics and practices were incorporated into interviewees' teaching, passing on the tradition. More controversial was an emphasis on competition prominent during the Soviet era. Additionally, the teacher-student relationship was described as family.

Imagination. From the earliest to later experiences, interviewees described the role of imagination in their learning of music and study of piano.

My first teacher was about imagination in the music. I continue to use this approach. (I12)

Russians have a way of playing that I learned in Austria—imagination, musicality, style—They use story to understand music. The psychology of teaching is to help student to bring life to the story. (I1)

Sound and Tone. Russian pedagogues Neuhaus and Lhevinne stressed the mastering of tone as essential to the substance of music (1973, 56–57, and [1924] 1972, 25) and that emphasis continues.

Russians have an anatomical way of playing. Sound is everything. (I11)

(L) taught in the "Russian style," which emphasizes technique, a beautiful singing tone, and unbelievable technical virtuosity. She knew classical repertoire beautifully. She strongly believed in technical virtuosity. (I20)

The creation of sound and tone is associated with the physical playing of the instrument.

> Russians tend to play with somewhat flatter fingers and higher wrists, for example Rubenstein. Germans tend to use more curved fingers. But that is detail. (I14)

> (V) worked a lot with the wrist and focused on the use of the forearm. I use this approach for small-framed people if there is a large area to cover. Otherwise, I emphasize the floating of the wrist; inhale wrist up; exhale wrist down. (I15)

Technical Virtuosity. Emphasis on perfect technique as a means to express the ideas of the composer characterized the early "Russian School" and continued during the Soviet era (Lhevinne [1924] 1972; Hechinger 1968; Gelfand 1986–1987; and Sonderland 2006).

> The Russian, or rather Soviet, approach is to focus on the notes. The Moscow Conservatory was very strict—hit a wrong note and you are a criminal. Professional musicians are to run like a perfect machine. It is not about a great personality. (I12)

Competition. During the Soviet era, an emphasis on competition, even in the early years, also emerged. Winning was important.

> It was difficult to sign up a child for music school. It was not possible to study an instrument in school. You had to compete and take an exam. Six to 10 children competed for one spot. I did not make the cut the first year. Eventually I did. (I5)

> The emphasis is on competitions, first place prize. Everyone is likely to play perfectly. You do not want to annoy the judge by creating a unique interpretation. Unique annoys them. Ethical is what is properly correct. The main way to a career is to win a competition. You get two years of concerts. Then it depends on those helping you—whether or not you get more concerts. (I12)

> Before I entered the conservatory, I participated as the youngest participant in the Fifth Tchaikovsky Competition. I tied for 4th place. The competition was my ticket to the conservatory; I entered without any exams. (I9)

The interaction between an emphasis on technique as "correctness" and competition, while a part of the musical education of several interviewees, raised issues in the context of their own teaching, in practice.

Teacher-Student Relationship. Within or outside Russia, whether the teacher was male or female, interviewees described the teacher-student relationship within the Russian tradition as family.

> When she (K) taught, she radiated love and understanding, and all children felt they were in a family. Neuhaus' wife was always kind and made us feel welcome in their house. There was always a very special, light and creative atmosphere. (I14)

> He (K) became a great mentor; he led me to a bigger world. We had a close relationship, like family, with his wife and kids. This is an especially Russian tradition. (I12)

> Her (O) studio is like a family; it makes a huge difference. (I19)

The "Russian School" was not the only tradition experienced by interviewees; references were also made to the French and German schools. Moreover, an interviewee's teacher or the interviewee, him/herself, might have studied with teachers trained in different traditions. Nevertheless, the Russian school, by way of example, illustrates how tradition may contribute to the teaching approach of a contemporary pianist, demonstrating continuity and change. While aspects of tradition may be passed on, others may be modified, in practice, to accommodate differences in cultural and societal expectations of parents and students and changing perspectives on effective teaching.

Pedagogical Training

Studies in piano pedagogy were also identified as a possible contributing factor to the development of an approach to piano teaching. Exposure to formal courses in piano pedagogy varied. Opinions as to the value of these courses differed. Interviewees also reported informally studying pedagogical literature and reviewing piano teaching materials.

Formal

Country of study, time period, age, career expectations, and personal inclination affect opportunities to pursue pedagogy courses. Such courses were part of the required curriculum in the former Soviet Union. Among interviewees who studied primarily in the United States, requirements and opportunities for formal pedagogical study varied.

In the former Soviet Union and countries within its sphere of influence, pedagogical training began early in the specialized music studies and continued through the conservatory.

Teaching was part of my training in precollege and the conservatory—pedagogical practice. You had a course on methods of piano teaching and read books, for example, Neuhaus. Pedagogy is a necessary part of musical training. It is assumed that anyone graduating from a good music institution will teach. Most training is to teach children. (I5)

At the conservatory, I had courses in pedagogy as part of the curriculum. (I7)

Interviewees usually taught, after graduation, while pursuing a performance career. That is, "You could not escape teaching unless you went into the accompanying field; the great thing is to do both, in combination" (I5).

After completing the conservatory, I was supposed to teach or accompany. I received all As—solo, chamber, accompanying, and pedagogy—and received all four qualifications from the state committee. You were assigned to work by the committee. The examiner from the K Conservatory invited me to do post graduate work. I spent two years there doing post graduate work. I wrote papers, performed solo, and taught. (I5)

I knew eventually I had to teach as part of my career. In my last year at the conservatory, I had an assistantship with a teacher, had a few students. I taught in T at the conservatory for 10 years. (I9)

Only one interview who attended the Moscow Conservatory reported not having to take courses in pedagogy—"My specialty at the conservatory was performance. It was possible to study pedagogy, but I did not" (I14). She did not begin teaching until coming to the United States.

Formal pedagogical training was less common among U.S. interviewees. Pedagogy might be a required course in a music program. One interviewee pursued undergraduate and graduate programs in piano pedagogy.

I decided to teach late in college. I was a piano major from the start, but added a pedagogy concentration later. I was lucky that they had pedagogy and I could study it as an undergraduate. My master's degree is in piano pedagogy and performance. I spent two years learning how to teach piano. (I2)

The undergraduate courses focused primarily on teaching beginning students, including such topics as maintaining lesson time, lesson planning, how to introduce pieces, and how to introduce a child to the piano. Graduate studies furthered and extended this training to more advanced levels.

From my formal education, I learned that piano teaching is a serious job and planning and thought go into a lesson. To find a piece for a student, it is

necessary to consider the issues in the piece, personality of the student, and that
it be fun for the student. (I2)

More typical was the interviewee who took one or more courses in
pedagogy as part of a program. Although this exposure did not precipitate
a change in career path from performance to teaching, the assessment of
the quality of the courses was positive. Interviewees described the information as useful and helpful when developing an approach to teaching later in
their music career. Useful and helpful course content included instruction on
teaching methods, developmental psychology, learning styles, and how to
teach beginners.

> I took an undergraduate pedagogy class one semester. We had to go to a music
> store and review three series with different philosophies, for kids. I went back
> and used this approach when I started teaching. (I3)

> At the university and conservatory, my courses in developmental psychology
> and teaching methods gave me a very strong grounding in understanding more
> about teaching. (I18)

> Pedagogy courses are of great value. They enable you to see lessons for begin-
> ners, if teaching a beginner. From them you can learn methods. (I1)

> I took courses in pedagogy in graduate school. The classes were helpful. (I19)

> I was classically trained and I continued to study applied piano for another five
> years. I also studied with a Taubman[1]-trained teacher for a number of years and
> attended the Taubman Institute for three summers. I use many of their move-
> ment patterns to teach today. (I16)

Others interviewees, even those who were younger and had studied at a
university or conservatory, had not pursued courses in piano pedagogy.

> I did not take pedagogy courses. (I17)

> I have never taken a pedagogy course. (I10)

Additionally, not all those who studied piano pedagogy found the course to
be useful.

> I was pedagogy minor, but classes provided little information and little real
> training. (I6)

While outside the scope of the current study, the mixed opinions as to the benefits of piano pedagogy courses raise questions about the content and quality of such programs. Nevertheless, interviewees were usually able to glean some beneficial information from courses in pedagogy or found other pedagogical tools that were useful in developing an approach to teaching.

> I recently began to read a lot about piano pedagogy, seeing that teaching will be a big part in my career. (I10)

Such tools might be used to complement, or instead of, formal pedagogical training.

Informal

Among the informal pedagogical tools cited were reading texts of historical and contemporary pedagogues, watching videos on teaching piano, studying the various piano teaching series, and attending conferences.

> I had courses as part of the curriculum, but I was interested in pedagogy. So, I read the books of the people who were important in the piano world. For example, Neuhaus's book[2]—it was fascinating; Hofmann about piano playing[3]; and works by Leschetizky. (I7)

> I have never taken a pedagogy course. Recently, I read Seymour Bernstein's *20 Lessons in Keyboard Choreography*. There are videos of his teaching on YouTube. (I10)

> I was pedagogy minor, but classes provided little information and little real training. Once I had my own studio, I began going through the methods books. (I6)

These resources are not only available to new teachers but those who are already teaching. Reading and attending academic conferences reflect the theme of continuous learning.

> I continue my education through conferences, etc. (e.g., on pre-thinking and planning). I like to see a lesson given; that is the way I learn. (I2)

Learn by Doing: Experience as Teacher

While acknowledging the emphasis on formal training in piano pedagogy in the United States today—these days, they are big on pedagogy courses (I17)—interviewees emphasized the importance of learning by doing. Learning by doing encompasses everyday experiences as a teacher, other teachers, earlier experiences as a student, and even learning from one's students. That is not to disallow the contribution of the other factors previously discussed but to underscore that piano teaching is an ongoing process of continuous learning. Whether from the former Soviet Union, South Korea, Australia, or born in the United States, the general consensus among interviewees was that experience was the greatest teacher.

> Once I started teaching, I used what I learned from my teachers and my own everyday experience. Now—I am learning every day—reading; listening; and, as a teacher, learning from my teaching. Each student is different. I learn from them. (I14)

> Training to teach was more through experience. I made conscious choices, including to teach young children, consciously selecting methods and pieces, determining what is good for certain levels, and to teach adults. I learn by doing. Every student is your teacher. You learn what works and what does not work. The biggest teacher is experience. (I6)

> It is hard to be a good piano teacher out of the box. You have to have seen; it is better if you have seen a lot. I followed my teacher. I learned on the job by doing a lot and watching. (I17)

> I have grown and evolved as a teacher by just doing the job, gaining experience, additional training, attending conventions and workshops, and involvement with professional organizations. (I16)

> I observed: taking the advice of (O); a life of taking piano lessons; and being observant about what happens, as I got older. (I19)

Experience is defined to include the challenges experienced by the interviewee. A teacher's limitations and challenges as a student can be the source of knowledge that informs one's teaching. What was helpful to a teacher, as a student, may provide the key to reaching a student. Empathy with a student can be an important part of the teacher-student relationship.

> I have found that my limitations as a young student have become my strengths as a teacher. As a young student I was able to play if I stayed in an intuitive space but because distraction was an issue, I would easily be thrown off without a range of tools beyond playing the notes in front of me. (I18)

> I also learned from personal struggles as a student—for example a late start. Because of my own struggle, I had to build a technique; it made me aware of

the process. I developed a good analytical ability because I had to deal with my own struggle. I learned on the job. I learned by doing a lot; I learned by watching. (I17)

What was helpful for my students is what I found helpful and effective for myself: look at what students are missing—the teacher has not addressed or the student has not absorbed the structural elements. Learn to play and how to approach. Get the student to notice a piece on a number of levels. (I19)

Teaching from one's own experiences as a student further underscores the importance of matching the student to the teacher.

Fundamentally, teaching is perceived to be a process of continuous learning and education. Accordingly, the contribution of each identified factor may not only vary among interviewees but over the course of an interviewee's teaching career as his/her approach continues to evolve. The lessons learned from experience are explored further in later chapters, as the interviewees describe being a piano teacher. The next section considers the confluence of factors contributing to an individual's teaching approach within the arenas of the lesson, beyond the lesson, and promoting the general culture.

ARENAS: CONTEMPORARY APPROACH
TO TEACHING PIANO

In practice, an interviewee's approach to teaching piano was eclectic—reflecting several sources, although one might be dominant. Accordingly, identifying the unique influence of a particular factor may be difficult.

It should be difficult for a teacher to isolate those elements of his/her approach that derive from a unique influence. Our teaching principles and devices reflect a rich accumulation of everything we have been taught that we have accepted, everything with which we experimented and found successful, all that we have heard and admired, all that we have read and tested. (Abram 1996, 1)

Nevertheless, an interviewee often not only associated specific factors and experiences with the development of aspects of his/her piano teaching approach (e.g., technique and the mechanics of playing the instrument) but also being a piano teacher—developing as a person and teacher. Teaching approaches were also pragmatic, continuing to evolve in response to new circumstances, challenges, and continuous learning over time. The traditions, techniques and skills, love of music, and wisdom of teaching experience are passed on to the next generation of pianists through the lesson, beyond the lesson, and the promotion of the general culture.

The Lesson

As the primary arena in which the study of piano occurs, it is within the one-on-one piano lesson that the specific contributions of teachers, tradition, and pedagogical training are evidenced. Interviewees identified specific ways in which their respective piano teaching approach—philosophy and practice—reflected the convergence of factors within the lesson.

From Teachers

The contribution of teachers to an interviewee's approach to teaching within the lesson was reflected in technique, character, and interactions with students, providing evidence of continuity from teacher to student/teacher. At the same time, there was an awareness of the need to change and develop an approach to teaching that did not encompass the detrimental practices of one's teachers. Of particular concern was the consideration of the psychological well-being of one's students.

Technique. Teachers provided examples not only of how to achieve a certain result in performing a piece but ways to communicate to the student how to produce the desired result.

> Physical position: You have to feel the weight of your body up from your behind—the armpit to the finger tip. The instrument is your body as well as the piano. (I15)

> Sound/tone: Watching myself react to the difficulties of this or that student . . . I notice my stress on musical direction or "flowing line," an alertness to having one tone move smoothly out of the decay of the previous tone. This must be V. based. (I15)

> I went to graduate school not to pursue a degree, but to study with a particular teacher. He was an amazing musician. He had a dramatic impact on my life musically. He opened my ears to sound, the production of sound. (I6)

Character. Teachers not only influence the how but the who within the context of the lesson. Positive and negative experiences helped to form attitudes on how, and how not, to relate to a student in the context of the lesson. The character of a teacher might be reflected in the tone, criticism, intensity, and patience conveyed to the future teacher, as student, within the lesson.

Tone: Never in her life did she raise her voice during a lesson. She never exerted any kind of pressure on her pupils. (I14)

Critique: She (I14) would always find something positive to say, not just a negative. She would first say something positive and then a negative. (I12)

She made me feel badly about myself. I try not to make students feel badly, but to motivate them. (I3)

Intensity: She did not yell. She was insistent. When you came out of a lesson, you felt as if she had put you through the mill. (I17)

Patience: Patience is needed to teach the steps that the student needs to know. (I1)

Interaction with Students. Fundamental to teaching piano is the interaction between teacher and student within the lesson. Examples of how to communicate with and bring the student into the learning process learned from a teacher include:

Playing as example: Her own piano playing was a significant part of the lessons, and somehow, we were all affected by it and remembered it for a long time, sometimes forever. (I14)

Our lessons would last three hours. He would give me a performance of the piece at the end of the lesson. (I12)

Choosing repertoire: She encouraged students, even at an early age, to choose their own repertoire. (I14)

Keeping a notebook: I learned to use a notebook to keep track of lesson assignments. (I16)

Motivation and Psychological Well-Being. Menahem Pressler underscores the need to understand the psyche of the person to whom you are transferring the knowledge, when teaching piano (Brown 2009, 37). Viewed through a contemporary mental health lens, positive motivation and the psychological well-being of one's students are areas vulnerable to "bad" piano teaching, especially given the "maestro model" as the traditional prevailing approach to piano teaching. Recognizing the effects of such negative experiences, interviewees sought to create a positive environment for their students within the lesson.

Motivation: The lessons were not much fun; there was no laughing. My teaching style was not influenced by her style. All of my students laugh. I try to motivate them, keep it light-hearted. If I notice a student has serious talent, then I push them. Otherwise, I see it as a leisure activity. (I3)

Psychological well-being: Psychological strain on the student is something that should be avoided. Attention to the psyche is as important as developing pianistic skill. (I15)

From Tradition

Tradition is observed in interviewees' teaching but filtered through experience. As Harold Schonberg noted in *The Great Pianists*:

Americans until only a short time ago were studying with foreign-born teachers whose roots were in the nineteenth century. . . . Among the teachers . . . were foreign born . . . and if not, they had studied abroad. One would have thought that American products of such teaching would automatically respond to the same kind of literature that their mentors had represented. But it did not work out that way. (Schonberg 1987, 495–96)

The importance of the Russian tradition to the study of piano in the United States has been a recurring theme throughout the book. An emphasis on imagination and sound/tone, for example, may be passed down from teacher to student.

My first teacher was about imagination. I continue to use this approach. (I12)

When she played Rachmaninoff's *Moment Musical* in E minor, I remember how incredibly her left hand moved, the immense power of her sound, and the clarity and intensity. (I14)

While reflected in the teaching approach of interviewees, tradition is not the sole explanation for how they teach.

From Pedagogy

Studies in pedagogy may enhance teaching within the lesson. Courses and written material provide information on technique, approaches to teaching technique, communicating skills and techniques to different student populations, and understanding of learning styles.

Resource. Pedagogical materials have historically provided tools for transmitting the how of playing the piano.

When I started teaching I looked at the different methods available and picked the best. Over two to three years I developed a system that I am able to use with almost 90 percent of my student population. (I3)

At conservatory we dissected the various teaching methods, which has been very useful in determining which books to give students. (I18)

Communication. Understanding how to teach different populations can be conveyed through courses. For example, courses on teaching beginning students lay out how to plan lessons and introduce a child to the piano.

Even if you had a good teacher as a beginner, you need to learn how to teach a beginner because by the time you are ready to teach, you are advanced. Pedagogy courses enable you to see lessons and learn methods for teaching beginners. (I1)

Learning Styles. Drawing on social science disciplines, courses on piano pedagogy may provide insight into the working of the brain, learning styles, and learning strengths and challenges of different populations.

Different people have different learning styles. At the university, we studied the developmental psychology of Piaget and the psychology of Bruner, which gave me incredible insight into understanding the range of possibilities in learning and the limitations that children may have at earlier ages. (I18)

For most interviewees, formal or informal pedagogical training was complementary to their development as students and experience as musicians.

Beyond the Lesson

At any stage, a teacher may have demonstrated, by example, that teaching piano extends beyond the lesson. Musically, the study of piano involves not only practicing and learning pieces but also listening to the music and investigating the life and times of a composer. Learning extends beyond music to art, literature, and history. Beyond music and the arts, students may be taught about being a "good person"—about integrity and responsibility. The tradition that is passed on is more than the technique needed to play the instrument; it is about being a human being.

Appreciation of Music

Teachers might instill appreciation for music by taking students to concerts. These experiences create memories and models. This practice was observed across traditions.

> She regularly took her pupils to concerts. It was with her that I heard Sofronitsky[4] for the first time. He played Liszt and Schubert-Liszt, and the impression of that recital has never faded from my memory. (I14)

> Dr. E was serious, rigorous, but warm. She brought the seriousness of the craft, reverence for music; we are the servants of music. She had a big impact—she cared; took me to my first Carnegie Hall concert and to Austria, to the composers' places. (I10)

Beyond Practicing

Experiences outside the lesson extend beyond practicing and music to the arts, literature, and life generally.

> I cannot categorize what I learned from my teachers. It was not a matter of playing the piano, but being in the world of music, their galaxy. I was living in the reflection of their artistic and musical glow. I learned the technicalities of the piano, but also opera and ballet. My teacher could quote Pasternak. It was museums—the Hermitage—visual arts. I would travel to see a Vermeer, but perhaps to hear a great pianist. (I9)

> Outside the lessons she treated me like her daughter. I was a fresh immigrant. She helped me to immerse in the American life style. She showed me life outside practicing, like an American mother. She was not married and did not have her own children. She took on the challenge of grooming three students with care and attention. All three of us happened to be Korean. My parents were appreciative. They trusted and respected her. They never doubted what she said to do. They handed me over to her to help me musically and to become more well-rounded. It was not all about practicing. (I6)

As part of teaching about life, in general, the relationship between teachers and students might become more like a family. Russian teachers, in particular, were reported to foster such relationships.

Being a Musician and a Person

The responsibility of the piano teacher extends beyond the piano, the music, and arts and literatures to overseeing the personal growth and development of the student. That is, teaching piano extends beyond transmitting the skills and technique required to play the instrument to fostering the development of the student as pianist, musician, and human being.

> Many teachers were role models. What they showed me was that integrity to music-making comes first and dedication—each was totally dedicated but in different ways. When I see a student, I try to instill a sense of responsibility, dedication, integrity, and honesty with themselves and with music. (I11)

Promoting the General Culture

The responsibility of the piano teacher reaches beyond teaching the best and the brightest to the average student. The end is not just the individual but society. Recognizing the responsibility of promoting the general culture is not new or not American. As Neuhaus observed:

> One cannot create talent, but one can create culture, which is the soil on which talent prospers and flourishes. (1973, 171)

Interviewees expressed awareness of the importance of teaching the appreciation of music to the next generation, not only to the professional musician to be but the average child and even adults.

> I became interested in teaching. As I moved into my adult years I saw the good part of teaching. You were creating, educating a new generation to appreciate music. A student might not become a professional musician, but teaching gives you feedback that what you do is helpful to the future. (I9)

> Teaching children is a chance to inspire love of music. (I10)

Even the young, future pianist may learn to recognize a responsibility to the larger society and culture.

> I was not just playing piano, but I was an ambassador to a world of culture. (I8)

SUMMARY AND CONCLUSION: CONTEMPORARY APPROACHES TO TEACHING PIANO: ECLECTIC AND PRAGMATIC

The New York Times's music critic Harold Schonberg characterized American pianism as eclectic and pragmatic (1987, 495–96). This characterization aptly describes contemporary U.S. approaches to piano teaching, as illustrated by interviewees' experiences and observations. Rather than simply teaching as they were taught or following the example of a single influence—an individual teacher, tradition, or graded piano instruction series—interviewees describe a confluence of factors that, with thought, reflection, and work, evolves into the pianist's approach to teaching—eclectic. The requisites (fingering, pedaling, sound/tone, daily practice, and artistic image) and arenas (the lesson, beyond the lesson, and promoting the general culture) are constants; however, viewing piano teaching as a process of continuous learning, an interviewee's approach was not stagnant or conscribed within a specific or single time period but continued to evolve—pragmatic.

While eclectic and pragmatic and given the diversity of interviewees' backgrounds and educational experiences, it is perhaps surprising that common perspectives on teaching piano are evidenced. Although the contribution of a particular factor or combination of factors might vary, early and later teachers; tradition; formal or informal pedagogical training; peers and colleagues; and, especially, learning by doing generally played a role in the development of an interviewee's teaching approach. Within each educational arena, the traditions, techniques and skills, and love of music handed down to the next generation of pianists reflect the understanding that the lesson is more than passing on skills; teaching the student extends beyond the lesson time; and the responsibility of the piano teacher reaches beyond the individual student to the advancement of the general culture of the society. In response to experience and personal development, as a pianist and teacher, and changing circumstances (e.g., immigration and changing student populations), an interviewee's approach to teaching piano continued to develop over time. Perhaps openness to change and flexibility in pursuit of effective teaching explains the similarities in interviewees' perspectives on piano teaching, wherever and within whatever tradition each had studied, as will be discussed further in chapters 9 and 10.

NOTES

1. Dorothy Taubman was an American music teacher, lecturer, and founder of the Taubman Institute of Piano.
2. Neuhaus (1973).
3. Hofmann ([1920] 1976).
4. Vladimir Sofronitsky (1901–1961) became a legend in Russia and was one of the signal forces in Soviet pianism (Dubal 1989, 248).

Chapter 9

Being a Piano Teacher
Professional Life and Qualities

Continuing the musical journey, this chapter and the next focus on being a contemporary piano teacher. Piano teaching takes place within the music profession, generally, and the piano teaching profession, specifically. While many of the challenges experienced by the piano teacher have remained constant, specifics vary with a particular time and place. Viewing the interviewees as experts on contemporary piano teaching, this chapter begins with their observations about the music profession and teaching piano, as it affected and continues to affect their personal experiences as a professional musician and piano teacher. Situating contemporary piano teaching within the professions sets the stage for the discussion of the qualities of a good piano teacher, relevant today, presented in the second section of this chapter. Although the specifics of a particular quality may change over time and differ across geographic boundaries, the qualities, extrapolated from the literatures and interviews, provide a framework for constructing or perhaps reconstructing the image of the contemporary piano teacher. Chapter 10 then considers contemporary piano teaching, in practice.

CONTEMPORARY PIANO TEACHING: THE MUSIC PROFESSION AND PIANO TEACHING ENVIRONMENT

The demands of the music profession may precipitate, but do not end with, the decision to teach piano. The challenges of sustaining a career in music continue as the pianist engages in multiple roles. Moreover, piano teaching, itself, also requires diversity in the where and whom necessary to maintain a sufficient cadre of students. Interviewees' perceptions of the contemporary

187

music profession and piano teaching environment provide perspective on the relevant qualities of a good teacher necessary to meet such challenges.

The Music Profession: Protean Career

Without exception, interviewees began the path to a career in music with the expectation of becoming a performer. There were expectations of success.

> Growing up, I believed you could have a career and give concerts if you practice, win competitions, and get management. I practiced, won competitions, and got management. (I8)

All pursued education and training and began their careers as solo performers, successfully. Nevertheless, interviewees described the changes in the music profession that impacted the sustainability of a career performing as a classical pianist.

> Classical piano careers are declining. (I1)

> I have had a success as a concert pianist, but the music profession has changed. Solo opportunities are shrinking, but there are more musicians. The power of the competitions had limitations, but what has replaced it is worse. (I8)

> The scarcity influences the way the art is practiced. That is—there is a scarcity mentality and increased competition. One plays louder, looks shinier, and brags more. (I10)

> After finishing school, I liked to perform. I went to schools and gave concerts with BG (flautist). Despite his reputation, there might be ten people in the audience and no money. It beats you down because you are donating your time and working for free. (I3)

Given the limited solo performance opportunities, factors other than quality of performing come into play. The literature on the sociology of work points to structural barriers, including race, ethnicity, and gender, which may affect the selection and pursuit of a career. Cultural bias may affect performance opportunities or venues of opportunities, although conditions in the United States may not be as restricting as in other countries.

> The culture in the United States is very Euro-centric. We (Hispanics) feel it is more difficult to break into the world. Society has stereotyped Hispanics—Puerto Rican music is salsa, not classical. Classical music is not associated with someone from Puerto Rico, from a Latin background. There is a bias. (I11)

> For an Asian woman, the situation in the United States is not as bad as in Europe, where, for example, you hear such comments as Asians do not have artistic imagination. (I10)

Other factors are outside the control of the performer, as well.

> I realized that there were other factors. There is not a real direct link: If I play well, I succeed, and get more concerts. I accepted that I could play, be artistically edifying, and people would not like it. You can have rave reviews and they will not ask you back; and they can ask you back when you do not have rave reviews. Other factors that seemingly are not in your control and have nothing to do with playing affect whether you are asked to perform. You have to have the ability to have people want to help you. (I8)

Recognizing the realities of the music profession requires adjustments to personal expectations and dealing with disappointment.

> It is an awful profession—the reality—it is a tough career with built-in challenges and disappointments. You have to work out how to deal with the challenges and disappointments, how to respond so as not to be defeated. (I17)

Responding to the challenges, interviewees continued to persevere by engaging in two or more paths within the music profession—a protean career. The second, although not secondary, path was teaching piano while still performing. Three interviewees were composing in addition to performing and teaching (I18, I19, I20) and a fourth was composing, teaching, but no longer performing (I1). Pursuing multiple paths helped to fulfill the pianist's needs, not simply financial but also personal.

Piano Teaching Environment: Diversification

Although described in the literature as attractive because of the regular income, regular hours, and a level of artistic and administrative control (Bennett 2016, 108), a contemporary piano teaching career may require diversification in the teaching environment and/or types of students taught. As the one-on-one lesson remains the pillar of piano teaching, interviewees primarily taught students individually, rather than in a classroom or group setting. Nevertheless, to insure a sufficient number of students, interviewees might teach in a number of venues—one or more institutional settings, including music schools, colleges and universities, conservatories, summer programs, or a private studio. Typically, the piano student described in the literatures is a young child or nascent pianist, but the student population within today's settings may be diverse in age, level of keyboard skills and accomplishment, and interest in the study of piano.

Because of the interrelationship between teaching venues and types of students, it is difficult to differentiate between the two. That is, within the same or across different teaching venues, interviewees teach students of varying ages, abilities, and accomplishment. An interviewee's students might range in age from the very young child through ninety years.

I have taught all kinds of students and in all kinds of teaching environments. Currently, my teaching at C University usually includes doctoral or masters students and non-music majors; at L School I teach adults and little kids; and privately, I teach kids. (I11)

My youngest student is 5. I have 14 private students ranging in age from 5 to 16. I teach three classes of adults at the evening division. (I10)

Because of my background, I teach mostly pre-college students, ages 12 to18. At L School, I am teaching much younger students. I began teaching one young student, whose brother and a friend wanted to take lessons. Now I am teaching quite a few younger students. (I7)

Each adult student is different, so there has not been one style. I have had engineers, actors, stay-at-home moms, opera singers, and a wide range of others from complete beginners to professionals. (I18)

In a university, college, or conservatory, students are primarily preprofessional and professional piano majors but may include nonmajors in other fields requiring piano study.

My students are college age 16 to 25 years old, even older. Now I am teaching bachelors, masters, professional, and doctoral students. I taught pre-college for several years. (I14)

As an associate teacher at two conservatories, students are more professional and career-oriented. I have to prepare them for exams. I assisted (I14) in the college division; there, the students are only professional. (I12)

At C University, my students are usually doctoral or masters students who are very serious. I have some students for whom music is secondary—non-music majors. (I11)

At H University, I teach beginners; music majors; and students of voice and other instruments, who are required to play piano. Music education majors are required to take four semesters and non-music education majors two semesters of piano. (I15)

Nevertheless, over the course of a piano teaching career, an interviewee usually had taught students of different ages, levels of ability, and interest in the study of piano.

As in the music profession, generally, changes in economic conditions, musical preferences, and competing interests may affect opportunities to teach.

Lack of job opportunities: There are hundreds of applicants for a modest number of academic positions. I'm lucky because I have more teaching than I can handle. (I10)

Changing interests in music styles (classical to rock or hip hop), instruments (e.g., guitar and violin), and other activities (e.g., sports and computer games) affect the demand for piano lessons. The advent of the adult piano student may offset a decline in the number of younger piano students. Nevertheless, changes in the piano teaching market present challenges. The teaching needs of different populations vary. Additionally, teaching contracts may restrict opportunities to teach at other institutions, simultaneously, or provide lessons privately to a student from one's institutional cadre. During the summer, interviewees may teach at a "camp" or "summer institute," often in a different part of the country and directed toward different types of piano playing—solo, four-hand, or chamber music.

> I teach in New Hampshire in the summer. The focus is chamber music, at all levels. (I10)

> I have coached chamber music at the (State) Music Festival during the summer. (I5)

The specific teaching situation and the way in which each interviewee resolved the challenges, posed by both the diversification required to sustain a career in music and teaching piano, varied. Nevertheless, common themes emerge regarding the qualities needed to do so.

QUALITIES OF A GOOD PIANO TEACHER

The qualities of a good piano teacher, identified from the literatures and explored from the perspective of the interviewee, include personality and temperament; motivation to teach; having a method, or not; repertoire; knowing each student; recognizing the individuality of each student's playing; and beyond the instrument. Two additional qualities were extrapolated from the analysis of the interviews—hard work/diligence and perseverance. The definitions and descriptions as to what is meant by a particular quality reflect contemporary views on education, generally, and music education, specifically. The qualities of the teacher encompass intellectual and emotional attributes:

> Someone who can advise, especially on technique, but is not overbearing on the musical side—guidance and expertise, but not too strict. (I19)

The relative importance of a particular quality—for example, personality and knowledge of the repertoire—may, however, vary with the stage of the musical development of the student, as documented in the extant research (e.g., Sosniak 1985a and 1988).

Personality and Temperament

Personality and temperament are consistently identified among the qualities of a piano teacher, although the particular traits encompassed within this quality vary not only by time and place but practice. What was accepted 150 or even fifty years ago has changed not only in music but in U.S. society, generally. Such examples from the early pedagogues as the "leçons orageuses" of Chopin are not to be emulated. Nevertheless, well into the twentieth century, the piano student, including many interviewees, might experience difficult personalities and, while frowned upon today, such practices may persist.

Notwithstanding the dramatic portrayals of the early pedagogues, first and foremost among the array of personality traits identified in historical literature is patience. Türk emphasized that with most pupils calm dignity will avail more than angry reproaches and the like ([1789] 1982, 18). That has not changed. Reflecting their years of experience as both piano student and teacher, interviewees consistently identified certain desired personal traits intrinsic to the teacher, as person, and relational between teacher and student. These traits, which included empathy, flexibility, and interest in human beings, in addition to patience, were considered to be important whether the student was a child; future professional musician, or not; or adult.

Patience

Paramount among the qualities of the good piano teacher is patience. Although interviewees may not have experienced patience during their own studies, patience was a quality that they sought to realize in their own teaching with all students.

> Be kind and patient. (I7)

> No matter what the age of the student—patience is a necessary quality of a good teacher of piano. Patience is needed when a student does not "get it" or when a student does not practice as much as he/she should. (I2)

Patience may not, however, be an innate quality of the individual but learned behavior, especially through the experience of working with piano students of different abilities and background.

> I am able to work with a range of students from many different backgrounds. Over the years I have worked with a number of students with different kinds of challenges. This experience has taught me patience and thinking outside of the box. (I18)

The diverse music education backgrounds of U.S. students pose challenges, especially when contrasted to the common backgrounds of students trained under the more structured system of the former Soviet Union. At the Russian conservatory, all students come with and have the same background (I9). To teach different types of students effectively involves both the recognition of and adjustment to the differences.

> U.S. and Russian students are different. Patience—American students need a lot of encouragement. There is no need to encourage Russian students. (I5)

While acknowledged as an important attribute of the piano teacher, maintaining one's patience may be difficult. As most teachers will admit, some students are more challenging.

> Being patient can be difficult when a student does not understand an issue at the usual rate. Or, when I have run out of ways to explain the issue, it is a challenge. But, sometimes these students are the most rewarding because it is a big deal when they do "get it." (I2)

Additionally, the workload necessary to maintain a living may strain a teacher's patience.

> Some are tired, because they are over teaching. They don't have patience with students. If you are tired, you don't have patience with students. (I1)

Yet, whether attributable to fatigue or teaching style—yelling at a student was considered to be ineffective with most students although there might be exceptions.

> There is nothing to yell about. What do you accomplish when you yell except to get a sore throat? (I15)

> No I don't yell at my students; I almost never do. Times have changed. (I17)

> I do not believe in raising my voice. I believe raising one's voice is a sign of a helpless teacher. If a teacher starts to yell, it is because the teacher does not know what to do. (I14)

Here again, behavior may change with experience teaching and the maturing of the teaching approach.

> I used to yell, as a result of three influences on my teaching style: my high school teacher, martial arts background, and dance—experiences at the dance studio. I do not do it anymore. I learned that it does not work for everyone and

can backfire. It may work with certain students—you have to learn to what the student responds. (I18)

Empathy

Closely related to patience is the ability to empathize with one's students; that is, being able to see things from the perspective of the student.

> One cannot be a good piano teacher without empathy—how the student is responding to what you are telling, showing. Some teachers just teach music, not the person. That is not what I do. I see where they are vulnerable and what their issues are and teach to them. (I17)

Whether the student is an adult, child, or college student, from the standpoint of the student, life is often challenging.

> Mostly, I acknowledge that the life of the student is complicated. With college students I do not judge. It is always possible to learn a piece over, if needed. (I15)

Empathy with the student, especially children and teenagers, may mean addressing parental expectations and even recommending that the child not pursue further studies.

> Hypothetical: A student is taking piano because mom said to do it. That can be a problem especially for boys. I spend time to make the child think about whether he/she wants to try. If they come in on the fence regarding the piano, I try to push them over to the side that this is something that I want, enjoy, and want to keep doing. If the child is not interested, I have a conversation with the parent. If the situation presents, I explain to the parent that I expect from my experience that this will end well for anyone. (I2)

Ultimately, it is the teacher who sets the mood and establishes the environment within which the lesson takes place.

> I learned to be positive with students. I try to say positive comments. Consider—what did you like? Then, make suggestions. The teacher sets the tone. (I1)

Setting that mood may require flexibility and being able to adjust one's expectations and approach to different populations and personalities.

Flexibility

Related to the personality traits of patience and empathy is flexibility. As will be discussed later in this section, not all students learn in the same way.

To be able to teach—reach—a particular student or student population may necessitate adjustments to a teacher's approach and expectations. Making such accommodations to difference—age, personality, musicality, or culture, for example—calls for flexibility as "one size does not fit all."

Flexibility does not, however, mean not having a general approach to teaching piano. To be able to play the instrument involves technique. Nevertheless, how one communicates to convey that information may vary from one student to the next.

> There is not just one way to teach a student. You have to use different language with different students. Some understand when you say—make it beautiful. You have to take different approach with each student. For some, you can explain and they understand; some you have to show. (I15)

Flexibility may mean adjusting one's approach to the same student in a particular situation.

> You make plans for the student, but you have to be able to change them or teach the student in a different way if the student does not "get it." (I2)

Flexibility assists the teacher in responding to individual differences among students, part of knowing each student.

The wide age range and different levels of accomplishment—from beginners to advanced students—among interviewees' students may require modifications in approach. Teaching young children presents particular challenges.

> With children you are leading them—from "darkness"—giving direction. Most are not going to be professional musicians. You are preparing them, giving students something to continue playing for the rest of their lives. You have to make sure they want to. In some respect, you are giving them a sense that with ability they can become competent at anything. (I19)

> When I was growing up, you would be given a piece or movement and learn it by the next lesson. I have learned that for young kids the way I was taught is overwhelming. Instead, you need to organize the child's practicing. It drives me crazy when a student does not practice using the organization I have given them. (I6)

> To teach children, you must learn child psychology. (I4)

Teaching college students, whether in a music school, college, university, conservatory, or privately poses other types of challenges for both the teacher and student, especially balancing academic course work and music studies.

With college students, when they do not have time to practice during exams, rather than beat themselves on the head I teach them tricks—playing on the table—to use when they cannot practice on a piano. (I15)

University students have a bigger academic load; there is more emphasis on academics. Conservatory students can be better; expectations are higher. It's the reality. (I11)

I suppose I like to teach college students—that is why I am doing it. Kids can be wonderful, so can adults. With college students, I can influence their lives, but that is not really true except in a professional sense. I teach advanced students—graduate students, but the question is what they are going to do to use their education. I feel guilty because there are no jobs. (I17)

Variations in the abilities, experience, and current life situation among adult piano students not only present challenges for the piano teacher but can also be rewarding.

Teaching adults is more problematic. They bring baggage with them. An adult's piano playing reflects his/her professional work style. I see how they work by how they play the piano. But, they enjoy playing. (I1)

Adults are completely different from children. Most adults know their agenda. It is a process of steering them if their agenda is too or not ambitious. You help set goals, but usually they have a clear picture of what they want to do. (I19)

They want to be there. There are no pressing career ambitions; they appreciate the time. They practice better than the college students. They can engage at an adult level. They may know more about a composer. (I10)

Responding to these differences requires flexibility, on the part of the teacher, in expectations and the tools and approaches used to teach adults.

Nevertheless, adult students are not a discrete population, except, perhaps, to be distinguishable by age. Abilities and level of playing differ—some are beginners, some are advanced, and others are somewhere in between. Experiences range from those who might have become professional musicians but chose other careers—doctors, lawyers, dentists, or even political scientists—to those who began piano studies in later years.

Adults are fun. They have been pursuing piano studies longer and may have made a career elsewhere. Sometimes you cannot push adults physically. (I10)

Adult students have different reasons for continuing to study piano. Some adults take lessons to be able to play the piano simply for pleasure and personal enjoyment whatever their level of proficiency; others seek personal achievement by participating in performance courses or juries; still others

explore music wherever it may take them; or, a student may seek to attain more than one objective. Yet, all are pursuing a personal musical journey.

> I like working with adults because they are learning as a choice. I have worked with beginners and professionals. I find joy in seeing them open up. (I18)

Addressing the needs and objectives of each adult student requires flexibility.

Cultural differences between teacher and student may require flexibility and adjustment in teaching approach. Interviewees who had studied and taught in the former Soviet Union noted having to adapt to cultural differences between Russian and American piano students.

> Russian teachers are intrusive with respect to posture. Russian kids are used to it. American students are not. You don't want to make children hate you. Teaching Russian students is simple; just give. You have to be more flexible with American students. (I5)

Cultural demands continue to present challenges to the piano teacher, as new groups of immigrants join the population of piano students. For example, a relatively recent phenomenon observed by interviewees is the growing number of piano students whose families have emigrated from China. Differing views between teachers and parents, reflective of cultural differences (e.g., the benefits of frequently changing of teachers or simultaneously studying several instruments), may create tensions in the teaching relationship. Awareness and understanding of such differences, rather than arguing with the parent, prevent the loss of the student.

Within contemporary U.S. society, perspectives on the role of the piano lesson, itself, may present challenges.

> I have become frustrated working with families who have their children take piano lessons more as an alternative to babysitting, where the actual investment in education is not part of their interest. (I18)

The quantity and diversity of structured activities that devour the time of the average U.S. child, including sports, dance classes, guitar lessons, video games, and television, compete not only with the piano lesson but also with practice time.

> Sports and playing video games and hand held devices including the cell phone activity have taken over. (I16)

> More and more children opt out of music lessons for sports or spend much of their free time with technology. Children do much better when they have peers who also study classical music and if they have other disciplines. They tend to

stay with lessons longer when there are recitals, continuity, and a sense of the longer arc of learning. (I18)

The competition between piano lessons and other childhood activities is portrayed in the children's literature (e.g., Delton 1994 and Macmillan 1943). Although new activities—video games, for example—have been added to the litany of youth activities that interfere with playtime pursuits, the child's lament is the same.

Interest in Human Beings

The passion for music and, specifically, the motivation to share the love, knowledge, and traditions of music was identified as a driving force underlying both the initial decision to teach and continuing to do so. The motivation and love extend beyond the music to the person of the student in the context of the one-on-one lesson. Interviewees underscored interest in human beings and love of students, particularly, as necessary to being a good teacher.

> Interest in human nature—make people better. One-on-one with students can make a student a better person—be honest at the piano and a good citizen. (I1)

> I enjoy people in general. I love children, especially very intelligent children with a good heart and soul. (I6)

> To teach children music, you have to love both—children and music. Kids instantly feel; they can't help it. If they like you, you can teach everything. I love adults; half of my students are adults. (I5)

Focusing on the other person expands the role of the piano teacher beyond the transmission of skills and training of the future professional pianist, shifting the purpose of teaching and learning to the development of the person.

> The study of piano can be part of life, whatever you do. That is, you do not have to become a professional pianist. When "piano lessons" or music study teaches both identification with the physical force of nature and the positive aspects of being human, the student has gained a philosophy of life. (I15)

> It is the process of creating a personality and a musician, not about piano playing. (I9)

Developing an understanding of the student, as person, places additional demands on the teacher. As Neuhaus suggested: teaching which sets itself such an objective ceases to be mere teaching and becomes education (1973, 22).

Personality, Temperament, and Teaching Piano

While each teacher, as each student, is an individual, interviewees identified patience, empathy, flexibility, and interest in human beings as personality traits of the good piano teacher. Notwithstanding the love of students and teaching piano, like the historical pedagogues, contemporary piano teachers are only human with personal preferences and "pet peeves" that test their patience and strain flexibility. Cultural differences, including treating the piano teacher as a babysitter or parental over or under involvement in a child's lesson and practicing, may create tensions. The student who does not listen—fails to follow the recommended approach to practicing—or refuses to make a necessary adjustment—"I learned it that way"—is frustrating and confounds piano teaching. As for preferences, some interviewees particularly enjoy teaching children; others prefer teaching adults. For the most part, interviewees like, even love, teaching students of any age but prefer students, of whatever age, who work hard and take studying piano seriously.

> I like to teach kids who are serious; I do not want to waste my time, their time, or their parents' money if they are not serious. (I11)

> Adults can contextualize and get out of the parent-child relationship and move to an adult to adult relationship of mutual respect. (I8)

The desired personality traits help to ameliorate the challenges of teaching and also contribute to the actualization of other identified qualities of a good piano teacher. For example, interest in human beings underlies, in part, the motivation to teach. Patience and flexibility support the knowing of each student—responding to the differences among students and student populations. These personal traits are reflected in interviewees' practice of teaching.

Motivation to Teach

Motivation as a quality of a good piano teacher has been defined to include three components: (1) a drive toward music, (2) the ability to motivate students to learn, and (3) the motivation/commitment to teach. Underlying each is a love of music, students, and the profession.

A Drive toward Music: Love of Music

The love of music is not only fundamental to the decision to pursue music as a career but lies at the heart of teaching piano.

> Teaching is part of my make up as a musician. I need to impart my knowledge. (I11)

When I was 16 . . . My whole life was music. Mostly, at that time, I had elementary-level students. (I20)

Beyond the desire to pass on music traditions and skills to the next generation is the realization of the powerful effect music has on one's life (Madsen and Kelly 2002, 330). The effect extends not only to the future professional pianist but to a larger population of children and adults who share the love of music. Music and piano study was believed to contribute to the life of the student, whatever professional path he/she would choose.

Studying music awakens how it feels to be alive. (I15)

If music is taught well, it is influential in whatever career they choose. They learn it in music. Two of my students are going to Brown University. Even if they do not continue studying music, they have a good standard of expectations. (I11)

Ability to Motivate: Love of Students

In the context of teaching piano, motivation extends beyond the desire of the teacher to share skills, tradition, and especially the love of music, to inspiration. Interviewees underscored the importance of being able to inspire students.

To inspire is the greatest quality. Be inspiring, stimulating—do not just tell the student how to do—do this or do that—or to memorize. (I12)

A teacher should be able to inspire, encourage, and stimulate. (I11)

If the student does not have the motivation, it is your job, as the teacher, to instill it. It is all about discovery. (I18)

While inspiring a love of music is fundamental, how one inspires varies with the student's age and experience. Teaching children offers the chance to inspire love of music. (I10)

For the beginners, it is important to be willing to be silly, to do ridiculous things to get a point across. (I2)

If I notice a student has serious talent, then I push them. Otherwise, I see it as a leisure activity. I try to motivate them, but I guess my standards are not high. My standard is: Are you enjoying this? The goal is not so much to learn the piece perfectly, as nothing is perfect, but that the lesson is a positive experience. (I3)

For the more mature student, inspiration includes exemplifying artistry and being an artist.

At the conservatory, one must be a great artist—have a body of work and level of playing that inspires students. (I9)

Different teachers have different ways of conveying, but artistry is what is needed. (I10)

Whatever the age of the student, a teacher can kindle the desire to learn more about the music, the piano, context of piece, and beyond.

I want to be contagious, give the student the fever to want to learn more. (I9)

The inspiration of a teacher encompasses more than music but reaches into the core of the person. Describing a professor, then colleague, who had greatly inspired her, an interviewee observed:

She was wonderful—inspiring, helpful, technical, humane, supportive, and generous with her time. (I12)

The professor was also interviewed. When asked to identify the qualities of a good piano teacher, she responded: "To be a good person first of all" (I14). Clearly, she had inspired her student.

Motivation/Commitment to Teach: Love of the Profession

The third component of the motivation to teach piano is the love of the profession. Although teaching piano may provide a more regular income, regular hours, and a level of artistic and administrative control (Bennett 2016, 108), interviewees underscored the importance of love of teaching as the primary motivation.

You have to love teaching. You cannot feel that you are doing it because you have to earn money and every student is taking your energy. The keys are love and professionalism. Be knowledgeable and very professional. (I14)

Teaching allows you to pass on the tradition—it is a great thing, rewarding. (I12)

That love underlies the motivation to continue to teach.

My mom forced me and the head of the T Conservatory invited me to teach. He said I should take on just a few students. He said it would be better for my own playing. Twenty five years later, I now know the attachment. (I9)

Nevertheless, actualizing the love of teaching involves dedication and self-discipline.

Teaching piano requires dedication. (I1)

A teacher has to have and impart to the student incredible self-discipline, love, and dedication to craft. (I11)

As love of music underlies the commitment to pursue a career in music, love of the profession underlies the commitment to piano teaching, which sustains the decision to teach piano.

Having a Method, or Not

The question of whether having a method is necessary for teaching piano pervades the historical pedagogical literature, as discussed in chapter 2, with no definitive answer. The broader term "approach," used throughout this book, encompasses but is not limited to teaching keyboard skills. Interviewees were methodical in their teaching of the requisites needed to play the instrument—methods—including basic skills, hands and fingers, and pedaling.

> *Basic piano skills*: I place strong emphasis on the student acquiring basic piano skills and incorporate anything in which the student is interested. (I3)
>
> *Hands and fingers*: Once one understands that music is flowing, one understands that at the piano hands have to be flowing, always in route. We choreograph hands and fingers, feeling the flow—the breeze—it is not a matter of just pressing down. You have to make sure that the hand does not fall when the "short" thumb plays. You have to accommodate different shaped hands. (I15)
>
> *Pedaling*: Pedaling, for example, is not down here and up here. You have to get further—different percentages.[1] (I11)

One interviewee, with colleagues, developed a comprehensive series of books to be used in teaching students the necessary skills associated with progressive levels of playing (Levine Music 2017).

Interviewees also considered how to communicate the necessary information effectively, for example, to children.

> *Children need structure*: You have to establish structure and consistency; repeat yourself; and be careful not to give the student too much at one time. (I10)
>
> *Communication*: Asking the student questions can lead to great discussions in learning and teaching. They have opinions if asked. And some if not asked. So listen so that a dialogue created to impart knowledge can occur. (I16)

Interviewees' approaches to teaching piano, in practice, are discussed further in the next chapter.

Repertoire

The social science literature and interviewees specify "knowing the repertoire" as a quality of a good piano teacher. Participants in the Mills and Smith study identified wide repertoire among the hallmarks of good teaching at the higher education level (2003, 9). Interviewees' responses emphasized the need for a strong background and ability to play the repertoire.

> Have a great education in music and an extensive background. (I20)

> Be a fantastic pianist, including style, technique, training, and have performed. (I1)

As a quality of good piano teaching, knowing the repertoire may be considered on two levels—knowing how to play and being able to teach a piece of music. Knowing how to play the repertoire may serve to inspire, as a way of motivating students, as previously discussed. Performing and teaching a piece are, however, not the same. In the context of teaching, knowing the repertoire means being able to identify piece that will motivate, inspire the student.

> Be able to find repertoire that will excite them and that is within a range of what will both challenge them and help them achieve success. (I18)

Being able to teach the repertoire includes identifying what the student needs to know and how to communicate that to the student. The "what" to be communicated includes technique and understanding of a composer's intention in order to realize the composer's intent. Knowing the repertoire is important to setting expectations and understanding student concerns and challenges with respect to learning, playing, and performing a piece—empathy.

> It helps to know how to play. There have been good teachers who do not perform, but actively performing changes your perspective on what to expect from a student and identify with what they are doing. (I17)

> Having performance experience gives insight into how difficult it is to play the piano. (I3)

> I try to teach my students to do a performance. It's personal; everyone is nervous. It's human—it's impossible not to be nervous, but the reasons why are different. (I1)

Knowing the repertoire may be viewed as the intersection of performing and teaching. While not all teachers perform and not all performers teach, or can teach, interviewees viewed teaching and performing as complementary,

generally trying to achieve a balance between the two—being able to play
and teach the repertoire, as will be discussed in the next chapter.

Knowing Each Student

The need to know each student is a recurring theme in the historical and
contemporary pedagogical literatures. For the historical pedagogues, knowing encompassed not only the student's capacity to play the piano but also
physical and psychological characteristics, personality, and interests outside
of music. For example, Leschetizky was interested in personality and Curcio
wanted to know her students very well musically, pianistically, and personally (Newcomb 1921, 96 and 131 and Ashley 1993, 18). The contemporary
literature on piano teaching identifies knowing the needs and goals of the
individual student and tailoring piano teaching as a valuable part of the one-
on-one experience (Carey and Grant 2015, 7–8).

View Each Student as an Individual

In the current study, considering the quality "knowing each student" raises
the question: From the perspective of contemporary piano teaching what
constitutes knowing each student? How does the teacher go about learning to
know the student? Interviewees underscored the need to know each student as
a unique individual, not only his/her musical capability but as a person, and
to incorporate this knowledge into the teaching of that student.

> Each student is an individual. Every student is different. Every student should
> be approached as an individual. (I20)

> You have to take each student individually; each is different. You get to each
> student through difference entrances. Cultivate where the student is, not where
> the teacher wants to go. (I7)

> At the conservatory, one must be dedicated and care for the well-being of one's
> students and their individual gifts. (I10)

> Different students have different needs. Some students do better with less
> direction and others need more of a framework with the specific steps in their
> preparation. (I18)

Analyze a Student's Capabilities and Weaknesses

To understand the piano student's individuality and determine the appropriate
response require that the teacher analyze the needs of the particular student.
Deppe appears not only to have analyzed a student's difficulties but believed
in his ability to correct limitations, according to Fay's memoirs (Fay [1880]

2011, 287). During a lesson, Curcio would frequently demonstrate, sitting next to the student and practicing the troublesome spot together; a physical problem would be analyzed until the student could do it (Ashley 1993, 17–18). Menahem Pressler prides himself in being able to teach his technical principles, the same principles, to different people differently (Brown 2009, 47).

Of the contemporary teacher, knowing the student requires analytical acumen—being able to analyze the capabilities and the person.

> Every teacher has to be a psychologist—especially if teaching the young. Factors to consider are family situation and how and where the student was brought up. You have to be accommodating and understanding. (I12)

> Analytical ability is paramount. (I17)

Analysis encompasses assessing a student's capabilities—strengths and weaknesses—to determine the appropriate teaching approach and foster the development of that student. An interviewee's personal experience may provide insight into the need and skills for such an analysis, as well as contributing to the awareness that each student requires a tailored response.

> I developed a good analytical ability because I had to deal with my own struggle. (I17)

> A teacher should be able to analyze what a student's weaknesses are to bring from point a to point b. (I11)

> What is most important is the ability to recognize the positive potential aspects of the student and to help the student discover and develop them. I do not believe all are the same. I do not take the same approach. My favorite question is: What is the piece about? It is parallel to looking at a Monet painting inside out. Some students are about nuts and bolts—so the approach is more about the technical (e.g., how to hold the hand). It is necessary for all, but some need more. (I8)

Selecting the appropriate piece of music to be studied involves both analyzing the particular student's capabilities and knowing the repertoire.

> Sometimes students struggle with technique—scales, reading—which can be painful. You have to give the student pieces that are within the realm of possibilities—what the student is ready to learn, what is right for the student. (I1)

> Different students learn at different speeds. (I6)

Selecting a piece for a child or an adult may involve different considerations.

Child: To find a piece for the student, it is necessary to consider the issues in the piece, the personality of the student, and that the piece be fun for the student. (I2)

Adult: With the adults, I like to have them work on pieces of different levels: one piece that the student can learn in one sitting; one piece that takes three or four sittings and can be worked on over a week; and one piece that will take more than one week. Most do so, except the beginners. (I3)

Additionally, analysis is essential to teaching a piece—analyzing the music to identify what the student needs to know and problem areas, to help the student learn the piece.

I am analytical. I break up the piece clearly, especially with technique—break it up into concrete steps to improve technical ability. (I19)

An interviewee may have learned from experience the importance of being able to analyze a piece to be able to teach it, but pedagogical courses may also help to hone analytical skills.

In graduate school, one of my projects was to create my own curriculum for a 12-week course. For teaching at the intermediate level, we had a list of fifty pieces. To teach the pieces, we had to learn each piece, analyze the piece, learn to teach it, and determine what the student would need to know to learn the piece (e.g., rhythm, fingering, and sharps and flats). (I2)

Knowing the student is defined to encompass more than musical capability. Personality and personal circumstances also affect learning and how best to teach the student.

Personality and Person of the Student

As the historical pedagogues recognized, a student's personality and psychology play a role in musical development. Leschetizsky was more interested if he saw a student was doggedly trying to overcome a difficulty (Newcomb 1921, 131). Curcio believed that to grow as a teacher, it was necessary to know the student musically and psychologically, as caring for the student opens the teacher's vision of what is the best approach for each individual (Ashley 1993, 30). The principle remains that understanding the personality and psychology of the student is part of knowing the student and affects the learning and teaching of piano. Teaching piano is about teaching the person, whatever the age of the student.

Some teachers just teach music, not the person. That is not what I do. I see where they are vulnerable and what their issues are and teach to them. (I17)

Have a strong feeling of trying to help the student to advance personally and musically. (I20)

Each student is a universe, unique. As a teacher you need to tune into the student—choose what to say in a way that they will understand and pique their interest. You need to plug into the world of the student—get a sense of their experience and problems at home. Determine what music to give and how you speak to the student—even jokes. There is not just one way to teach a student. (I15)

While a piano teacher may have to function as a psychologist or social worker, without professional training in these fields there are boundaries.

I taught in the home for years. It was helpful because I learned family style (e.g., the student whose parents listened to reggae music). Teaching in the home, I had the benefit of knowing the families. The challenge is determining how much do you really want to know? You need to ask the question. (I18)

Whether the student is a child or an adult, the challenge for the teacher is how to apply, in practice, knowledge of student.

Recognizing the Individuality of Each Student's Playing

Communicating the composer's meaning and inspiration is fundamental, but there is room for individuality. Different pianists may play the same piece differently, while maintaining the composer's intent.

If you look at the students of teachers such as Neuhaus, for example, you can never tell that the student studied with the particular teacher because these teachers treated each student differently. (I7)

Perhaps one of the greatest contributions of modern technology—CDs, DVDs, and YouTube—is the opportunity to listen, almost simultaneously, to the same piece played by different pianists. Doing so opens one to the experience of hearing different interpretations of a piece, sometimes even by the composer. The contemporary piano teacher is able to

demonstrate the differences to students, using the technology to look up the pieces from more than one artist and compare and contrast them. (I16)

The tension between imitation and individuality is part of the teacher-student relationship. The goal is independence (Sherman 1997, 62). Moreover, in later stages of the development of the talented young pianist, the music—the expression and interpretation of valuable works of art—was all that mattered (Sosniak 1985a, 66).

When a student is learning and I feel something is there. . . . One day the student sits and plays and it happens—musicality comes. I wait for it. Sometimes it takes years—wait for it. You have to get him/her to discover what he/she feels about music. It is a spiritual journey. They do not need a therapist—just go to the piano. (I1)

When the student-teacher relationship is right things click, communication is received, and progress happens. The ability to help someone learn to express themselves throughout the piano repertoire has no words. It transcends what is concrete and orderly. It enters the godly realm. (I16)

Individuality in playing is affected not only by the teacher-student relationship but also the influences of competitions and technology. The emphasis on individuality of playing suggests not only a rejection of a cookie cutter approach to teaching but also a response to the perceived effects of competitions—they all play the same—and the influences of technology—why go to a live concert when you can sit at home and listen to a perfect recording? Sameness in playing, whatever the source, would seem to be in sharp contrast to the artistic image—a requisite essential to the creation of beautiful piano music—identified by the historical pedagogues.

Beyond the Instrument

Teaching piano is not just about conveying the skills necessary to play the instrument. As many of the early pedagogues knew and as interviewees observed, activities "beyond the instrument" foster a student's musical growth as a musician.

It is more important to raise a musician than a piano player—playing correctly. (I9)

As part of contemporary piano study, "beyond the instrument" may mean teaching about the composer and historical background of the piece being learned and having a student engage in related activities—listening to other compositions of the composer and music outside the context of the lesson. Interviewees identified a range of activities, illustrating how each engaged with students beyond playing a piece of music.

I try to connect the student with the classical composers, by having them listen to other works of the composer. For example, if they are studying a piece by Debussy, I will have them listen to "Afternoon of a Faun." (I3)

To foster students to love music, I encourage them to go to concerts, read about the composer, and listen to classical music—become familiar with the music, make it part of life. (Note: She will provide CDs to students who cannot afford them.) (I1)

Reflecting on their own experiences as piano students, interviewees recalled being taken to a concert by a beloved teacher, having dinner with a teacher and his/her family, being introduced to musicians and other artists at social functions arranged by a teacher, as well as recitals and other opportunities to perform (e.g., I17, I14, I20, and I11). Carrying on this tradition, interviewees might arrange functions for their students.

> I have music parties where the students play for each other. At the 92nd St Y we held Halloween concerts. Students would dress up as the composer they were playing. (I15)

Such efforts were not always welcomed by colleagues.

> My first year at M I started class recitals, like Moscow. I did not know that American teachers taught within set hours. I would stay until 11 o'clock at night. It was a fantastic recital. The President of the school called me. He said the recital was incredibly good, but did not want me to do it again. Others were not doing it and did not want to, because it required additional time without pay. I stopped. Later, I started to "fit in" group performances at my home, before juries. The students would play for each other. (I14)

Creating opportunities beyond the instrument broadens the purpose and goals of music education, and, specifically the piano lesson for the individual student.

ADDITIONAL QUALITIES: HARD WORK AND PERSEVERANCE

Two additional qualities of the contemporary piano teacher emerged from the interviews—hard work/diligence and perseverance. Identified as factors that contribute to the development of the young pianist and the decision to teach piano, these qualities pervade interviewees' experiences becoming and being a piano teacher. Both are essential to sustaining a career in music and piano teaching. Both are necessary to respond to the challenges described at the beginning of this chapter. Perhaps because such qualities are so personal to the teacher rather than the relationship between teacher and student, interviewees did not identify either as qualities of a good teacher. Yet, these qualities were exemplified in their own teaching experiences and practices. Accordingly, the author would be remiss in not highlighting them.

To teach piano well requires talent but being a piano teacher, even for the "natural teacher," entails hard work and diligence. Actualizing other qualities of the good teacher—knowing the student and having an extensive repertoire, for example—involves work to plan each lesson and select the appropriate pieces for each student. Hard work includes learning to reach and trying to keep each student interested in the study of music and the piano. The historic literature describes how early pedagogues developed resources to support their teaching—Chopin composed etudes and Czerny wrote exercises that have been handed down and are played by contemporary students. Interviewees not only spent time reviewing methods books in preparation to teach (I6, I3), but one published a comprehensive series of books on keyboard skills and sight reading (I1) and another composed pieces that served as teaching tools (I19). Interviewees' hard work is reflected in their piano teaching, in practice.

Continuing to teach and sustain a piano teaching career also requires perseverance. While economic need may precipitate the decision to teach piano, maintaining a cadre of students is necessary to sustain that decision. Interviewees were typically associated with an institution in addition to teaching privately. Teaching in a music institution or university setting may offer access to students more readily than private teaching, but there may be a price to pay (i.e., one only receives a percentage of the tuition paid by the student). Once having found the students, the cadre has to be maintained, which can require flexibility and adaptability. Maintaining a cadre of students involves balancing economic interests and quality of teaching—considering not only the number of students one can teach but teach well. Different student populations, changing student populations may call for different ways to reach and encourage students to continue studying piano, reflecting other qualities or traits (e.g., knowing the student or flexibility). The quality of perseverance and that of hard work are reflected in interviewees' piano teaching, in practice, as evidenced in chapter 10.

SUMMARY AND CONCLUSION: RECREATING
THE IMAGE OF THE PIANO TEACHER

Piano teaching takes place within the music profession, which impinges on the teacher and teaching. The life of a musician has historically not been easy, usually requiring the pursuit of more than one path—the protean career—to sustain a career in music. Interviewees' experiences demonstrate the demands and vicissitudes of the music profession today. All were engaged in at least one other aspect of the music profession—performing, composing, or writing, in addition to teaching. Moreover, the challenges of teaching piano are not new, although the specifics vary by time and place. Today, sustaining a cadre of students usually involves teaching different types of students—children, precollege adolescents, undergraduate and graduate students, and adults—in different educational settings, often simultaneously. The current situation in the music and piano teaching professions is reflected in the desired qualities of a contemporary piano teacher described by interviewees.

As presented in this chapter, the descriptions of the qualities of a good piano teacher, identified from the historical and social science literatures, underscore continuity and differences in beliefs. Although the fundamentals of good teaching remain constant, the emphasis and description of a particular quality may differ as to what works—the how—reflecting the time (when) and place (where) piano teaching occurs. For example, the personality and temperament characteristics of patience and flexibility contrast with the images portrayed in many of the fictional and nonfictional accounts, even some of the historical student memoirs. Over the next decades, the specific qualities of the piano teacher can be expected to change, as U.S. social and cultural values and parenting practices change. Moreover, it is also important to note that in practice even the best teacher is not necessarily the best teacher for a particular student.

> Even the best teacher is not the best for everyone. There is a personal relationship and you can't fit everyone. That is not to say that there are not bad teachers. (I8)

The close personal one-on-one relationship between piano teacher and student involves matching teacher and student.

> It's about matching the human qualities, the character. Talent and gifts develop. (I14)

Chapter 10 explores the contemporary piano teacher and approaches to piano teaching, in practice, which generally reflect the identified qualities of a good piano teacher.

NOTE

1. The damper pedal can be depressed to varying degrees—quarter, half, full—to create different effects.

Chapter 10

Being a Teacher of Piano

In Practice

Continuing to explore the professional life of the contemporary piano teacher and piano teaching through a social science lens, this chapter focuses on being a piano teacher, in practice, describing overall approaches and challenges and rewards of piano teaching today, as well as offering advice to prospective teachers of piano. Individual differences notwithstanding, from the interviews emerge common themes, underlying approaches to contemporary piano teaching and reflecting the qualities of a good teacher, as described in chapter 9. Although not generalizable to the population of teaching pianists, interviewees' observations regarding the challenges and rewards posed by the music profession and demands of teaching today's piano student are illustrative of contemporary piano teaching. Generally not advising others to pursue a career in music or piano teaching, interviewees, nevertheless, express satisfaction with their personal career choice and, with prodding, offer advice to future piano teachers. While challenging the images often found in literature and film, which are at worst demonic and at best tepid, the intention of this chapter is not to romanticize either the person or the profession but to present a portrait of the contemporary piano teacher and piano teaching, grounded in qualitative social science.

CONTEMPORARY APPROACHES TO TEACHING PIANO IN PRACTICE

As diverse personal experiences with piano teachers, traditions of study, and pedagogical courses or readings contribute to each interviewee's approach to piano teaching, variations, in practice, are no surprise.

Approaches are different—it's not about good or bad. (I14)

The purpose of this section is not to resolve differences, advocate a particular approach, or provide a guide to teaching piano but to demonstrate that contemporary approaches are thought-out, deliberative, and deliberate. Moreover, differences notwithstanding, common themes emerge. Reflecting continuity in piano pedagogy, contemporary approaches encompass (1) individualizing the approach to the student; (2) developing each student's musical growth through activities beyond the instrument, a piece, or the lesson; and (3) promoting the general culture. Additionally, interviewees provide advice to students.

Overall Approach: Thought-out, Deliberative, and Deliberate

Music theory, technique, and the selection of pieces are generally considered fundamental to teaching piano. Nevertheless, by now it should be clear that there are different paths to teaching how to play the piano repertoire and create beautiful music. The overall approaches to teaching piano, presented by way of illustration, were described by two interviewees from very different backgrounds—the first was educated in the United States and the second in Russia. Although the approaches differ, each reflects a well-thought-out, deliberative, and deliberate process.

> In general, I try to work on theory, technique, and pieces. In theory, I try to take the student from "here" to the next step. In technique, I try to take the student from "here" to the next step. With regard to pieces, I try to have each student work on some type of classical piece and something the student wants to play, which could be anything. (I3)

> My approach to teaching depends on what is coming up, for what the student is preparing: (1) a solo recital, competition, or jury or (2) new repertoire. I want the student to be conscious of what is going on and not just repeat the piece a million times. I want the student to first, become familiar with, sing, and understand the image of the piece, and second, little by little begin to work with touch. Even little children can learn to do it. The approach is not mechanical; you have to understand the harmonic structure and format of the piece and it gives good results. (I14)

Interviewees' approaches to teaching piano may differ, but all extend beyond the transference of skills to play the instrument well. Like the historical pedagogues and as identified in the contemporary studies on piano teaching, approaches emphasize the need to analyze, recognize, and adjust one's teaching approach to the individual differences of each student; engage with students beyond the lesson; and promote the general culture. Interviewees' consideration of each of these aspects of piano teaching is well-thought-out, deliberative, and deliberate, as will be evidenced in the discussion to follow.

Individualizing Teaching: Teach Each Student Differently

The importance of considering the individual student, musically and personally, has been a recurring theme throughout the book. While interviewees' approaches to teaching piano differ, knowing and treating each student as an individual and using analysis to develop that understanding was a generally accepted aspect of each approach. That is, piano teaching is not rote, "one size fits all," or rigidly following the sequence of books in a particular music education series, as is so characteristic of the horror stories of piano lessons.

> I take a different approach with each student. For some you can explain and they understand; for some you have to teach technical details; others you have to show. I use different language with different students. Some understand when you say—make it beautiful. You have to make the student aware of possibilities. (I15)

Knowing each student includes identifying strengths and weaknesses that may affect musical development.

> A good teacher has to be like a doctor—analyze the student's good points and weaknesses, then establish a plan to develop them. To see progress is the most important thing. (I8)

Given the diversity of today's piano student population, treating students as individuals and adjusting one's teaching approach can be challenging.

Diverse Student Populations

Modifications to an interviewee's teaching approach may be in response to the needs of a particular group of students. Age is perhaps the most frequent source of difference. In practice, adjustments may include using different types of resources, engaging in different conversations within the lesson, or working differently with the music, itself.

> I try to have each student work on some type of classical piece and something the student wants to play, which could be anything. With adults, I like to have

them work on pieces of different levels: one piece that the student can learn in one sitting; one piece that takes three or four sittings and can be worked on over a week; and one piece that will take more than one week. Most do so, except the beginners. (I3)

My approach depends on the student and the level, for example:
- Children: I use good method books. Kids like having a book—to complete this page, this book. I use stickers to reward and check that they did the work. Some have just learned to read. But you have to make known that they are expected to practice, finish the assignment, and show more progress at the next lesson.
- College students: We can talk interpretation and psychology. I can use my performance experience with them. (I10)

Now comprising a significant number of contemporary U.S. piano students, considering characteristics and needs of adult students is part of individualizing an approach to teaching piano. Adult piano students are not, however, a homogeneous population, as discussed in the previous chapter.

Adults are interested in learning and trust the teacher. Sometimes the egos have to be left behind. You have to win them over by letting them experience the ease of playing. Most adults are committed and have a love of music. (I6)

For adult beginners, you have to find a starting point. (I18)

Sometimes you cannot push the adults physically; centering the body is important for adults. (I10)

Beyond the diversity of groups of students are students with special, individual needs.

Special Needs

Children and adults, who love music and want to learn the piano but confront particular physical or learning difficulties, require creative teaching and sometimes damage repair. Several interviewees lamented the effects of "poor teaching," particularly the resulting physical damage that can occur. Correcting and preventing further damage may require teaching the student to play the piano differently.

Adults have different experiences. An adult may have to unlearn. (I18)

In the United States, local piano teachers are poor teachers. We see the damage at the conservatory (e.g., the tension in children's hands). (I4)

The lowest level on the teaching ladder is Mrs. Jones in the suburbs. L School does recovery. (I1)

"Bad habits" can also present serious problems for the aspiring pianist. Changing the habits of an advanced student may be difficult, even met with resistance.

Most of my students are college students, the majority graduate students. If they have bad habits, addressing them is long and complicated. If the habit is unhelp-ful—change, but that means going back. The challenge is on two levels. First, getting the student to be aware that what he/she is doing is hard. Second, the student may know full well what he/she is doing, but is convinced it is right— "what I learned." (I8)

A teacher who has confronted similar challenges may not only empathize with the student but be able to draw from personal experiences to help the student overcome the problem.

Twenty eight years ago I had finger problems. I changed my playing. I became aware that you cannot change one thing without changing everything else—all are part of the package—head, hand, and energy flow. I bring this awareness into my teaching. (I8)

In recent years, general understanding of learning issues associated with autism, dyslexia, and dyscalculia has grown. Teaching piano to children and adults confronting such challenges may require a different way of thinking and an alternative approach.

I have had to think outside of the box in teaching; for example, some students have challenges in reading. In these cases I have emphasized improvisation, singing, and ear training as the primary source of learning, which then leads to reading. (I18)

The field of music therapy has emerged, broadening further the scope of music education.

Individuality and Motivation

Individuality is about supporting the development of each student's musical capability. Using the student's interests and other talents facilitates commu-nication and individual growth.

I ask: what will make this student shine? The dancer—dance with the hands. The gymnast—who had weak sound—pretending to be sitting on the horse changes the center of gravity and improves sound. The boy with tiny hands—pretending to swat a fly creates sound and power. It is possible to do these things even when a student is not advanced. (I18)

Perhaps the greatest motivator and key to teaching to the individuality of the student, however, is the music itself.

Be attentive to each student as an individual and look for music you know they will enjoy. By far the best motivator of playing is good music of interest. (I16)

The good teacher works from the student's image of the music to make it flow. Even with beginners I give them a piece and have them play it in different moods. I ask: what did you do differently? What did you do to create different moods? It's a combination of the mystical and the practical to turn it into the magical. (I15)

(K) encouraged students, even at an early age, to choose their own repertoire. Since then, with my students, I always ask them first what it is they want to play. (I14)

Encouraging the experience of music, not only within but beyond the lesson, is the responsibility of the contemporary teacher and encompassed in approaches to teaching piano.

Beyond the Instrument, Piece, and Lesson

Recognizing that teaching piano extends beyond the skills necessary to play the instrument, piece, and weekly lesson, interviewees provided examples of activities to support a student's musical and personal development. Among the activities were those that reflected the tradition of piano teaching (e.g., recitals, juries, and going to concerts) and others now available through modern technology (e.g., listening to performances on YouTube or learning about composers through Internet searches).

In the context of learning a piece, a student might be encouraged to read about the composer, listen to the piece performed or other pieces by the composer, or study the historical period in which the piece was composed.

Try to know much more than just your piano pieces. You have to know about the composer, the composer's other works—symphonies, quartets. (I14)

Read about the piece; learn what happened to the composer when he was writing the piece; and listen to orchestral pieces written during the same period. Watch movies such as *Fantasia* and *Mr. Beethoven Lives Upstairs*. (I12)

Interviewees also organized traditional activities such as recitals or other settings in which students could share their music.

I especially like having piano recitals where all of the families get together at my house for a potluck and music. I prefer this informal setting because it is less intimidating and it gives the families a chance to get to know each other in a non-competitive environment. This serves as a marker where the students and their families can see a progression. (I18)

I arranged a recital for my students. Each student prepared two pieces—one Bach and one modern to show innovation. They loved it. Not every student played both pieces; only one student did not play. (I1)

Not only young children, but adults and college age students participate in activities beyond the lesson.

I started to add activities outside of class. For example, to celebrate Tchaikovsky's 175th anniversary I organized a program of his lesser known pieces. Everyone was assigned a piece. (I9)

I hold music parties with my students at H University. They share music with each other. (I15)

My adult students perform for each other in December and May. All the adult students know each other. (I5)

Activities extend beyond the confines of the studio, practice room, or recital hall. A student may participate with the teacher and other students, in the tradition of the early pedagogues. Or, they may engage in musical activities with friends or parents.

My students are pre-professional, in the Pre College Division (Ages 9 to 15). They go to concerts and competitions. Several will not become professional musicians, but will love music. (I12)

I tell my students to find ways outside of your piano lessons to enjoy music. Listen to live music. Listen to the masters. Play in an ensemble. Surround yourself with other creative and arts-minded people. It helps generate enthusiasm for your work. (I18)

Playing the piano is about more than good fingers. Go to the theater, to museums. You have to be the personality of a professional. (I14)

Through such activities, interviewees sought to instill in their students a love of music and the piano, in particular.

Do it for the love of music. Understand that it is a great responsibility and it takes discipline and practice. (I6)

Nowadays, things are different; the music field is in transition. Love of music is most important. Whatever you do—love, respect, venerate, and treasure like a gift that not everyone has. (I11)

Experiences beyond the lesson reflect interviewees' early musical journeys, described in chapter 6, and helped to shape their own love of music and personality as a musician, which they pass on as teachers.

Promoting the General Culture

Teaching piano is perceived to be not simply about training future professional musicians but contributing to the culture of the community and society. Having learned from their teachers, interviewees actively incorporated this perspective on teaching into practice.

(U) was a big influence. He instilled a sense of discipline; piano is part of music and music is part of culture. (I8)

Continuing the tradition of service, a teacher may engender in his/her students the responsibility and desire to engage with the community.

Think Community: Create a social environment for the student that encourages reaching out and bringing pleasure to other people. (I1)

Carrying out the responsibility to contribute to the community and general culture is manifested in interviewees' teaching of diverse populations. Not all students will become concert pianists; most will not. Nevertheless, each child can still experience the love of music and the arts.

Younger students can use musical education in different ways, not professionally, but as doctors, accountants, and in other careers. Studying piano teaches discipline and skills that are transferable. I do not feel guilty about teaching them because it is not about a job. Studying piano raises an individual's understanding of the arts and life; sometimes that is enough. (I17)

If music is taught well, it is influential whatever career they choose. They learn it in music. (I11)

In the tradition of her teacher, an interviewee described the relationship between teaching the average student and the development of the culture of the society.

I try to work at the level that is right for the student. I use a different approach for the talented and the middle student. We need the middle, average student; it is not possible to have a class of just professionals; it is impossible to teach a few geniuses. It is important to pay attention to the middle, average student to raise the general level of humans. (I14)

Instilling the love of music in children and promoting the continued development of adult students, wherever their musical journey takes them, contributes not only to the life of the individual student but to the culture of the society in general.

Advice to Students

Interviewees were generally not quick to respond, but with prodding, offered examples of advice they give to students. Sometimes the advice reiterates that of the early pedagogues, demonstrating continuity; for example, "listen to yourself play." Advice includes keep a notebook, be patient and persist when practicing, and engage in music-related activities beyond playing pieces. The ultimate goal is that the student plays for the love of the music.

Listening

The literature on developing the talented young musician (e.g., Sosniak 1990, 154) and interviewees' experiences with music in their early years underscore the relationship between listening to music and the pursuit of the study of piano. Listening to performances of the pieces the student is learning, other compositions by the composer, and music in different venues fosters the love of music and musical growth. Listening is essential to piano study.

> Listen to more music, explore.

> I try to connect the student with the classical composers by having them listen to other works of the composer. (I3)

> I always encourage them to listen, to go to concerts, to hear the greatest musicians. For the younger students, I try to find cooler ways—clips on I pod, YouTube. Today you have to be cool. (I7)

> Go to concerts. Read about the composer. Listen to classical music—become familiar with the music, make it part of your life. (I1)

> Listen to live music. Listen to the masters. Play in an ensemble. Sing your favorite songs on a regular basis. (I18)

Interviewees also sought to encourage both students and parents to listen to music more.

Echoing the advice of the early pedagogues, perhaps most important is that the piano student learn to listen to his/her own playing: "Listen to yourself play!" "Listen to what you are playing!" Teaching the student to listen is the responsibility of the teacher.

> A teacher has to get a student to listen to him/herself. Listening is the only way to be aware of difference. A violinist has to listen to him or herself because of intonation. Intonation is not an issue for the pianist and therefore a pianist does not learn to listen to him/herself. The issue is not hearing what is there. The real difference—the real student—listens to him/herself and adjusts. (I8)

Fleisher underscores the importance of listening to one's playing, suggesting that the performer have three personae at all times. Achieving communication among the three is the struggle of the musician.

> Person A hears, before he/she strikes a single note, exactly what he/she wants. Without a clear idea of what you're going for, everything that happens is an accident. . . . Person B is the player occupied with pressing the keys, attempting to achieve what A wants. And Person C is sitting a little apart, listening, judging, and trying to hear whether B is getting what A intended and helping him or her adjust if not. (Fleisher and Midgette 2011, 214)

He goes on to describe a state of ecstasy that results when communication among the three works and absolute frustration when it does not.

Keep a Notebook

Keeping a notebook to track assignments is helpful for a child. As the student progresses, even for an adult, recording instructions and insights from the lesson can be useful.

> I have all students keep a notebook. In the notebook are the goals of each week. What the goals are, vary. It might be some practicing on a piece, working on a phrase or passage, or memorizing a point. It is individual—whatever it takes to get them through to the next baby step. (I3)

Recording lessons is another mechanism employed by some teachers to help the student retain the advice and examples provided within the lesson.

Practicing: Patience and Persistence

As did the early pedagogues, contemporary teachers hold different views on the extent of time to be devoted to daily practice and how to go about practicing. Nevertheless, a general theme that emerges from the interviews is that the student be patient, as well as persistent, about practicing.

I encourage students to be "persistent" about practicing, learning pieces that they don't enjoy but that will help them later on. Be patient about practicing. Practicing is a lot of repetition, not mindlessly. Don't repeat the same mistakes. (I2)

Be patient as classical works are hard to master. Take time to learn how to move properly at the piano to make the music easier to play. Be persistent and do not give up. Take small passages of challenging works and perfect them and move on. Learn how to practice effectively as people have less time today. (I16)

Be patient. Know that nothing great comes without perseverance and dedication. Stick to a routine and discipline. Love what you are doing. Play music that you like but also music that will help you progress. (I18)

Love of practicing comes from the love of music. How to instill that love is the biggest challenge. Of 100 students, 2 to 5 may become professionals, but I don't want the others to hate it. I want them to listen. I want them to have good memories of lessons. (I7)

If practicing is not going well, students are advised:

When frustrated—step away, eat a snack, do something else, and come back to the piano later. Chances are it will be better. (I2)

Similarly, an adult might be advised—have a cup of tea—and then go back to practicing.

Additionally, interviewees underscore that practicing is not simply a task that the student is sent off to do but a reciprocal relationship between the teacher and student.

We (the student and I) understand together. I do not say—"Go Practice"—they do not know how. I do it with them to understand the piece of art—I teach them to understand. My method comes from my teachers. (I14)

To be effective, it may be necessary to tailor practicing to a particular student or circumstances.

You need to organize their practicing for them. (I6)

I usually recommend practice on a piece for 20 minutes each day, but that approach does not always work. For example, I had a student who was having difficulty with a Bach piece. I suggested that he work on it 5 minutes a day for a month and then play it for me. He did so. At the end of the month he had learned the piece well. (I1)

Don't Compare

Focusing on the individuality of the student, the paramount directive is: Do not compare yourself to other students! The advice is passed from teacher to student.

> Teach students to be themselves, not compare themselves to others, and accept where they are in their training at that moment and that each moment is an opportunity to grow and to learn. Mrs. B. used to say that we should climb our own mountain and not compare ourselves to others. I have tried to work with students in a way that will help them feel the most power in their own learning. (I18)

Continuity and Change

Contemporary approaches to piano teaching and advice to students echo themes identified in the historical memoirs and pedagogical treatises. While specifics may vary, the illustrative examples of contemporary piano teaching approaches are systematic and deliberative, focus on the individual student, extend beyond the lesson, and promote the general culture. The advice to students reflects not only today's social and cultural environment but timeless fundamentals of learning the piano.

CONTEMPORARY PIANO TEACHING: CHALLENGES AND REWARDS

The challenges and rewards of the music profession and teaching piano student, today, in part, shape the career of the teacher and teaching of piano, in practice. While presenting challenges, piano teaching in the context of the music profession, especially the need to pursue more than one path, is not without its rewards. Teaching piano in the one-on-one setting is not only challenging but can be the source of both personal and practical rewards. Interviewees were not strangers to these issues, although how each pianist is affected and responds differs.

Pursuing a Career in Music: Challenges and Rewards

The message is clear—pursuing a career in music, as a pianist, poses professional and personal challenges, including the limited number of positions, long hours—not 9 to 5—of preparation, low salaries and few paid benefits, and difficulty in balancing work and personal life. To meet the overall challenge of sustaining a career in music, interviewees usually engage in teaching piano and performing. Accordingly, the discussion of challenges and rewards within the profession focuses primarily on balancing these two paths, by way of example.

Challenges of a Protean Career: Teaching and Performing

Given the pursuit of a career both teaching piano and performing, the question arises: What is the relationship between teaching and performing? Do they complement or compete with each other? What are the challenges in practice? Interviewees generally describe them to be complementary with some challenges.

Complementary. Acknowledging that not all performers teach and not all of the great pedagogues were performers, being able to do both, while not absolutely necessary, is considered to be beneficial.

> Some of the most famous teachers did not perform. A teacher may have the technique, master it all, be a fantastic performer, but unable to go public. It is better if a teacher has at least some knowledge of what goes on on stage, performing. (I14)

> My belief is that you cannot be a good teacher if you are not a good performer; or you cannot be a good performer unless you at least know how to be a good teacher. (I2)

> I do not believe it is necessary to be a performer to teach, but performing provides insight. (I8)

Interviewees consistently describe performing and teaching as complementary.

> Teaching and performing go together well. Practicing, myself, clarifies my thoughts on teaching. (I1)

> Playing and teaching complement each other 100 percent. I prefer performing and teaching—equally. (I6)

> It's like the left hand and the right hand. (I9)

> Teaching and performing are complementary. I'm alive in the way I talk to students. (I15)

Teaching and performing support and reinforce each other.

> Performing and teaching are symbiotic. As a teacher you gain more insight into your performing when you teach and vice-versa. (I18)

On the one hand, performing contributes to teaching by enabling the teacher to understand the challenges confronted by the student in learning a piece. Examples of what may go wrong and advice on how to respond can be imparted to the student. Performing can energize teaching.

> I use performance in teaching to understand the challenges for students, identify what I might do and what I can tell the student to do to meet those challenges, and determine how to interpret a piece. (I2)

> It is beneficial to have had performance experience. The amount of effort and concentration to get on stage is what happens to the student playing before someone. (I3)

> Performing and teaching complement each other. What a performer learns from performance—what to do on stage and what went wrong—can be applied to teaching. (I11)

> What I use with them are things I discovered with my playing—various things. (I15)

> Working with students who are performing takes experience playing; it informs how you teach. (I19)

> I talk to my students about safety nets, damage control. I am a performer. I give practical advice: Try not to turn lapses of memory into collapses. I do not pretend to be the best teacher, the best for all students, but I try to help. (I8)

> Preparing for performances can give a person the extra focus to improve and achieve goals on a higher level. I find this is true both for students and myself. I tend to bring more energy, light and directness to my teaching when I am also performing. (I18)

Composing adds another dimension. Interviewees might compose pieces for teaching piano and/or use their compositions in teaching.

> I was doing a lot of teaching, especially beginners. I improvised duets for them and then turned them into pieces of varying complexities. (I19)

> Composing is a separate pursuit. I have taught some of my compositions. (I20)

On the other hand, teaching experience can contribute to performing. Specifically, teaching can help to clarify thinking about a piece, enhance focus, and reinforce habits and skills.

I learn from teaching and apply to performance. (I8)

Teaching complements the study of music. When you are telling a student about a piece and see it from the outside, the music becomes clear. (I7)

Teaching reinforces skills and sharpens one's own habits as a performer—playing pieces or arpeggios more carefully. Practice smarter—if I teach it, then I should do it too. (I19)

Similarly, teaching can reinforce composing.

Teaching reinforces composing, the understanding of the process; studying the music, you analyze your writing. (I19)

Challenges of a Protean Career. That is not to say that maintaining the teaching and performing paths simultaneously does not pose challenges. Both demand time and energy, demands which compete, presenting challenges, when pursuing both simultaneously.

Teaching and pedagogy conflict because of time. For performance you just work at the piano. Teaching involves working with students. Now I am trying to find a balance between the number of students and the number of performances. My goal in life is to find a balance. (I7)

The relationship between teaching and performing is not an easy one. It is hard to practice after spending time teaching. (I8)

Performing and teaching conflict—scheduling is difficult. Performing takes away from teaching when performing, but you find a way to make up. (I11)

Teaching and performing both require concentration and energy. To shift between teaching and performing may be difficult for the pianist, particularly the practicing required to prepare for a performance. Interviewees meet this challenge in different ways.

Going from teaching to performing takes a major shift in gears, because teaching intrudes on practicing. (I8)

The week before I give a concert I cannot teach. My concentration narrows to the program. Teaching disturbs my concentration. The festivals are difficult because you have to teach eight hours before the performance. I have two brains—teacher and pianist. The two are separate. I cannot think as a teacher when I am preparing for a performance. (I12)

When teaching full-time, it is almost impossible to perform because the students are taking from you. On a day when I have taught all day, it is like I have played for five hours. I do not have the energy to practice. I have to take time off teaching to perform. (I14)

For the teacher/composer, the time and energy required for composing vie for limited personal resources.

Sometimes teaching, performing, and composing compete; time is very valuable. (I20)

Need to Balance. Engaging in teaching and performing involves a complex balancing act—determining the number of students and scheduling teaching, performances, and practice time.

I have found challenges in balancing the number of students that works best in order to give them my full attention. I also need to have enough energy and time to work creatively as a composer and performer. This has been a challenge financially. I think most teachers who are creative have the same challenge. (I18)

Balancing teaching and performing is a challenge. Both take energy and time. I have to schedule practice time. Sometimes I have to cancel teaching to travel to perform. Teaching can be rescheduled; it is not impossible. (I10)

I have a balance: I teach every day; accompany, mostly routine; and go to the (State) Festival in the summer. (I5)

Pursuing both paths and having a family adds the dimension of balancing career and a personal life.

Other challenges are the real life obstacles—family and children. (I10)

The decision to have a family has ramifications and affects other career choices. How interviewees meet the demands of family life vary. A family of origin—parents of the pianist—might provide support, especially when both the pianist and spouse are musicians.

My husband and I both have supportive parents. They help watch the kids when we travel. (I10)

Or, a spouse might share responsibilities, as in other two-career marriages.

Difficulties are the time and scheduling; there is so much to do. I go to bed at 1 or 2 AM. Have to run the house. My second husband was a dentist/artist—always art; taught art. We shared the household responsibilities. (I15)

The desire to have a family, and doing so, might contribute to choices made in the professional life of the pianist.

I spent fifty one years at ACE because people should have a sense of place. We wanted to build professional work where we lived, not tour, because we had small children. We wanted to maintain family and professional lives. We attracted some of the best chamber musicians in the New York area. (I15)

Challenges confronted by pianists who immigrated to the United States with a family were different from those experienced in the country of origin.

I emigrated from Russia to the United States in 1996. I came here without any idea of a job, without the language, not driving, with two children and divorced. My little daughter was born in the United States. I was prepared in teaching, performing, and accompanying. (I5)

The decision to have a family appears to have affected male and female interviewees differently. Male interviewees may have experienced concerns regarding family responsibilities but did not voice them within the interviews. The complexities of the role of gender in the pursuit of a career as a pianist, including both performing and teaching, merit a separate study.

Rewards: Teaching in the Context of the Profession

Despite the challenges and desire to create a balance not only in one's career but in life, interviewees found being a piano teacher within the context of the music profession to be rewarding.

I joined L School in 1998. I have a home studio on the side and I accompany here widely. During the last five years, I have coached chamber music at the (State) Music Festival during the summer. I am happy and fully realized. (I5)

It is a struggle to be both a performer and a teacher, but it is a fun challenge and rewarding. (I10)

I am a performer by disposition. I am not performing now, but I practice every day. I am a virtuoso pianist. I do need to practice. Composing is new. I am a happy person. I practice, compose, and teach almost every day. (I1)

The rewards are both practical and personal.

A career teaching piano generally offers the practical and concrete benefits of a regular income, regular hours, and a level of artistic and administrative control (Bennett 2016, 108), which can provide a stable base for the ups and downs of a performing career.

> Teaching is financially stable. (I10)

Teaching piano also has the advantage of portability. As demonstrated by the experiences of interviewees who had immigrated to the United States, teaching piano is transferable, although differences in social, cultural, and parental expectations of the piano teacher may require changes to one's teaching approach.

Interviewees did not perceive the pursuit of both performing and teaching piano to be a disadvantage. Rather, while recognizing the challenges of balancing the demands of both careers, interviewees described the personal fulfillment of doing both.

> Performing and teaching piano are compatible, complementary; one feeds the other. Both are essential to me. (I17)

> I think for me both are important. (I16)

> Sometimes teaching and performing help—try to find fulfillment in both pursuits. I have been able to succeed in that. (I20)

Perhaps the necessity and reward of pursuing both paths are reflective of the two sides of passion (Duckworth 2016, 143). Whereas performing is primarily self-directed, teaching focuses on the well-being of others.

> It is nice to do both because you are developing different parts of your brain. Performing is a challenge. There is a fulfillment in playing, a high; you have to keep doing it. The integration of musical knowledge and technique is the hope. Performing helps you be a better teacher, on the practical level of playing. If you do not perform, you cannot tell the student what will happen when he/she performs. When one is a teacher, one does not think about oneself; the performer puts self first. It is a good symbiosis. (I10)

Doing both fulfills different personal needs.

Pursing the Teaching of Piano: Challenges and Rewards

While fundamental to the study of piano, teaching within the context of the one-on-one piano lesson is not without its challenges. The rewards described were primarily intangible or at least nonmaterial, stemming from the relationship between teacher and student and passing on of the tradition and love of music. Often overcoming a challenge is the reward—challenges and rewards may be two sides of the same coin.

Challenges

Drawing from years of experience teaching piano, the challenges interviewees identified fell into three categories—the teacher-student relationship, frustrations and demands of teaching students with varied abilities and interest in piano, and parents. The examples are not exhaustive, nor is any assessment made of the relative importance of each challenge to learning. Nevertheless, such examples provide insight into the environment of contemporary piano teaching.

The Teacher-Student Relationship. While the closeness of the teacher-student relationship is essential to teaching and learning to play the piano, it is also an area of professional and personal vulnerability. Fictional and nonfictional accounts of the horrors of the piano lesson underscore the inequality of power within the relationship, the vulnerability of the student, and the responsibility of the teacher to nurture and not abuse his/her position of authority over the student. Interviewees recognize the responsibility.

> The teacher is one of most important persons in life at that moment. The student is vulnerable, precious cargo. Even if not dramatic (e.g., suicidal), the relationship can have bad long-term consequences on the student. Emotionally, the teacher is in a position of power. The teacher-student relationship is the parent-child paradigm no matter what age the student—adolescent or adult. An adult can contextualize and get out of parent/child relationship, move to an adult/adult relationship of mutual respect. (I8)

While not raised as a problem experienced by any interviewee, there was an awareness of the current climate of concern regarding sexual harassment and mistreatment of children. Teaching piano in a one-on-one environment is particularly vulnerable to such issues because of the need to demonstrate how, which requires touch. Before demonstrating the physical position or technique necessary to create the desired sound, a teacher is compelled to ask whether a student minds a hand or arm being touched. That is not to say that the student does not bear some responsibility for dressing and behaving properly. Nevertheless, the onus is on the teacher as an adult and person in authority to ensure that the piano lesson is a safe place for a student's musical and personal development, whatever age. For both the teacher and student an advantage of having lessons within an institutional setting, rather than a private studio, is that the institution may ensure that potential teachers are subject to background checks.

Teaching the Student. Within the context of the lesson, interviewees enumerated specific challenges and frustrations associated with teaching the individual student, including instilling enthusiasm for music and the instrument, communication, personality conflicts, and culture conflicts.

Instilling enthusiasm: Many of today's piano students mirror the young piano student depicted in the children's literature. Not all are budding future professional pianists. Sometimes compelled by parents and usually conflicting with other activities, piano lessons may be approached with some resistance, even among those who will eventually experience the passion. The challenge for the teacher is to try to instill in each student an enthusiasm for music and interest in the piano, which fosters the passion and discipline necessary to succeed.

> The problem is to maintain the interest of the student who is not so interested or does not have time. (I19)

> If the student is intelligent and talented with discipline, it is ideal. The challenges are teaching students, especially the talented, who are not responsible, and those who lack effort and discipline. (I6)

> Not all students have the discipline to stick to the rigors of training. When they come to lessons unprepared there can be frustration that ultimately results in the cancellation of training. This is especially true for students who prefer to learn popular music and have impulse control issues. On the other hand, when students learn to stay with their training and are able to see the larger picture of developing their skill through discipline, they find much reward when they feel success as a result of their hard work. (I18)

The music, itself, may inspire interest. The charge of the teacher is choosing the appropriate piece for the student.

> The challenge is hunting for the right piece of each student. Knowing what the next step is for this student, one step at a time. (I3)

Even the talented student may need encouragement. Interviewees point to the problem of teaching the talented student who is not improving (I6). The challenge and frustration is how to help the student, when the problem is not within one's own experience.

> The biggest frustration is talented students who do not get better because of blocks in self that I cannot alleviate. For example, people with memory problems. I can deal with myself, but I'm not the student. I understand what they are talking about, but can't apply from myself. (I8)

The contemporary piano teacher is confronted by the changing culture of American society and general life style of young people.

> Students today are far too stretched in their activities. Very few, even talented, kids practice enough to get into a college to study music. Not enough dedication. While there are dedicated students, they plan to major in something else. I fully understand that. They want to make a living. (I16)

> We have a great societal challenge in keeping up the traditions of teaching classical music. More and more children opt out of music lessons for sports or spend much of their free time with technology. We live in a world where there is less discipline, where multitasking and immediate gratification are the norm. Parents are less likely to provide a structure for disciplined training. (I18)

Competition between athletics and music is not new, but computer games and other musical instruments, especially the guitar, also present a challenge to piano teaching itself—how to reach the child. Offering the opportunity for such group interactions as online gaming and playing in a band, in sharp contrast to the one-on-one piano lesson, these activities are powerful magnets for youthful interest, time, and enthusiasm, as any parent of a teenager or tween knows.

Communication: At its core, teaching involves communication. When teaching piano, communication includes not only conveying the skills and techniques necessary to play the instrument but love of music to diverse student populations. Variations in age and backgrounds, among other differences, complicate communication between the teacher and each student.

> The challenge is being able to communicate with students musically and personally. (I20)

> Challenges include trying to create imagination for the less imaginative and guiding the ear to listen for subtleties when the student is not used to listening. (I6)

Not being able to reach a student who does not "get it" is a source of frustration.

> Sometimes it is difficult when a student does not understand an issue at the usual rate. Or, when I have run out of ways to explain the issue, it is a challenge. (I2)

> The learning process is a challenge; you have failures and successes. You learn from failures. (I11)

Success in communicating with such a student is rewarding.

But, sometimes these students are the most rewarding because it is a big deal when they do "get it." (I2)

Personality conflicts: Heinrich Neuhaus observed that the fullest possible understanding between teacher and pupil is one of the most important conditions for fruitful teaching (1973, 170). In the previous chapter, qualities of a good teacher were identified, including personality traits, but teaching is a reciprocal relationship and the personality of the student may present a challenge.

Personalities can be difficult—the personality of student and teacher. They talk about teachers' personalities, but a student's personality can be difficult. (I11)

From the perspective of personality, some students may be easier to teach than others.

Personality wise, it is easier for me to teach the really talented. We can talk about concepts and interpretation. (I2)

Culture conflicts: Beyond the personality of the student are wider culture conflicts and language differences, requiring adjustments in teaching approach to overcome them.

In the United States, my formation as a teacher happened. It was a completely different experience than in Russia. At the Russian conservatory, all students have the same background. In the United States, students come from different places. I have to find a possible way to get to the heart, brain, or ear of each student. (I9)

The challenges identified are wide-ranging and require different types of solutions. Finding solutions involves qualities of a good teacher, especially patience, empathy, flexibility, knowing each student, and going beyond the instrument.

Parents. Early pedagogues, including Leschetizky and Vengerova reportedly complained about the parents of their students (Newcomb 1921, 81; and Rezits 1995, 84). Waterman is even reported to have chosen parents rather than pupils "to make sure that I am going to have the right cooperation" (Grindea 2009, 23). Interviewees might find parents to be meddlesome (I19), or worse.

Sometimes parents start children later—8 years old, with lady down the street. That is too late, generally. (I14)

The biggest challenge for children is the parents, especially if they do not understand the teacher or music and don't trust you. (I6)

One father would pace during the lesson. He had a short fuse; the child was anxious. He limited the child's learning. It was a toxic environment. I left the situation. (I18)

Parents say they will follow through with their kids like they do with school homework. But few actually do. (I16)

As reported in the literature (Sosniak 1985a, 24–29 and 54–58; and 1985b, 417–18; Howe and Sloboda 1991a, 43–44 and 51; and Davidson, et al. 1995/1996, 44), interviewees also noted the contribution of supportive parents to the success of the piano student.

Kids need structure. Kids are doing other things. Students whose parents make sure the child is at the piano usually do better. (I18)

Parents do the follow through—sometimes it is establishing the practice routine; sometimes they are musically cued in. Kids with no parent involvement are hopeless before age 11. (I10)

Reflecting variations in teaching philosophies and experiences, interviewees engaged differently with parents in the lesson and held different expectations of the parental role in the student's practicing. A teacher may encourage active involvement of the parent in the lesson and practicing.

As a teacher, the presence of the parents makes all the difference. Parents do most of the teaching during the week. I encourage parents to practice with the student. (I10)

Or, the teacher may set boundaries with parents to foster the teacher-student relationship.

I do not allow parents to sit in on the lesson. The teacher needs to set boundaries with the parents, especially in the home. In teaching, you want to develop an independent relationship with the child. If the parent has a different message, the parent's presence will give a mixed message; that is a problem. (I18)

The role of the parent changes over time with the musical development of the student.

Rewards of Teaching

Seeing a student succeed, overcome a specific challenge, or experience the joy of music in the lesson are the shared rewards of the reciprocal relationship between teacher and student. While not uncommon to teaching in other areas, such rewards are particularly powerful within the context of the one-on-one relationship essential to the study of the piano. Perhaps the greatest reward is the establishment of a positive relationship between teacher and student from which emerges a shared love of music. Such relationships, forged through music, are often lifelong.

When You See the Student Succeed. The most frequently and consistently mentioned reward of piano teaching is seeing a student succeed. Perhaps this is the essence of all teaching, reflecting passion, as purpose—the concern for the well-being of others (Duckworth 2016, 143). Success is usually described as progress in playing and heightened musical awareness.

> Generally the rewards are modest, but if the student gets better, the reward is enormous. (I8)

> When a student is learning and I feel something is there. One day the student sits and plays and it happens—musicality comes. I wait for it. Sometimes it takes years. (I1)

> AHA moment—seeing the satisfaction of accomplishment of a student. (I6)

> Seeing students progress and do well. (I19)

The reward of success can extend beyond the particular piece or event. The reward is an achievement for both the student and teacher.

> When a student plays with understanding and meaning . . . I am not happy if a student just hits the correct notes. I ask: What does it all mean? (I12)

> When a student reaches fulfillment and makes a great advance. I have been able to achieve that to a great extent. (I20)

> When a student connects to a piece; when it is established, the student takes it with him or her for the rest of his/her life. It is a gateway to the treasure out there. (I3)

> Helping another human being to be excellent in the field, as you have been. Joy in developing their talents; everyone is different. It's like a garden and flowers. (I11)

When a Student Overcomes a Particular Challenge. Students may confront particular challenges, for example, a difficult piece or performance anxiety. To see a student overcome such challenges—fear of performing (I6)—is rewarding for a teacher.

Seeing students master a piece, especially a piece that the student thought he/she could not master. (I2)

When students play recitals, I invite other teachers. A boy of 12 played an artistically well-done performance; he touched the teachers I invited. That is a reward. (I14)

When a Student Enjoys the Lesson. Among the challenges of teaching identified earlier in this chapter is instilling enthusiasm in a student. Perhaps the most immediate and direct evidence of having done so successfully is in the student's response to the lesson.

At the end of a lesson, the student says—we are done already? Why can't our lessons be longer? Working with kids "off the bench," for example working on rhythm, when the student says that was fun. They are excited, happy, and keep with it. (I2)

Relationships That Last a Life Time. Whether or not the student becomes a professional pianist, relationships forged in the sharing of music may continue for decades. Early pedagogues recognized that the outcome of good teaching can be lasting positive relationships, as do contemporary teachers.

The relationships are for a life time. My past students are in touch. We talk on the phone and visit. That is rewarding. I am in touch with so many former students. It is a rich life. Not everyone stays in touch, but a lot do. It is meaningful. As a piano teacher, you are able to change peoples' lives. It's a lifetime commitment. It is both a profession and a vocation—you would do it if they did not pay you! (I17)

A tangible reward is that lessons are one-on-one, which is rare, and a personal relationship develops. The students become attached and you can be instructive in the way they think about music and the instrument, itself. I see improvement. (I10)

The challenges and rewards of the music profession and teaching piano, specifically, are reflected in the types of advice offered by interviewees to prospective piano teachers. Ending on a positive note regarding both the profession and teaching piano, interviewees do not suggest that they would have chosen another path knowing what they now know. Nevertheless, they were generally not quick to recommend that others join them, particularly as full-time professional musicians and piano teachers.

ADVICE TO FUTURE PIANO TEACHERS

With some prompting, interviewees offered advice to the future piano teacher. Not a handbook or guide, but highlighting themes fundamental to the piano teacher as professional and educator, interviewees consider—the profession, preparation, teaching in practice, the need to network, life balance, and continuous learning. Underlying the advice is an understanding of the qualities of a good piano teacher, which interviewees not only sought to exemplify in their own teaching but to see emulated in the profession.

The Profession

Considering the demands and vicissitudes of an ever-changing profession, the first recommendation of several interviewees is not to pursue a career in music or teaching piano. A career in music is generally unstable financially. While a career teaching piano may be more stable than other paths in a music career, it too is usually not lucrative.

> I do not advise pursuing teaching classical music. You cannot make a proper living. For example, L School teachers only receive a percentage of the price charged for lessons. (I1)

> Don't do it. It takes too much. (I14)

> I'm not sure I would recommend this profession. Unless one can teach at the college level, the earnings do not keep pace with the cost of living. One needs a second income either from yourself or a spouse. Self employment is too expensive today. (I16)

Short of not pursuing a career in music, or at least having a second income, the recommendation is to teach in a limited way so as not to be financially dependent on either teaching or performing.

> For those who have the calling to teach. I say do it in your spare time as a hobby and do something else to pay the bills. This way you don't have to be under pressure to carry a certain load of students to pay the bills. The economy does not always cooperate with your vocation. (I16)

The advice to future teachers also reflects interviewees' personal motivations to pursue a career in music and piano teaching—following the passion, passing on the tradition, and contributing to the larger society and culture.

> I would really make sure teaching is what you want to do and that you are not just doing it out of necessity. Doing it out of necessity creates an army of

frustrated people and that is projected to the students. To be done well, teaching and performing, like anything else, have to be done not just out of necessity. To perform you have to have something to say. To teach, you have to have a vocation. (I7)

I see teaching as a service: How can I add to the culture of music should be the guiding question. (I10)

The inner quest is how to save society through culture. Why are sports coaches more respected, listened to, and have more authority over the family and kids than music educators? (I4)

Given that potential musicians and piano teachers would more than likely have similar motivations and, therefore, not heed the recommendation not to pursue such a career, interviewees provided suggestions on how to follow the path.

Preparation

Advice on how to prepare to teach piano today draws not only from inter-viewees' early pedagogical development (chapter 8) but also lessons learned as teachers and working in the profession. Recommendations to future teach-ers to pursue training or an academic degree, as well as to observe good teaching, underscore interviewees' belief that teaching piano is a profession.

The profession needs more good teachers, trained teachers. There is a debate over whether there should be certification before one can claim to be a piano teacher. I do not have a strong opinion on certification, but I believe there should be a required level of training rather than just the little old lady down the street, who is not a particularly good teacher. (I2)

Get a degree from a reputable university in music or in music education, depending on whether you plan to teach and perform or just teach. If just teach-ing, earn a degree in music education. (I3)

Observe good teaching. Learn the profession from watching and observing. (I17)

This advice stems, in part, from the quality of teaching and lack of preparation that interviewees observe and even experienced. As one interviewee noted,

The problem in the United States with regard to teaching piano is that it is not "professional education." Teaching piano is "not just to make a little money" for young ladies with a few years of education. (I4)

Reflecting interviewees' beliefs about the process of developing as a piano teacher (chapter 8), advice regarding preparation to teach encompasses the development of the teacher, as a musician and as a person.

> Develop your own playing and pursuit of the art, craft in your way. Out of that will come what you have to offer students. (I10)

> Be able to play and be interested in human beings. (I1)

Before setting out to teach, the future teacher is asked to reflect on the question:

> Do you know, are you prepared enough (technically, ethically, humanity) to take up the responsibility of teaching others? (I4)

Teaching

Interviewees provide a wide range of piano teaching-specific recommendations. From their vast experiences, the cumulative advice includes activities within the lesson, personal qualities, the teacher-student relationship, and responsibility to the profession.

Within the Lesson

The advice within the lesson mirrors a number of the challenges to teaching addressed earlier in this chapter—preparation, communication, and individualizing the approach.

Preparation.
Take the time to develop a system of teaching. Go to a music store; there are so many methods series published now. Pick the three best and develop your system. (I3)

> Prepare lessons for students: Plan how to teach the piece, prepare for where the student is at the time—acceptance, have a goal for the student. The reward is in the performance. (I1)

Communication.
There are words that I do not use with students, because they discourage them: don't, difficult, hard. I also make sure that that the piece is possible for the particular student to learn. (I1)

> With regard to the technical, you are not to do or say certain things. But know what to do overall. (I7)

Individualization.
The teacher's responsibility is to give the student a technical framework to express oneself and play the music they want to learn. (I19)

As a teacher, you need to choose what to say in a way that the student will understand; pique their interest; plug into the world of the student—get a sense of their experience and problems at home; and determine what music to give and how you speak to the student—even jokes. (I15)

Personal Qualities

Patience, flexibility, modesty, and love of people are qualities of a good teacher to be emulated. Accepting the talents of other teachers and especially those of one's students runs counter to the generally competitive societal and professional environment but reflects the shared and cooperative atmosphere necessary to foster creativity and support the recognition of the individuality of each student's playing.

You need patience, flexibility, willingness to try new things, and openness to change plans. (I2)

Qualities—modesty, humility. Recognize that you do not have all the answers. (I8)

To teach, you have to love people. To teach children, you must learn child psychology. (I4)

Don't be afraid of anyone's talents. A student may be more talented than the teacher. Accept each other's talents—other teachers—as well. (I1)

The Teacher-Student Relationship

The teacher-student relationship, while at the core of piano teaching and individualized music teaching, generally, has its challenges, as discussed earlier in the chapter. The relationship is also a source of the rewards of teaching. Nevertheless, interviewees offered cautions.

The relationship is not as a surrogate parent. I know some students as people better than others. There are certain things you need to know (1) recognize musicality and bring it out and (2) try not to get involved in the personal life of a student. If the student is 16 to 18 years old, not getting involved is harder. By 25, the student can compartmentalize. (I8)

Do not make a student feel not capable of doing certain things. If a student wants to learn a piece, I encourage them. I want them to learn, to be dedicated. (I12)

Responsibility to the Profession

Handing down the tradition of piano teaching includes acknowledging and conveying to future teachers awareness of the responsibility to the profession. Teaching piano is more than the transfer of skills.

> Be open. Learn your craft. Understand developmental psychology. See each student as a unique being. Teach them to teach themselves. Help them own their learning because they will feel a greater sense of accomplishment when they have made their own discoveries. Be willing to put an incredible amount of effort into exploring ways that will help students feel motivated to learn. Find repertoire that will excite them and is within a range that will both challenge them and help them achieve success. Be able to discern between students who do better with less direction and those who need more of a framework. (I18)

In the tradition of the early pedagogues and as developed throughout the book, teaching piano is about educating the student and promoting the general culture.

> Future teachers pass on a tradition. What is the tradition? Music is art. Art has a structure, components, language. Art is also to lift the human spirit; through music you create beauty, transform people. That is the self discipline. You are teaching self-discipline, love, inspiring, encouraging, and demanding. (I11)

The responsibility is formidable.

Networking

As in many other professions today, pursuing a career in music is not only a matter of talent and hard work but also involves the ability and opportunity to network with colleagues. Networking offers the possibility of a supportive environment, shared experiences, opportunities for collaboration, and constructive feedback.

> Be able to network; be a community person; be a kind and gentle person in society. Develop a network of colleagues. It keeps you alive and provides feedback. (I10)

> Affiliation with prep schools, a college, or music store helps to obtain students. The majority of teachers teach out of their home. Now they can set up a website on-line with information on fees, schedule of lessons, etc. (I3)

Interviewees were engaged in networks and relationships with other musicians, pianists, and teachers of piano, which are evidenced in institutional associations and personal relationships. Some relationships develop from the teacher-student relationship; peer relationship may be forged in graduate school; and still other relationships emerge from experiences as a teacher in an institution or through shared friendships.

> It was at a competition that I met (I8); he was a judge. Now I play for him and (I14) before I play a concert. (I12)

> Regarding the way I teach now—my last teacher (I11) had the strongest influence. I am still working with him. (I7)

Recommendations of other teachers to interview—the snowball technique used in this study—also point to the existence of such networking.

Life Balance

How to create a satisfactory work/life balance is much discussed in U.S. workplaces today. Creating a balance or balances in a music career—between work and personal life, between or among paths within music, and within piano teaching itself—was identified as a challenge earlier in this chapter. Interviewees not only recommend attaining balance but describe the negative effects on one's teaching of not doing so.

> Have a mixed life. For example, one of my colleagues is a composer, as well as a teacher. He is famous. He has to practice every day. (I1)

With respect to teaching, establishing the optimum number of students is part of that balance.

> I generally prefer to stay under 12 students per week, which is barely enough to live on. (I18)

The effects of not doing so may be detrimental to one's teaching.

> If you are tired, you don't have patience with students. Don't over teach. (I1)

Not unfamiliar to interviewees, the overextended, tired, and cranky piano teacher exemplifies how not to teach and traditions not to pass on to future teachers.

Continuous Learning

From experience, and as they teach today, interviewees stress that teaching piano is a process of continuous learning. Continuous learning includes but extends beyond conveying keyboard skills. The responsibility of the teacher is not only to develop the student, as a pianist, musician, and person but to continue to develop as a teacher and person—to never stop learning.

> Get as much training as you can and never stop training. Go to pedagogy conferences. I always look for new opportunities. After 8 years at L School, I teach completely differently. I learned from other teachers, at conferences and workshops, and through trial and error. As a department chair, I do faculty evaluations. I get ideas by observing colleagues teaching, even if it is just one thing. I am still changing. (I2)

> Never stop being a student of music. That is what is fun. (I10)

> Keep practicing. It makes you a better teacher, full of empathy and compassion. (I6)

Reflected in the advice given and the description of contemporary piano teaching, in practice, is the vision of piano teaching as more than conveying keyboard skills. Piano teaching is about being an educator.

SUMMARY AND CONCLUSION:
BEING AN EDUCATOR

The life of a musician has historically not been easy and pursuing more than one path to sustain a career in music not uncommon. Moreover, the challenges of teaching piano are not new, although the specifics may vary in today's educational environment. From the experiences of the piano teachers interviewed, as experts, emerges a picture of the contemporary teacher and teaching of piano in the United States. As did the historical pedagogues, the contemporary piano teacher passes on a tradition, but that tradition involves more than simply conveying the mechanics of playing the instrument well or teaching the genius and future concert pianist. The emphasis on individualizing one's teaching to the student, identified in the historical literature, resounds throughout the interviews. Teaching piano is about developing the student, as a person, and contributing to the culture of the society, as described by Neuhaus and articulated in the interviews.

> Our purpose is modest, and at the same time vast; it is to play our amazing, our magnificent piano literature in such a way as to make the hearer like it, to make him love life still more, make his feelings more intense, his longings more acute and give greater depth to his understanding. . . . Of course, everyone knows that teaching which sets itself such an objective ceases to be mere teaching and becomes education. (Neuhaus 1973, 22)

Moreover, given the diversity of interviewees' backgrounds and experiences, the discussion of contemporary U.S. piano teaching in this and the preceding chapter suggests an American piano tradition, characterized by a "melding" of different traditions and that is both eclectic and pragmatic.

Additionally, while not generalizable to the population of teaching pianists, interviewees' observations regarding the challenges and rewards of a career teaching piano—the music profession and teaching itself—are illustrative of piano teaching today. Interviewees recognized the necessity of pursuing a protean career, usually performing and teaching. While acknowledging the demands of balancing the two paths, interviewees generally viewed the two as complementary. Underlying the advice to future piano teachers—the profession, preparation, teaching in practice, the need to network, life balance, and continuous learning—is a portrait of the piano teacher as a professional and an educator.

Despite the challenges identified, men and women continue to choose to become piano teachers. To the question—Why teach piano and, especially, why continue to teach piano, given the challenges?—the answer is at least in part love of students and love of music. On the individual level, the paramount reward identified was seeing students succeed. In the broader context, teaching piano and the piano teacher contribute to the culture of the larger society, a key aspect of the tradition to be passed on. Ultimately, being a good piano teacher is to be an educator—to lead the student to knowledge. The next chapter presents the author's conclusions.

Conclusion

The piano remains a fixture of contemporary Western culture and society. The piano teacher and piano lesson—the medium through which the love of and skills necessary to play the instrument are passed to the next generation—are common childhood memories and can be expected to be so for generations of children to come. As one interviewee observed:

> The piano was invented hundreds of years ago. It is one of the greatest inventions. People love it now and there is no reason to believe that they will not love it one hundred years from now. For anyone to have exposure, to study, is valuable. (I3)

Given the pervasiveness of the weekly piano lesson and uniqueness of the relationship between teacher and student, the experiences of the piano lesson and teacher extend beyond the individual student, contributing to the culture of a society. Considering the historical, cultural, and social importance to a society, in general, the piano teacher is an appropriate subject for social science inquiry. Viewed through a social science lens, the current study set out to develop a portrait of the contemporary U.S. piano teacher and teaching within its historical and social science contexts.

VIEWING THE PIANO TEACHER
THROUGH A SOCIAL SCIENCE LENS

Portrayals of the piano teacher in literatures vary from the kindly older woman to the despicable man or woman who preys on the young student.

247

While colorful characters, even caricatures, in fiction and anecdotal depictions in nonfiction provide interesting reading, they present a skewed picture of the piano teacher. Nevertheless, these images have informed and continue to shape perspectives and expectations of the piano teacher. In contrast to the popular literature, viewing the piano teacher through a social science lens focuses on common themes and patterns rather than the idiosyncratic and anecdotal, enhancing our understanding of both the piano teacher and the profession.

Situating the piano teacher and teaching in its historical and social science contexts and drawing on the experiences of twenty contemporary piano teachers, as expert, this book has explored three topics: deciding to become, becoming, and being a contemporary U.S. piano teacher. Memoirs of students of historical piano pedagogues, treatises on piano pedagogy and memoirs of notable pedagogues, and contemporary research on the study and teaching of music establish the historical and social science contexts. Interviews with twenty pianists, experienced piano teachers, who are currently teaching piano within the United States, provide firsthand evidence. Grounded in the social science tradition that views those who have experienced a situation as meaningful experts, the personal experiences and perceptions of these teachers shed light on key factors that contribute to the choice and pursuit of a career teaching piano. Each journey, each path to teaching piano, is unique. Most are stories of resilience in response to the ebbs and flows of a music career, demands of piano teaching, and personal challenges. As a composite, they present a larger picture of the contemporary piano teacher and piano teaching profession in the United States.

EARLY YEARS: DEVELOPING AN INTEREST
IN AND PASSION FOR MUSIC

Interviewees' personal and background characteristics—gender, age, educational training, national origin, and country of piano study and training—are diverse. In many respects, however, the interviewees are similar to the participants in previous social science studies. While often not from a family of professional musicians, interviewees experienced music early in life, usually in a home environment where music was valued. Sometimes providing the spark, more often interviewees' first teachers were not dissimilar from the depictions in the children's literature or experiences of many children. But, the young pianist persevered. Perhaps most important in the earlier years, from wherever the inspiration, was the discovery of the passion—the love of music and the piano—that motivated and sustained continued study.

DECIDING TO BECOME A PIANO TEACHER:
BEYOND ECONOMICS—THE PASSION TO SHARE

After developing an interest in music and the piano, usually during the early years, the decision to teach piano could occur at any stage in the developmental history of the piano teacher. For some teaching began in adolescence; most were teaching by their college years; and three began teaching as mature professional pianists. Not all first teaching experiences were positive, sometimes leading to a hiatus, but by the time of the interview all had been teaching for more than a decade. Although economics usually played a role in deciding to teach piano, the explanation for the decision is more than simple economics at whatever stage or age the decision was made. Moreover, interviewees continue to perform, while teaching.

Adolescent Employment: Early Experiences Teaching Piano

Distinctive among interviewees' adolescent experiences with music was the opportunity to teach piano. Before age eighteen, about half had begun teaching other children. In contrast to the description of adolescent employment in the career choice literature, these young pianists were not engaged in noncareer related after school activities to earn money but a career-related experience that could provide income. Rather than negatively setting them apart, their ability to play the piano brought neighborhood children, even gang members, to the door. Interviewees, who studied under the Russian system, highlighted early preparation and expectations that they would teach. That is not to deny that a young pianist, especially boys, may be subject to teasing from their peers. Nevertheless, interviewees' experiences suggest that sharing and learning music peer to peer, child to child, may contribute to the musical development of the young student/teacher. Early teaching opportunities may awaken the passion to teach piano—moving the young pianist beyond self-directed interest in music to interest in the well-being of others. Such experiences, especially under the guidance of a teacher, may contribute to the decision to and continued pursuit of piano teaching as one path within a music career.

Challenging the Stereotypes: Economics
and "Those Who Can't"

The music profession, generally, has been described as protean—encompassing multiple careers to meet personal and professional needs. Teaching piano is one path. Perhaps the most frequent explanations for why teach—whether piano, other instruments, or teaching in general—are lack of talent—those who can't, teach—and economics—a steady source of income. For the interviewees in the current study, teaching piano is a chosen musical path. Teaching piano is not an afterthought, a temporary adjustment while waiting for one's performing career to take off, a way of staying in music when one does not have "sufficient" talent as a performer, or a means to make ends meet. While the challenges posed by a performing career may explain the choice of teaching piano for some, interviewees had had or continued to pursue active performance careers. While not denying that economics may play a role, often a precipitating factor, in deciding to teach piano, economic need is not sufficient to explain either the initial decision or continuance of a career teaching piano. Other choices are available—engaging in business; writing, as illustrated by the plethora of contemporary piano methods books; or other musical paths—composing or conducting.

Beyond the Stereotypes: Love of Tradition and Being Good at It

Attributing the decision to economic need misses the importance of the context and role of other factors in the choice to teach and continue teaching piano. Whatever an interviewee's background, economics—teaching for the money—was usually a part of the decision but not sufficient motivation to teach piano. Moreover, focusing on the monetary aspects was perceived to be potentially detrimental to teaching piano—as evidenced by the cranky and overworked early teachers of many. Whatever the initial impetus, teaching was embraced as part of the interviewee's identity as a musician, not as a temporary adjustment while waiting to achieve the ultimate definition of musician—performer. Interviewees were "realists" not "dreamers."

The decision to teach cannot be attributed to interviewees becoming tired of performing, as evidenced by their continuing to perform in a variety of venues. Unlike Manturzewska's Polish pianists, interviewees' increased pedagogical interest cannot be explained by a drop in energy, learning capacity, and artistic efficiency, usually accompanied by vacillating self-esteem, depression, and various psychosomatic symptoms (1990, 136). Despite the continued emphasis of performing as the pinnacle of a music career, interviewees did not view teaching as a second-rate profession. Emphatically, the decision to teach was not because an interviewee could not perform, as most continued to perform while teaching. Teaching and performing were two sides of a coin.

The overriding message is that at whatever ever age an interviewee began teaching, they taught because they could, were good at it, and loved doing it. Each interviewee was an artist and a pedagogue, with the different skills required of performing and teaching embodied in the same person. Following in the tradition of the early pedagogues, at the heart of the decision to teach piano is the desire to pass on the tradition and love of music—the passion—directed toward the benefit of others. Interviewees not only expressed a passion for music but a love of teaching piano and a love of their students. Perhaps that is the answer to the question: Why teach piano?

> You have to love teaching. You cannot feel that you are doing it because you have to earn money and every student is taking your energy. The keys are love and professionalism. (14)

> It's a lifetime commitment. It is both profession and avocation—you would do it if they did not pay you! (17)

BECOMING A PIANO TEACHER: ECLECTIC AND PRAGMATIC

An interviewee did not simply teach how he/she had been taught. Each developed an approach to teaching piano, drawing on multiple sources, including the factors extrapolated from the social science literature—early teachers, tradition, and formal pedagogical training—and additional factors, identified through the interviews—later teachers, peers and colleagues, informal pedagogical training, and learning by doing. Within the arenas of the lesson, beyond the lesson, and promoting the general culture, interviewees' approaches to teaching were eclectic and pragmatic. Despite the diversity of backgrounds and educational training, what is perhaps most striking about the interviewees' descriptions of their respective teaching approaches is the similarity.

Each approach was eclectic. While the source of a particular aspect (e.g., use of the wrist or letting the student select a musical composition to study) might be identified, more often isolating aspects derived from a unique influence was difficult. Reflecting personal experiences and consonant with earlier pedagogical traditions, interviewees' approaches to teaching piano typically extended beyond passing on the skills necessary to play the instrument within the lesson to activities beyond the lesson and promoting the general culture. Additionally, negative experiences might help to shape interviewees' approaches both by way of example of practices not to follow and providing the impetus to find a better way.

Contemporary approaches to piano teaching may also be characterized as pragmatic. Circumstances might necessitate adjustments to an interviewee's approach. Changes in a teacher's student population, for example, as a result of immigration (e.g., Russian and American students) or age (e.g., adults and children) call for different tools, language, expectations, and content. Addressing the needs of an individual student may require teaching differently. Interviewees' approaches were not stagnant but continued/continue to evolve in response to continuous learning from peers, colleagues, educational conferences, and new experiences.

Perhaps because experience was considered to be the greatest teacher and each interviewee had not only been teaching piano but teaching piano within the United States for more than a decade, teaching approaches reflect common themes. Whether learned from teachers, tradition, pedagogical courses, peers, or experience, interviewees articulated similar perspectives on teaching piano. While teaching within the lesson encompasses the transmission of the skills to play the instrument, interviewees emphasized the importance of developing a student's knowledge of music beyond the piece to music, the arts, and history. Perhaps most important, however, is fostering the development of a student as a human being. Teaching piano extends to experiences of music beyond the lesson—concerts and other shared activities—and promoting the general culture of society—teaching average students and engaging with the community. Interviewees' perspectives are reflected in their individual teaching, in practice—being a piano teacher—and taken together, are exemplified in contemporary U.S. piano teaching.

BEING A PIANO TEACHER: QUALITIES AND PRACTICE

While, perhaps, an effective literary device and reflective of some actual student experiences, the piano teacher depicted in literature and film is typically tepid, at best, and, at worst, malevolent. To create a portrait of a contemporary piano teacher, this study focused on the qualities of a good teacher and piano teaching, in practice. Here again, individual differences notwithstanding, from the interviews emerge common themes, underlying approaches to contemporary piano teaching and reflecting the qualities of a good teacher, in practice. For example, the emphasis on individualizing one's teaching to the student, identified in the historical literature, resounds throughout the interviews. Like the historical pedagogues, in practice, interviewees' teaching activities reached beyond the lesson, demonstrating continuity in piano teaching.

Qualities demonstrating both continuity and change include the motivation to teach, the personal quality of patience, and knowing each student. Love of music, love of students, and love of the profession—passing on the traditions—motivated historical pedagogues and continue to motivate contemporary piano teachers. As interviewees repeatedly observed, you cannot teach piano just to earn money. The greater rewards are intangible—seeing a student succeed and lasting relationships forged through music. The lack of financial rewards may be the root of many bad experiences—the tired and cranky teacher who lacks patience. Patience was consistently identified as a quality of a good teacher. While recognized in the historical literature, certain historical pedagogues were also known for their outbursts. In the current climate, yelling at one's students is generally not advisable. Knowing the individual student may, however, may be the quality most relevant throughout the development of the student and fundamental to teaching. Good piano teaching is not rote, rigid, or just relaying information but requires the teacher to be an analyst, psychologist, and educator.

In practice, the advice to students to "listen" and the broad definition of piano teaching approach to include beyond the lesson and promoting the general culture illustrate long-standing traditions. "Horen Sie Sich spielen," advised Deppe (Fay [1880] 2011, 287) or today—listen to what you are playing—the real difference—the real student—listens to him or herself and adjusts (8). Listening is essential to the ultimate objective—achieving a beautiful sound/tone.

Reflecting earlier pedagogical traditions and their own experiences as students, interviewees' approaches to teaching piano typically extend beyond passing on technical skills. Within the lesson, beyond may mean not only furthering the student's knowledge of the music studied but developing the student as a person, a good human being, as well as a musician. Beyond the lesson may mean participating in musical activities—going to concerts and listening to music—but also exposure to art and literature. Interviewees encouraged, even facilitated, students' participation in musical education beyond learning a piece or technique.

The role and responsibility of the piano teacher, as described by the noted Russian pedagogue Heinrich Neuhaus, extends beyond the transferring of keyboard skills to the individual student to the enrichment of the society to create a high level of musical culture (Neuhaus, 1973, 203). Contemporary approaches promote the general culture of the society—teaching the average student to appreciate music and apply the discipline to other activities, continuing the education of the adult who loves music, and raising the civic consciousness of the student to share his or her musical talents.

PORTRAIT OF A CONTEMPORARY
U.S. PIANO TEACHER

The book began with descriptions of the piano teacher drawn from contemporary fiction and nonfiction. The piano teacher of the children's literature is usually not a very exciting mature female, who rewards her students with stickers and chocolates. The piano teacher of the adult literature is more often a monster than an angel. By way of the selection criteria—gender, age, educational training, national origin, and country of piano study and training—interviewees were diverse. Considering the decision to teach piano; the development of an approach to teaching; the qualities of a good teacher; and piano teaching, in practice, the image of the piano teacher that emerges from this study is complex. As contemporary pianist and teacher, Blanche Abram observes, the piano teacher and teaching piano are complicated.

> Teaching is both an art and science colored by a complex interaction between the teacher and the student. Responding to the needs of each pupil, the gifted teacher instinctively reacts with empathy which is reflected in the voice quality used, the speed of speaking and the pitch of the voice, even the vocabulary—all in a natural manner geared to reach each individual student. . . . One is developing the student's musical sense and "hearing" ability while simultaneously training muscle coordinations that build a solid framework of intricate control that remains comfortable and, at the same time, teaching how to focus, how the brain works, how to practice, etc. etc. (Abram 1996, 1)

Ultimately being a good teacher of piano is to be an educator—to lead the student to knowledge. Like the early pedagogues, the challenge for the contemporary piano teacher is to lead the pupil to that degree of artistic insight, which his/her musical talent and mental endowments enable him/her to reach.

As exemplified by interviewees' musical careers, deciding to teach piano is not an either or choice, as the contemporary piano teacher, like many historical pedagogues, continues to perform or compose. Economics and the need to pursue more than one path to sustain a music career may contribute to deciding and continuing to teach piano, but financial gain does not explain the choice of teaching rather than another path. Being a piano teacher is about being a professional. Teaching approaches are eclectic and pragmatic, drawing from but not simply imitating early and later teachers, tradition, and pedagogical studies. In practice, teaching is thought-out, deliberative, and deliberate. To know each student, the contemporary piano teacher is often a psychologist. Professionally, being a piano teacher is an ongoing process of continuous learning. Not only patience but perseverance and hard work are reflected in interviewees' stories, although the latter were not mentioned as qualities of a good teacher.

While interviewees believed their teaching to be rewarding, the greater rewards were largely intangible—seeing a student succeed and lifelong relationships. Sometimes the greatest reward was the student who finally "gets it." It is not romanticizing to attribute the pursuit of piano teaching to love of music, of students, and passing on the traditions of the piano. Recognizing that piano teachers are human, subject to the foibles of all us, the portrait developed through the current study is very different from that presented in fiction and nonfiction.

FURTHER STUDY

The current study underscores the need for further social science research on the music profession, generally, and performers and teachers of piano. Questions regarding piano teaching and the profession, raised but left unanswered, are fertile ground for social science research: What are the effects of the stresses and strains of the profession on the piano teacher? What role might gender, race, or ethnicity play in the decision to teach piano? An essential component of many careers today, how might networking enhance opportunities within a musical career? Perhaps national and societal variations, affecting the employment opportunities available to musicians, may explain the differences in the reasons for mature musicians to consider teaching. Such comparative research could be very informative.

Additionally, the factors identified as contributing to deciding to become, becoming, and being a piano teacher may be used to explore the careers of teachers of other instruments, voice, and even conducting and composing. Are the patterns the same and if they differ, why? More broadly, are the factors identified relevant to the development of the fine artist as a teacher? Perhaps comparative studies of careers in sports, mathematics, medicine, and the sciences—similar to the Bloom project cited—might be undertaken, given sufficient resources. Much is to be learned by the application of social science approaches to the study of music and other fields.

CONCLUDING THOUGHTS

Interviewees' personal experiences and perceptions shed light on the factors that contribute to deciding to become, becoming, and being a contemporary U.S. piano teacher. Many are stories of resilience in response to the ebbs and flows of a music career or the challenges of piano teaching. While each journey is unique, taken together they provide a portrait of an educator and professional. Set in an historical context, these stories are part of a tradition of piano teachers. Situated within a social science context, the stories illustrate the choice, development, and pursuit of a career in music, specifically the piano. The overriding message, reflected in interviewees' approaches, is that teaching piano is about love of music—the passion—and the desire to share and pass on that love to the next generation. At the end of the day, the piano teacher bears the responsibility for transmitting the tradition to society in general. The need for the civilizing effect of music and the arts remains.

Appendix A

Selected Historical Piano Pedagogues

Table A.1 Selected Historical Piano Pedagogues

Pedagogue	Biographical Description
Muzio Clementi 1752–1832	Italy/England. Composer, keyboard player, teacher, orchestra conductor, publisher, and successful piano manufacturer. Published an influential text on playing the pianoforte.
John Freckleton Burrowes 1787–1852	England. Organist and composer. Author of a pianoforte primer used for nearly a century.
Frederick Chopin 1810–1849	Poland. Pianist, composer, and teacher. During the later part of his life, teaching became his predominant source of income.
Louis Plaidy 1810–1874	Germany. Pianist and teacher at the Leipzig Conservatory, 1843–1865. Wrote a textbook, translated as *The Piano Teacher* (Wier 1940, 404).
Carl Czerny 1791–1857	Austria. Student of Beethoven. Pianist, teacher, and composer. Teacher of Liszt and Leschetizky. Many of his technical pieces are still an essential part of pianists' training.
Ignaz Moscheles 1794–1870	Bohemia. Pianist, composer, and teacher. Principal professor at the Leipzig Conservatory. Published compositions for pianoforte.
Franz Liszt 1811–1886	Hungary. Student of Czerny. Composer, pianist, and teacher. Considered one of the greatest piano virtuosos of his time. Teacher, especially at Weimar.
Theodor Leschetizky 1830–1915	Poland. Student of Czerny. Pianist, teacher, and composer. Taught in St. Petersburg but primarily Vienna. Students included Austrian pianist, teacher, and composer Artur Schnabel and Polish president, pianist, and composer Ignace Paderewski. Over 1,200 pianists are known to have studied with him.
William Mason 1829–1908	United States. American pianist, teacher, and composer. Student of Liszt. His memoir provides an anecdotal account of lessons with Liszt at Weimar. Published numerous pedagogical works for the piano student.

(*Continued*)

Appendix A

Table A.1 Selected Historical Piano Pedagogues (*Continued*)

Pedagogue	Biographical Description
Ludwig Deppe 1828–1890	Germany. One of the foremost piano teachers in Europe. He developed a system of instruction involving careful attention to muscular movement; special study of pedaling; and use of a low stool to cultivate a soft, even, but penetrating tone.
Tobias Matthay 1858–1945	Great Britain. Twentieth-century British pianist, composer, and teacher. Founded a piano school in London in 1900. Expounding what he believed to be compliance with the laws of science, he evolved his own method of teaching, analyzing physical aspects of piano playing and stressing muscular relaxation and forearm rotation.
Hans Schneider 1863–1926	United States. Pianist, composer, and teacher. Published articles in music journals (Saerchinger 1918, 568). Founded the Hans Schneider Piano School, Providence, Rhode Island. He describes his methods in *The Working of the Mind in Piano Teaching and Playing* (1923).
Josef Lhevinne 1874–1944	Russia. Studied at the Moscow Conservatory. He immigrated to New York in 1919, where he taught privately and at the Juilliard School. His students included Adele Marcus. Published a text on principles of piano playing.
Josef Hofmann 1876–1957	Poland. Born into a musical family, he was a musical prodigy. Student of Anton Rubenstein. Regarded as without equal among Russian pianists (1910–1935). Immigrating to the United States, he was the director of the Curtis Institute from 1927 to 1938.
Isabelle Vengerova 1877–1956	Russia. Student of Theodor Leschetizky. Taught at the St. Petersburg Conservatory. Immigrating to the United States in 1924, she helped found the Curtis Institute, joined the Mannes College faculty in 1933, and taught at both institutions until 1956. Students included Samuel Barber and Leonard Bernstein.
Abby Whiteside 1881–1956	United States. Career centered around private teaching in Oregon and New York. Counters traditions. Concept of rhythm is at the heart of her ideas. Considers physical response of large playing units (torso, whole arm, buttocks) necessary for capturing rhythmic flow (Uszler et al. 1995, 345–46).
Heinrich Neuhaus 1888–1964	Ukraine/Russia. Began teaching at the Moscow Conservatoire in 1922 and served as its rector from 1934 to 1937. Students included noted Russian pianists Gilels and Richter. His reputation rested primarily on his teaching.
Maria Curcio 1919–2009	Italy. A student of Artur Schnabel. She settled in London in 1967, where her career as a teacher advanced (Ashley 1993, 2–12).
Louise Stroud 1913–2008	United States. A North Carolina piano and school music teacher (Stroud 1989, 1–6).
Menahem Pressler 1923–	Germany. Immigrated to Israel in 1939, and then the United States. Professor at Indiana University Jacobs School of Music (Brown 2009, 3).
Seymour Bernstein 1927–	United States. New Jersey-born, he began teaching piano at age fifteen. Maintains a private studio in New York and is an Adjunct Associate Professor of Music and Music Education at New York University (Bernstein 2002).

Source: Sadie, Stanley. 2001. *The New Grove Dictionary of Music and Musicians*. London: Macmillan Limited, unless otherwise noted within table.

Appendix B

Interviewees

Table B.1 Background Descriptions of Interviewees

Interviewee #	Gender	Age Range	National Origin	Country of Musical Education		Years Teaching Piano
				Early	Advanced	
1.	F	71 and above	Australian	Australia	Austria, U.S.	50
2.	F	31–40	Canadian	Canada, U.S.	U.S.	13
3.	M	51–60	U.S.	U.S.	U.S.	30
4.	F	71 and above	Russian	Russia	Russia	60
5.	F	51–60	Russian	Russia	Russia	35
6.	F	51–60	South Korean	South Korea, U.S.	U.S.	28
7.	M	31–40	Polish	Poland	Ukraine, U.S.	13
8.	M	61–70	U.S.	U.S.	U.S.	25
9.	F	51–60	Georgian	Georgia/ Russia	Russia	25
10.`	F	31–40	U.S., (Chinese-American)	U.S.	U.S. Netherlands	22
11.	M	51–60	U.S., (Puerto Rican)	U.S., (Puerto Rico)	U.S.	32
12.	F	51–60	Lithuanian	Lithuania	Lithuania, Israel, U.S.	38
13.	F	61–70	U.S.	U.S.	U.S.	40

(Continued)

Table B.1 Background Descriptions of Interviewees (*Continued*)

| Interviewee # | Gender | Age Range | National Origin | Country of Musical Education | | Years Teaching Piano |
				Early	Advanced	
14.	F	71 and above	Russian	Russia	Russia	41
15.	F	71 and above	U.S.	U.S.	U.S.	78
16.	F	51–60	U.S.	U.S.	U.S.	30
17.	M	61–70	U.S.	U.S.	U.S., Great Britain	46
18.	F	51–60	U.S.	U.S.	U.S.	30
19.	M	31–40	U.S.	U.S.	U.S.	10–12
20.	M	71 and above	U.S.	U.S.	U.S., Austria	67

References

Abram, Blanche. 1996. "Teaching and the Influence of Vengerova." (Unpublished), 1–2. New York.

Ashley, Douglas. 1993. *Music Beyond Sound: Maria Curcio, A Teacher of Great Pianists.* New York: P. Lang.

Barnes, Christopher, ed. 2007. *The Russian Piano School: Russian Pianism and Moscow Conservatoire Professors on the Art of the Piano.* London: Kahn & Averill.

Bennett, Dawn. 2016. *Understanding the Classical Music Profession.* New York: Routledge.

Bennett, Dawn and Andrea Stanberg. 2006. "Musicians as Teachers: Developing a Positive View through Collaborative Learning Partnerships." *International Journal of Music Education,* 24, no. 3: 219–30.

Bernstein, Seymour. 1981. *With Your Own Two Hands.* New York: Schirmer Books.

———. 2002. *Monsters and Angels.* Milwaukee, WI: Hal Leonard.

Bloom, Benjamin S., ed. 1985a. *Developing Talent in Young People.* New York: Ballantine Books.

Bloom, Benjamin S. 1985b. "Generalizations about Talent Development." In *Developing Talent in Young People*, edited by Benjamin S. Bloom, 507–49. New York: Ballantine Books.

Boissier, Madame Auguste. [1928] 1973. *A Diary of Franz Liszt as Teacher 1831–1832.* In *The Liszt Studies: Essential Selections from the Original 12-Volume Set of Technical Studies for the Piano*, edited and translated by Elyse Mach, ix–xxiv. New York: Associated Music Publishers.

Bomberger, E. Douglas. 2001. "The Conservatory and the Piano." In *Piano Roles*, James Parakilas et al., 124–34. New Haven, CT: Yale University Press.

Bonneville-Roussy, Arielle, Geneviève L. Lavigne, and Robert J. Vallerand. 2011. "When Passion Leads to Excellence: The Case of Musicians." *Psychology of Music*, 39, no. 1: 123–38.

Brée, Malwine. 1913. *The Leschetizky Method: An Exposition of His Personal Views.* New York: The University Society, Inc.

Brown, Duane. 2002. "Introduction to Theories of Development and Choice: Origins, Evolutions, and Current Efforts." In *Career Choice and Development*, 4th ed. Duane Brown & Associates, 3–23. San Francisco: Jossey-Bass.

Brown, William. 2009. *Menahem Pressler: Artistry in Piano Teaching*. Bloomington: Indiana University Press.

Buma, Lori, Frank C. Bakker, and Raôul R. D. Oudejans. 2015. "Exploring the Thoughts and Focus of Attention of Elite Musicians under Pressure." *Psychology of Music*, 43, no. 4: 459–72.

Burns, Amy Jo. 2014. *Cinderland: A Memoir*. Boston: Beacon Press.

Burrowes, J. F. 1840. *The Piano-forte Primer*. London: by author.

Caland, Elisabeth. 1903. *Artistic Piano Playing as Taught by Ludwig Deppe*. Nashville: Olympian Publishing Co. http://hdl.handle.net/2027/hvd.32044040898769.

Carey, Gemma and Cathrine Grant. 2015. "Teacher and Student Perspectives on One-to-One Pedagogy: Practices and Possibilities." *British Journal of Music Education*, 32, no. 1: 5–22.

Carhart, Thad. 2001. *Piano Shop on the Left Bank: Discovering a Forgotten Passion in a Paris Atelier*. New York: Random House.

Chambliss, Daniel F. 1989. "Excellence: An Ethnographic Report on Stratification and Olympic Swimmers." *Sociological Theory*, 7, no. 1 (Spring): 70–86.

Clementi, Muzio. [1801] 1974. *Introduction to the Art of Playing on the Pianoforte*. Introduction by Sandra P. Rosenbaum. Reprint, New York: Da Capo Press.

Conroy, Frank. 1993. *Body and Soul*. New York: Houghton Mifflin.

Couperin, François. [1717] 1933. *L'Art de Toucher le Clavecin*. Translation by Mevanwy Roberts. Reprint, Germany: Breitkopf & Hartel in Leipzig.

Czerny, Charles. [1837/43] 1982. *Letters to a Young Lady, on the Art of Playing Pianoforte*. Translated by J. A. Hamilton. Reprint, New York: Da Capo Press.

Davidson, Jane W., John A. Sloboda, and Michael J. A. Howe. 1995/1996. "The Role of Parents and Teachers in the Success and Failure of Instrumental Learners." *Bulletin of the Council for Research in Music Education*. Champaign, IL: University of Illinois Press on behalf of the Council for Research in Music Education, no. 127 (Winter): 40–44.

Delton, Judy. 1994. *My Mom Made Me Take Piano Lessons*. New York: Doubleday Book for Young Readers.

Dubal, David. 1989. *The Art of the Piano*. New York: Summit Books.

Duckworth, Angela. 2016. *Grit: The Power of Passion and Perseverance*. London: Vermilion.

Durrant, Colin. 1992. "Those Who Can't." *The Music Teacher*, 71 (February): 11–15.

Dwek, Carol S. 2006. *Mindset: The New Psychology of Success*. New York: Ballantine.

Eigeldinger, Jean-Jacques. 1986. *Chopin: Pianist and Teacher as Seen by His Pupils*. Translated by Naomi Shohet with Krysia Osostowicz and Roy Howat. Cambridge: Cambridge University Press.

Ericsson, K. Anders, Clemens Tesch-Römer, and Ralf Th. Krampe. 1990. "The Role of Practice and Motivation in the Acquisition of Expert-Level Performance in Real Life: An Empirical Evaluation of a Theoretical Framework." In *Encouraging the Development of Exceptional Skills and Talent*, edited by Michael J. A. Howe, 109–29. Leicester: British Psychological Society.

Fay, Amy. [1880] 2011. *Music-Study in Germany*. Reprint with introduction by Frances Dillon, New York: Dover Publications, Inc.

Fleisher, Leon and Anne Midgette. 2011. *My Nine Lives: A Memoir of Many Careers in Music*. New York: Anchor Books.

Freeman, Robert. 2014. *The Crisis of Classical Music in America: Lessons from a Life in the Education of Musicians*. Lanham, MD: Rowman & Littlefield.

Gardner, Roy R. 1901. "Leschetizky and His School." *The Musical World*, 1, no. 7 (August): 87–90.

Gaunt, Helena. 2008. "One-to-One Tuition in a Conservatoire: The Perceptions of Instrumental and Vocal Teachers." *Psychology of Music*, 36, no. 2: 215–45.

———. 2011. "Understanding the One-to-One Relationship in Instrumental/Vocal Tuition in Higher: Comparing Student and Teacher Perceptions." *British Journal of Music Education*, 28, no. 2: 5–22.

Gelfand, Yacov. 1986–1987. "Piano Education in the Soviet Union." Translated by Irina Lasoff. *The Piano Quarterly*, no. 136: 39–49.

Goldsworthy, Anna. 2010. *Piano Lessons: A Memoir*. New York: St. Martin's Press.

Grant, Katherine. 2014. *Sedition*. New York: Henry Holt & Co.

Greenspan, Deborah A., Becca Solomon, and Howard Gardner. 2004. "The Development of Talent in Different Domains." In *Beyond Knowledge: Extracognitive Aspects of Developing High Ability*, edited by Larisa V. Shavinina and Michael Ferrari, 119–35. Mahwah, NJ: Lawrence Erlbaum Associates, Publishers.

Grindea, Carola. 2009. *Great Pianists and Pedagogues in Conversation with Carola Grindea*. Reprint, London: Kahn and Averill.

Hechinger, Fred M. 1968. *The Big Red Schoolhouse*. Gloucester, MA: Peter Smith.

Hofmann, Josef. [1920] 1976. *Piano Playing with Piano Questions Answered*. Reprint with introduction by Gregor Benko. New York: Dover Publications, Inc.

Howe, Michael J. 2004. "Some Insights of Geniuses into the Causes of Exceptional Achievements." In *Beyond Knowledge: Extracognitive Aspects of Developing High Ability*, edited by Larisa V. Shavinina and Michael Ferrari, 105–17. Mahwah, NJ: Lawrence Erlbaum Associates, Publishers.

Howe, Michael J. A. and John A. Sloboda. 1991a. "Young Musicians' Accounts of Significant Influences in Their Early Lives. 1. The Family and the Musical Background." *British Journal of Music Education*, 8, no. 1: 39–52.

———. 1991b. "Young Musicians' Accounts of Significant Influences in their Early Lives. 2. Teachers, Practising and Performing." *British Journal of Music Education*, 8: 53–63.

Huhtanen, Kaija. 2004. "Once I Had a Promising Future." *Music Forum, Music Council of Australia*, 10, no. 3: 21–27.

Jellinek, Elfriede. 2010. *The Piano Teacher*. Translated by Joachim Neugroschel. London: Serpent's Tail.

Johnson, Monica Kirkpatrick and Jeylan T. Mortimer. 2002 "Career Choice and Development from a Sociological Perspective." In *Career Choice and Development*, 4th ed. Duane Brown & Associates, 37–81. San Francisco: Jossey-Bass.

Juilliard Catalogue. 2018–2019. https://catalog.juilliard.edu/index.php (archived).

Kelly, Steven N. 2016. *Teaching Music in American Society: A Social and Cultural Understanding of Music Education*, 2nd ed. New York: Routledge.

Kenny, Dianna. 2011. *Psychology of Music Performance Anxiety*. New York: Oxford University Press.

Kenny, Dianna, Tim Driscoll, and Bronwen Ackermann. 2014. "Psychological Well-being in Professional Orchestral Musicians in Australia: A Descriptive Population Study." *Psychology of Music*, 42, no. 2: 210–32.

Kenny, Dianna F. and Bronwen I. Ackermann. 2015. "Optimizing Physical and Psychological Health in Performing Musicians." In *The Oxford Handbook of Music Psychology*, edited by Susan Hallam, Ian Cross, and Michael Thaut, 633–47. New York: Oxford University Press.

Kochevitsky, George. 1967. *The Art of Piano Playing: A Scientific Approach*. Chicago: Summy-Birchard, Co.

Kofman, Irena. 2001. "The History of the Russian Piano School: Individuals and Traditions." PhD diss., University of Miami.

Kogan, Judith. 1989. *Nothing But the Best: The Struggle for Perfection at the Juilliard School*. New York: Limelight Edition.

Lee, Janice Y. K. 2009. *The Piano Teacher*. New York: Viking.

Levine Music. 2017. *Keyboard Skills & Sight Reading*. Washington, D.C.: Levine Music.

Lhevinne, Josef. 1921. "Practical Phases of Modern Pianoforte Study." *Etude*, 39 (March): 151–52.

———. [1924] 1972. *Basic Principles in Pianoforte Playing*. Reprint with introduction by Rosina Lhevinne. New York: Dover Publications, Inc.

Livingston, Alan W., Henry Blair, and Billy Bletcher. 1946. *Rusty in Orchestraville*. Los Angeles: Capitol Records.

Loesser, Arthur. 2015. *Men, Women, and Pianos: A Social History*. New York: Simon & Schuster, 1954. Reprint, New York: Dover Publications, Inc.

Mach, Elyse. 1991a. *Great Contemporary Pianists Speak for Themselves*. Reprint (Vol. I and Vol. II), New York: Dover Publications, Inc.

———. 1991b. *Great Contemporary Pianists Speak for Themselves*. Reprint (Vol. II), New York: Dover Publications, Inc.

MacKenzie, C. G. 1991. "Starting to Learn to Play a Musical Instrument: A Study of Boys' and Girls' Motivational Criteria." *British Journal of Music Education*, 8: 15–20.

Macmillan, Dianne M. 1943. *The Curse of Rafferty McGill*. Park Ridge, IL: Albert Whitman & Co.

Macmillan, Jenny. 2004. "Learning the Piano: A Study of Attitudes to Parental Involvement." *British Journal of Music Education*, 21, no. 3: 295–311.

Madsen, Clifford K. and Steven N. Kelly. 2002. "First Remembrance of Wanting to Become a Music Teacher." *Journal of Research in Music*, 50, no. 4: 323–32.

Manturzewska, Maria. 1990. "A Biographical Study of the Life-Span Development of Professional Musicians." *Psychology of Music*, 18: 112–39.

Marcus, Adele. 1979. *Great Pianists Speak with Adele Marcus*. Neptune, NJ: Paganiniana Publications, Inc.

Mason, William. 1901. *Memories of a Musical Life*. New York: The Century Company.

Matthay, Tobias. 1905. *The First Principles of Pianoforte Playing*. New York: Longmire, Green, & Co.

———. [1912] 2012. *The Nine Steps towards Finger Individualization through Forearm Rotation A Supplement to The First Book of The Pianist's First Music Making and The Child's First Steps*. Reprinted in *England's Piano Sage: The Life and Teachings of Tobias Matthay*, Stephen Siek, 413–17. Lanham, MD: The Scarecrow Press, Inc.

Merriam Webster Dictionary. https://www.merriam-webster.com/dictionary/pianist.

Miller, John and David Baker. 2007. "Career Orientation and Pedagogical Training: Conservatoire Undergraduate Insights." *British Journal of Music Education*, 24, no. 1: 5–19.

Mills, Janet and Jan Smith. 2003. "Teachers' Beliefs about Effective Instrumental Teaching in Schools and Higher Education." *British Journal of Music Education*, 20, no. 1: 5–27.

Mortimer, Jeylan T. and Monica Kirkpatrick Johnson. 1998. "New Perspectives on Adolescent Work and the Transition to Adulthood." In *New Perspectives on Adolescent Risk Behavior*, edited by Richard Jessor, 425–96. Cambridge: Cambridge University Press.

Mortimer, Jeylan T., Ellen Efron Pimentel, Seongryeol Ryu, Katherine Nash, and Chaimun Lee. 1996. "Part-Time Work and Occupational Value Formation in Adolescence." *Social Forces*, 74, no. 4 (June): 1405–18.

Moscheles, Charlotte, ed. [1873] 1970. *Recent Music and Musicians, as Described in the Diaries and Correspondence of Ignatz Moscheles*. Adapted from German by A. D. Coleridge. Reprint, New York: Da Capo Press.

Music Dictionary. 2008. Milwaukee, WI: Hal Leonard.

Neuhaus, Heinrich. 1973. *The Art of Piano Playing*. Translated by K. A. Leibovitch. New York: Praeger Publishers.

Newcomb, Ethel. 1921. *Leschetizky, As I Knew Him*. New York: D. Appleton & Company.

Nicholas, Jeremy. 2006. *Chopin: His Life and Music*. Salfords, Redhill, UK: Naxos Books.

Olmstead, Andrea. 1999. *Juilliard: A History*. Champaign, IL: University of Illinois Press.

Parakilas, James. 2001. "A History of Lessons and Practicing." In *Piano Roles*, edited by James Parakilas et al., 110–24. New Haven, CT: Yale University Press.

Parakilas, James et al. 2001. *Piano Roles*. New Haven, CT: Yale University Press.

Pecen, Ellis, David J. Collins, and Aine MacNamara. 2018. "'It's Your Problem. Deal with It.' Performers' Experiences of Psychological Challenges in Music." *Frontiers in Psychology*, 8 (January): 1–17.

Persson, Roland S. 1994. "Concert Musicians as Teachers: On Good Intentions Falling Short." *European Journal of High Ability*, 5, no. 1: 79–91.

———. 1996. "Studying With a Musical Maestro: A Case Study of Commonsense Teaching in Artistic Training." *Creativity Research Journal*, 9, no. 1: 33–46.

Pitts, Stephanie. 2012. *Changes and Choices: Exploring the Impact of Music Education*. New York: Oxford University Press.

Plaidy, Louis. 1875. *The Piano Teacher*. Translated by John S. Dwight. Boston: Oliver Ditson and Company.

Polisi, Joseph W. 2006. *The Artist as Citizen* (revised edition). Milwaukee, WI: Amadeus Press.

Presland, Carole. 2005. "Conservatoire Student and Instrumental Professor: The Student Perspective on a Complex Relationship." *British Journal of Music Education*, 22, no. 3: 237–48.

Rainbow, Bernarr. 2009. *Four Centuries of Music Teaching Manuals 1518–1932*. Woodbridge, UK: Boydell Press.

Randel, Don Michael. 1978. *Harvard Concise Dictionary of Music*. Cambridge, MA: The Belknap Press of Harvard University Press.

Rego, John A. 2012. "Skryabin, Rakhmaninov, and Prokofiev as Composer-Pianists: The Russian Piano Tradition, Aesthetics, and Performance Practices." PhD diss., Princeton University.

Rezits, Joseph. 1965. "Lessons with Vengerova." *The Piano Teacher*, 8 (November–December): 2–5.

———. 1979. "Can a Second Generation Method Be Successful: The Teaching of Isabelle Vengerova." *The Piano Quarterly*, 106 (Summer): 16–25.

———. 1995. *Beloved Tyranna: The Legend and Legacy of Isabelle Vengerova*. Bloomington, IN: Daniel Music Publications.

Sadie, Stanley. 2001. *The New Grove Dictionary of Music and Musicians*. London: Macmillan Limited.

Sadler, Michael E. and Christopher J. Miller. 2010. "Performance Anxiety: A Longitudinal Study of the Roles of Personality and Experience in Musicians." *Social Psychological and Personality Science*, 1, no. 3: 280–87.

Saerchinger, César, ed. 1918. *International Who's Who in Music and Musical Gazateer*. New York: Current Literature Publishing Company. https://books.google.com/books?id=qIEFAAAAMAAJ&printsec=frontcover&source=gbs_ge_summary_r&cad=0#v=onepage&q&f=false.

Sand, Barbara Lourie. 2000. *Dorothy DeLay and the Making of a Musician*. Portland, OR: Amadeus Press.

Schneider, Hans. 1923. *The Working of the Mind in Piano Teaching and Playing*. New York: Schroeder and Gunther.

Schonberg, Harold C. 1987. *The Great Pianists: From Mozart to the Present*. New York: Simon & Schuster.

Shanahan, Michael J., Jeylan T. Mortimer, and Helfa Krüger. 2002. "Adolescence and Adult Work in the Twenty-First Century." *Journal of Research on Adolescence*, 12, no. 1: 99–120.

Sherman, Russell. 1997. *Piano Pieces*. New York: North Point Press.

Siek, Stephen. 2012. *England's Piano Sage: The Life and Teachings of Tobias Matthay*. Lanham, MD: The Scarecrow Press, Inc.

Sloboda, John A. 1990. "Musical Excellence – How Does It Develop?" In *Encouraging the Development of Exceptional Skills and Talent*, edited by Michael J. A. Howe, 165–78. Leicester: British Psychological Society.

Sloboda, John A. 1996. "Acquisition of Musical Performance Expertise: Deconstructing the 'Talent' Account of Individual Differences in Musical Expressivity." In *The Road to Excellence: The Acquisition of Expert Performance in the Arts and Sciences, Sports and Games*, edited by K. Anders Ericsson, 107–26. Mahwah, NJ: Lawrence Erlbaum Associates Publishers.

Sloboda, John A. and Michael J. A. Howe. 1991. "Biographical Precursors of Musical Excellence: An Interview Study." *Psychology of Music*, 19: 3–21.

Soderlund, Sandra. 2006. *How Did They Play? How Did They Teach?: A History of Keyboard Technique*. Chapel Hill, NC: Hinshaw Music.

Sosniak, Lauren A. 1985a. "Learning to be a Concert Pianist." In *Developing Talent in Young People*, edited by Benjamin S. Bloom, 19–67. New York: Ballantine Books.

———. 1985b. "Phases of Learning." In *Developing Talent in Young People*, edited by Benjamin S. Bloom, 409–38. New York: Ballantine Books.

———. 1985c. "A Long-Term Commitment to Learning." In *Developing Talent in Young People*, edited by Benjamin S. Bloom, 477–506. New York: Ballantine Books.

———. 1988. "Changing Relationships between Teacher and Student in the Development of Talent." *Education and Society*, 6, no. 1 &2: 79–86.

———. 1990. "The Tortoise and the Hare, and the Development of Talent." In *Encouraging the Development of Exceptional Skills and Talent*, edited by Michael J. A. Howe, 149–64. Leicester: British Psychological Society.

Stolz, Barbara. 1985. *Still Struggling: America's Low Income Women Confronting the 1980s*. Lexington, MA: Lexington Books.

Stroud, Louise. 1989. *Music Antic-notes: Fond Recollections of a Piano Teacher*. Burnsville, NC: Celo Valley Books.

Subotnik, Rena F. 2000. "The Juilliard Model for Developing Young Adolescent Performers: An Educational Prototype." In *Developing Talent across the Life Span*, edited by Cornelis F. M. van Lieshout and Peter C. Heymans, 249–76. East Sussex, UK: Psychology Press Ltd.

———. 2004. "Transforming Elite Musicians into Professional Artists: A View of the Talent development Process at the Juilliard School." In *Beyond Knowledge: Extracognitive Aspects of Developing High Ability*, edited by Larisa V. Shavinina and Michael Ferrari, 137–65. Mahwah, NJ: Lawrence Erlbaum Associates, Publishers.

Subotnik, Rena F., Paula Olszewski-Kublius, and Karen D. Arnold. 2003. "Beyond Bloom: Revisiting Environmental Factors That Enhance or Impede Talent Development." In *Rethinking Gifted Education*, edited by James H. Borland, 227–38. New York: Teachers College Press.

The 5,000 Fingers of Dr. T. [1952] 1996. Burbank, CA: Columbia Tristar Home Video.

Tsay, Chia-Jung. 2016. "Privileging Naturals over Strivers: The Costs of the Naturalness Bias." *Personality and Social Psychology Bulletin*, 42, no. 1: 40–53.

Tsay, Chia-Jung and Mahzarin R. Banaji. 2011. "Naturals and Strivers: Preferences and Beliefs about Sources of Achievement." *Journal of Experimental Social Psychology*, 47: 460–65.

Tunstall, Tricia. 2008. *Note by Note: A Celebration of the Piano Lesson.* New York: Simon & Schuster.

Türk, Daniel Gottlob. [1789] 1982. *School of Clavier Playing.* Translation, introduction, and notes by Raymond H. Haggh. Reprint, Lincoln: University of Nebraska Press.

Uszler, Marienne. 1982–1983. "The American Beginning Piano Method View and Viewpoint Part 1: Roots and Branches." *Piano Quarterly,* 120 (Winter): 12–19.

———. 1983. "The American Beginning Piano Method View and Viewpoint Part 2: Crisscrossing Threads." *Piano Quarterly,* 121 (Spring): 15–32.

———. 1992. "Research on the Teaching of Keyboard Music." In *Handbook of Research on Music Teaching and Learning,* edited by Richard Colwell, 584–93. New York: Schirmer Books.

Uszler, Marienne, Steward Gordon, and Elyse Mach. 1995. *The Well-Tempered Keyboard Teacher.* New York: Macmillan.

Vishnevskaya, Galina. 1984. *Galina: A Russian Story.* Translation by Guy Daniels. New York: Harcourt Brace Jovanovich, Publishers.

Whiteside, Abby. 1961. *Indispensables of Piano Playing,* 2nd ed. New York: Coleman-Ross, Co.

Wier, Albert E. 1940. *The Piano: Its History, Makers, Players, and Music.* New York: Longmans, Green, & Co.

Index

Note: Page references in *italics* denote figures and tables.

About the Author

Barbara Ann Stolz is a political scientist/criminologist and amateur pianist. The daughter of a pianist/organist, she continues to study piano, while pursuing a career in criminal justice policy in academia and government. Her professional life has included academic positions at American University; the University of Illinois at Chicago; and Yaroslavl State University, Russia. She has carried out research for the legislative branch of the U.S. government. Currently, she is an adjunct professor in the McCourt School of Public Policy at Georgetown University and studies piano with Carlos Rodriguez at Levine Music in Washington, D.C. Her publications include two books, *Still Struggling: America's Low-Income Women Confronting the 1980s* and *Criminal Justice Policymaking: Federal Roles and Processes*; journal articles on diverse criminal justice issues (e.g., capital punishment, U.S. drug policy, U.S. intelligence policy, Russian criminal law, and human trafficking); and numerous government publications. She received her bachelor's degree from Fordham University and her doctorate in politics from Brandeis University.